Living with the Planet

Living with the Planet

Making a Difference in a Time of Climate Change

Catherine von Ruhland

This book is dedicated to the next generation: my nephew and niece, Zac and Eve von Ruhland, with much love, hope and prayer that their future on this small planet might be a Green and pleasant one.

A Lion Book
an imprint of
Lion Hudson plc
Wilkinson House, Jordan Hill Road,
Oxford OX2 8DR, England
www.lionhudson.com

ISBN 978 0 7459 5255 0 (UK)
ISBN 978 0 8254 6251 1 (USA)

First edition 2008
10 9 8 7 6 5 4 3 2 1 0

A catalogue record for this book is available from the British Library

Distributed by:
UK: Marston Book Services Ltd, PO Box 269, Abingdon, Oxon OX14 4YN
USA: Trafalgar Square Publishing, 814 N Franklin Street, Chicago, IL 60610
USA Christian Market: Kregel Publications, PO Box 2607, Grand Rapids, Michigan 4950

Typeset in 10/12pt Original Garamond
Printed and bound in Singapore
Printed on recycled paper

Contents

Acknowledgments

Writing this book has been a real privilege, and my heartfelt thanks go to the following who were with me for at least part of what turned out to be a fascinating but sometimes tough journey: Huw Spanner, who was there at the beginning and who helped set me off in the right direction; Gordon Harris, librarian, and Astrid Foxen, information manager at the development agency Tearfund, for helpful access to its book collection; Morag Reeve, my editor at Lion, for her support, encouragement and patience, and especially for extending the deadline when the hottest British summer on record – and global warming – stymied work on the book; the staff of Guy's Hospital Renal Satellite Unit, for helping maintain my health in the light of many coffee and ice cube overdoses, oh, and the blood I sweated…; my friends and family, who endured my bouts of high anxiety over the fate of the planet; Café Craft, Hampton, for providing a much-appreciated change of scene away from the computer and the newspaper cuttings (I recommend the lemon cheesecake…); the UK's *Independent* newspaper and *New Scientist* magazine for consistently excellent coverage of environmental issues; and deep respect too for the world's geography teachers.

Disclaimer: Such is the nature of the book's very subject that some things will have altered by the time of publication. Not too much, we all hope.

Catherine von Ruhland

Foreword

In this very useful work, the author surveys the continents and oceans of the world and deals with the various stresses that climate change and humans' actions are inflicting upon ecosystems and environments. The total picture is alarming and may seem hopeless, but we are relieved from complete despair by suggestions for positive actions that we can carry out. The aim is to follow the dictum of that pioneer ecologist E. F. Schumacher, to 'think globally; act locally'.

The grim reality, of course, as the author frequently points out, is that even large-scale collaborative efforts by individuals can only scratch the surface of this, the greatest challenge facing mankind. Only concerted governmental action throughout the world stands a chance of averting global catastrophe.

I can remember as a student in the 1960s learning many of the facts presented in this book. It was already recognized that major changes were occurring to our planet, for which we were responsible, but the chief fears then were of resource depletion and the accelerating effects of the population explosion. Today global warming has been rightly added to the set of threats facing mankind, and it is in many ways the worst since it could give us a planet that is incapable of sustaining large-scale human life. However, we tend to forget that the other mortal threats have not gone away. An uncontrolled population explosion must lead to mass starvation since the increased agricultural productivity of the planet is coming up against the constraints of limited land, diminishing water resources and loss of farmland to biofuel production. Yet there is no sign that the lesson of overpopulation, learned in the 1960s, is being remembered. Similarly, the gigantic industrialization effort under way in China and India, as well as being a major source of greenhouse gases, is destined to fail since there are simply not enough resources in the form of oil, coal and minerals to support fully developed industrial powers with such huge populations.

It is a frightening thought that resource depletion and overpopulation may cause economic catastrophe and mass starvation before global warming has had time to make our planet uninhabitable. Which horror do we prefer? Our fate is not yet sealed. We are rational creatures, replete with scientific knowledge, fully capable of controlling our own numbers and our footprint upon the world, and of creating an environment that can be sustained indefinitely. Are we wise enough to use these powers of reason before it is too late and before our accompanying vices of greed and stupidity ensure that ours is the most serious species failure in planetary history? The answer is up to each of us.

Peter Wadhams
Professor of Ocean Physics
Department of Applied Mathematics and Theoretical Physics
University of Cambridge

Introduction

When I was first asked to write this book, I knew what type of book I did *not* want to write: a 'put-your-bottles-in-the-bottle-bank' type list book to help readers 'act locally, think globally'. After all, I had already done that back in the early 1990s,[1] and I saw no point in repeating myself. And almost twenty years later, in the latest cycle of environmental publishing, there are again plenty of those types of books on the market more or less suggesting the same sort of thing: save energy, reuse and recycle, cut your carbon footprint...

Very much aware of how easy it is to wake up one day and wonder why you are going to such an effort to be Green – especially if you can see your neighbours happily getting on with their lives without feeling *they* have to – I sought instead to remind readers why we are attempting to live more simply in the first place. To take people on a journey from the outside in, from a small blueish marble spinning in space down to the continents and oceans, and ultimately to give account of the impact – for better or worse – that we are making to our planetary home. To help retain a sense of the Bigger Picture.

Initial chapters cover the Earth's atmosphere, the planet beneath and the waters that cover 71 per cent of the globe. The remaining seven chapters are each devoted to a different continent, beginning with the largest, Asia, down to the smallest, Australasia – or Oceania, as it is alternatively known. An influential environmentalist from each region is identified, and coverage is given to the notable issues affecting that particular part of the world. Each of

these chapters culminates with 'Lost and Found', a success story about a species no longer endangered, or of a new species discovered, followed by a list of suggestions for 'Taking Action'.

The intention is to place our individual actions in their global context to show that actions such as taking a quick shower instead of a bath, picking up litter, travelling by public transport instead of by car, or leaving a wild section in your garden to allow small creatures to thrive have their own intrinsic value. Such Green practices express a level of respect for the world around us and the communities in which we live. They are about *taking care*, and they should help us humbly recognize our role of coexistence alongside the other people, flora and fauna with whom we share this planet.

While our individual actions do have value – switching off lights in empty rooms, for instance, saves energy and money, and allows a better view of the night sky – they cannot in themselves either halt climate change or prepare us for the impact it will have. This demands action at business, national and international levels too.

It is the very recognition of our global interconnectedness that supports us here. We must relearn how to live *with* the planet rather than against it. Certainly that means aiming to attain a more simple and life-affirming existence that is in tune with our environment. But we can also support and join others working to make a positive and vital difference – many of their activities around the world are identified here.

Force of nature: waves bring joy to surfers and are a renewable source of energy – but can create devastation as tsunami.

The Earth's

'Climate change is the most severe problem that we are facing today, more serious even than the threat of terrorism.'

DAVID KING,
UK GOVERNMENT CHIEF SCIENTIFIC ADVISOR

Atmosphere

CHAPTER 1

The Earth's atmosphere is a layer of gases approximately 480 km (300 miles) thick, consisting of 78 per cent nitrogen, 21 per cent oxygen, 0.9 per cent argon, 0.03 per cent carbon dioxide and traces of other gases. Each layer of the atmosphere contains different properties, from the innermost layer, the troposphere, to the tropopause, the stratosphere, the mesophere, the ionosphere, and the farthest from the planet, the exosphere, which fades out into Space.

Without the Earth's atmosphere, all life forms that share the planet would be extinct. While preventing the Earth's own heat from dissipating into space, the gaseous blanket of the planet's atmosphere also protects the planet from the extremes of the sun's ultraviolet (UV) radiation.

The atmosphere evolved out of such physical processes as the Earth's volcanic exhalations and the contribution made by the Earth's life forms. Planetary degassing released gases, including carbon and sulphur dioxides, nitrogen and water vapour, to form the atmosphere between Space and the Earth.

The atmosphere is circulated primarily by solar heat. Because the sun is stronger at the Earth's equator than at the Poles, the difference in temperature fuels the movement of air in circulatory cells, transporting heat to the higher latitudes of the planet's polar regions. Further circulations of air and winds are created by the Coriolis effect,[1] the tendency of all moving bodies – including the atmosphere and oceans – to be deflected by the Earth's rotation ('as the crow flies', therefore, is not a straight line).

Approximately 80 per cent of the Earth's atmosphere is within 16 km (10 miles) of the planet's surface. The troposphere is the lowest band, reaching up approximately 17 km (11 miles) from land and water level. This is where our weather circulates, and where planes are able to fly. The tropopause divides the troposphere and stratosphere. The stratosphere extends outwards to 50 km (31 miles) and contains the ozone layer, which absorbs much of the sun's UV energy. The thinning of the ozone layer and the development of widening holes above the North and South Poles have caused considerable concern at

Previous spread: New dawn: Edinburgh's skyline is shrouded in fog at sunrise.

Opposite: The Earth's atmosphere is subdivided into five layers.

the impact the increase in solar radiation might have on the Earth's life forms and climate.

Beyond the stratosphere is the mesosphere, which is characterized by plummeting temperatures the farther it is from the Earth. It extends 80 km (50 miles) beyond the planet. In the thermosphere, by contrast, the temperature increases with altitude: the ionosphere and the outer exosphere together form this warm layer, beyond which is Space. The ionosphere is where the visual spectacle of auroras occurs, and it is the layer that allows radio waves to bounce around the curvature of the Earth. It is hundreds of miles thick and is so named owing to the numerous ions contained within it. Between approximately 640 km (400 miles) and 1,280 km (800 miles) from the Earth's surface exists the exosphere, the atmosphere's outermost layer. Beyond is Outer Space.[2]

Climate Change

Climate change refers not simply to temperature rise or fall but also to a range of phenomena, including raised sea levels, changes in precipitation patterns and cloud and snow cover. These in turn have a huge impact on water and food resources, and can harm habitats and those dependent on them. Climate change in itself is not necessarily harmful since ecosystems can adapt accordingly. However, if it occurs too rapidly – as is happening now – then the consequences tend to be detrimental.

Natural climate change occurs in cycles, whereas man-made – that is, anthropogenic – climate change occurs beyond natural climate variation patterns. The last ice age ended approximately 12,000 years ago, and since then there have been fluctuations such as the 'Medieval Warm Period' or the 'Little Ice Age'. A rise in land and sea temperature of between 0.4 and 0.6°C has coincided with the widespread burning of fossil fuels spurred by the Industrial Revolution that began in Britain and has since spread around the globe. The latest decade has been the warmest on record.

The Intergovernmental Panel on Climate Change (IPCC) was established in 1988 by the World Meteorological Organization (WMO) and the United Nations Environment Programme (UNEP) 'to assess on a comprehensive, objective, open and transparent basis the scientific, technical and socio-economic information relevant to understanding the scientific basis of risk of human-induced climate change, its potential impacts and options for adaptation and mitigation'.[3] Rather than carry out research, the IPCC bases its regular assessments of the

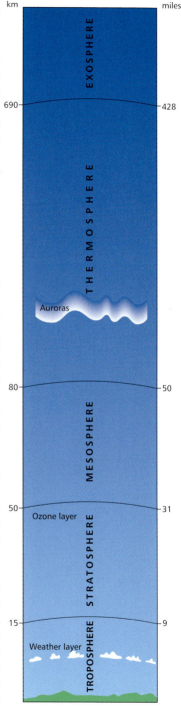

state of knowledge on climate change on peer-reviewed and published scientific/technical literature. In 1990 the First IPCC Assessment Report was to play an important role in the adoption, in 1992, of the UN Framework Convention on Climate Change (UNFCC), the policy framework for addressing climate change, which entered into force in 1994. Likewise, its 1995 Second Assessment Report paved the way for the 1997 Kyoto Protocol. In 2001, the Third Assessment Report (TAR) highlighted the scientific basis for climate change.

The IPCC's Fourth Assessment Report was due to be completed in 2007. A preliminary report issued in February 2007 examined the human and natural drivers of climate change. Scientific progress and advances in data analysis enhanced TAR's previous findings. Warming of the climate system was deemed 'unequivocal, as is now evident from observations of increases in global average air and ocean temperatures, widespread melting of snow and ice, and rising global average sea level'.[4] Not only were the increased greenhouse gas concentrations very likely due to human activity but 'discernible human influences now extend to other aspects of climate, including ocean warming, continental-average temperatures, temperature extremes and wind patterns'.[5]

Levels of future climate change are difficult to predict owing to a range of variables. For example, the 2001 IPCC report on climate change highlighted changes in cloud cover as a dominant uncertainty in any calculations.[6] Solar activity and changes in vegetation also challenge any future projections. Solar variation theory suggests that there is a correlation between solar cycles and major climate change on Earth, including recent global warming trends.[7] However, while the solar cycle accounts for around half the temperature rise since 1900, it cannot explain a rise of 0.4°C since 1980 – which suggests the impact of the Greenhouse Effect.[8]

Scientific debate hinges primarily on the net impact of greenhouse gas emissions in warming the atmosphere and to what extent climate feedbacks such as water vapours and clouds might or might not cancel them out. Yet no climate model has been produced that does not predict that atmospheric temperatures will rise in the future. However, some have proposed that any global warming is within the range of natural variation, so needs no explanation, or that the atmosphere is only warming in contrast to the previous cool period of the Little Ice Age. Some even suggest that global warming is not occurring at all.[9]

The Kyoto Protocol, part of the United Nations' Framework Convention on Climate Change, which had been agreed in 1997, came into force on 16 February 2005 in a bid to stall climate change.[10] The Kyoto Protocol was a major step forward internationally in signatory countries' recognizing the need to act on climate change. Its aim was to make thirty-nine signatory countries of the developed world commit to reducing their greenhouse gas emissions – particularly atmospheric carbon dioxide (CO_2) from vehicle emissions and industry – to legally binding limits of 5.2 per cent below 1990 levels by 2012. A year on, 160 parties had ratified the treaty.

While influential nations including the United Kingdom, Russia and Japan signed, neither the USA nor Australia did, citing economic harm. In the meantime, the USA remains the world's biggest polluter, while Australia's population produces a staggering 30 per cent more CO_2 emissions per capita than the USA. (However, Dubai in the United Arab Emirates overshadows such environmental harm by its over-development of millions of air-conditioned holiday apartments, and by building ski-runs and golf courses in the desert, for example.)

The economies of Western countries have benefited substantially from long-term investment in fossil fuel burning, so unless they reduce their own emissions and lead by example, it will remain difficult to convince developing countries that they should do so too. In fact, the global South's historic contribution to greenhouse gas emissions has been small, and at a per capita level still remains well below that of developed countries.

Many environmentalists regarded the cited reduction targets as too low to make any major impact. If the global average warming reached 2°C, millions of people around the world would face increased risks of hunger, malaria, or flooding, while billions of people would not have enough water.[11]

To avoid a 2°C temperature rise, scientists have calculated that concentration levels of CO_2 in the atmosphere must remain below 500 parts per million (ppm), and ultimately return below 400 ppm (according to Sir Nicholas Stern's report on the economics of climate change, published October 2006, the level stands at 382 ppm[12]). This would require global carbon dioxide levels to be cut by half by 2050, meaning the world's industrialized nations would need to cut theirs by 80 per cent. A concentration of 550 ppm, the upper stabilizing level cited in the Stern report,[13] has in fact a 68–99 per cent chance of exceeding the 2°C threshold.[14]

A year after the Kyoto Protocol came into force, it was noted that governments were behind on actions necessary to meet the legally binding targets of 2012. Emissions from Italy, Canada and Austria were all rising.[15]

In November 2006, The UN Climate Change Conference met in Nairobi in a bid to thrash out a more stringent treaty than Kyoto that would also take account of such rapidly industrializing countries as India and China, and support developing countries adapting to the impact of climate change.[16] Yet

> *'If we have any hope of keeping temperature increases under control while we still have time, governments around the world must do more to improve energy efficiency, clean up our use of fossil fuels and invest more in sustainable, safe renewables.'*
>
> CATHERINE PEARCE,
> FRIENDS OF THE EARTH INTERNATIONAL

its failure to produce a plan to agree a global target for reducing greenhouse gas emissions, or an adequate timetable to reach agreement on cuts displayed a 'staggering complacency', suggested Andy Atkins, Advocacy Director of UK Christian relief and development agency Tearfund. He said:

'We are limping along the road to adequate global CO_2 emissions cuts when giant steps are needed. The emissions cuts agreed under the first phase of the Kyoto Protocol were what countries thought they could manage, not what the world needed. The same must not happen in the second phase.'[17]

Poisoning the Atmosphere

While water vapour and CO_2 are the leading naturally occurring greenhouse gases, the phenomenon of global warming is largely the result of human activities, which both add to existing greenhouse gases, and contribute entirely new ones. Carbon dioxide emissions get an especially bad press for their contribution to global warming, but far more potent chemical substances

The Greenhouse Effect

For many people, 'Greenhouse Effect' is a term primarily associated with negative connotations of atmospheric pollution and artificial heating. Yet in reality, the Greenhouse Effect is the benign maintenance of the Earth's temperature via appropriate levels of water vapour, carbon dioxide (CO_2) and other gases in the atmosphere. Like a greenhouse, the atmosphere lets solar (short-wave) radiation shine through to warm the planet, and absorbs thermal (long-wave) radiation from the Earth's surface. Without the Greenhouse Effect, the long-term annual average temperature would be 32°C lower than at present[18] – that is, about -18°C[19] – and the oceans would freeze.

Greenhouse warming (a term that, in recent years, has become interchangeable with 'global warming') occurs when concentrations of greenhouse gases such as carbon dioxide, methane, chlorofluorocarbons (CFCs) and water vapour increase above natural atmospheric levels. It was the 1903 Nobel Laureate, Swedish chemist Svante Arrhenius, who, by measuring infrared absorption of CO_2 in an attempt to explain ice ages, calculated that increases in greenhouse gas concentration would result in higher global mean temperatures, and decreases would lead to lower global mean temperatures.[20]

Controversy regarding greenhouse warming relates to how the recognized rise in greenhouse gases due to human activity might merge with or obstruct measurement of natural cyclical changes in the Earth's climate or of contributors to global temperatures such as volcanoes or the El Niño phenomenon.

have exacerbated the problem. Not only is HFC123a, used in car air conditioning systems, the leading non-natural greenhouse gas, but it is more powerful on a molecule per molecule basis by a factor of ten thousand than CO_2.[21] Methane (CH_4) is almost as abundant in the atmosphere as CO_2 but is approximately twenty times as potent in its ability to foster global warming.[22] However, methane has a lifespan of twelve years compared to carbon dioxide's longevity of over a century, while greenhouse gas SF_6, the compound notably used in air cushion-soled trainers as well as the electrical industry, remains in the atmosphere for 53,000 years.[23] The world's livestock – the fastest growing agricultural sector – generates more greenhouse gas emissions than transport; 18 per cent as measured in CO_2 emissions. Livestock generates 65 per cent of human-related nitrous oxide (N_2O), a greenhouse gas 296 times as warming as CO_2, while it accounts for 37 per cent of all human-induced methane, and 64 per cent of ammonia, which contributes significantly to acid rain.[24]

As with carbon dioxide levels, the amount of methane in the atmosphere significantly increased with Britain's Industrial Revolution. Today, about two-thirds of that produced is from synthetic sources such as the extraction and transport of fossil fuels, and accidentally while drilling for natural gas, as well as from cattle ranching. Natural levels of atmospheric CH_4 are affected by phenomena like the El Niño ocean current and volcanic eruptions – such as Krakatoa, Mount St Helens and, potentially, the US's mega-volcano in the heart of Yellowstone Park – so vary annually.

As global methane levels had apparently stabilized since the 1990s, scientists and environmentalists emphasized the need to curb CO_2 emissions. A 2006 research study, however, indicated that the apparent levelling off of methane in the atmosphere was due to both draining and climate change drying out the world's wetlands, one of the major natural sources of CH_4, during the 1990s.[25] Decomposition of organic matter injects methane into the air, though it quickly breaks down. But methane production from this source plummeted. Unfortunately, this masked the vast increase in man-made contributions, particularly those that resulted from the Asian economic boom in China and India.

Whether or not the world's wetlands can recover, atmospheric levels of CH_4 are likely to rise simply because of the increasing human demand for energy, meat and milk across the world. Additionally, a rise in ocean temperatures in line with global warming is likely to enable the release into the atmosphere of once-frozen natural methane, or clathrates, previously stockpiled beneath the ocean floor. By heating up and reverting to gas its volume increases dramatically, forcing it through the seabed to potentially devastating effect – such as initiating a tsunami – but more significantly raising atmospheric temperatures by 1°C. The world's clathrates have been calculated to contain the equivalent of as much as 12 trillion tonnes of carbon – or double the carbon content of remaining global reserves of oil and coal.[26] The melting of Siberia's permafrost, site of the world's largest frozen peat bog, could produce a warming effect greater than the United States' man-made emissions of carbon dioxide.[27]

Controlling Greenhouse Gas Emissions

According to a 2006 UN report, a turn-around in the previous economic slow-down in Russia and the former communist states, which accounted for most of the 5.6 per cent decrease in greenhouse gas emissions from 1990 to 2000, sent global emissions up again.

The UNFCCC's 2006 'Greenhouse Gas Data' report states that total emissions from forty-one developed nations rose 2.4 per cent between 2000 and 2004, while former Soviet bloc countries together saw an emissions increase of 4.1 per cent during the same period.[28] As well as carbon dioxide, emissions of methane, nitrogen dioxide and other pollutants had all increased. According to Yvo de Boer, UNFCCC executive secretary, 'This means that industrialised countries will need to intensify their efforts to implement strong policies which reduce greenhouse gas emissions.'[29]

The UN data did not include fast-industrializing nations such as China, India and Brazil, so figures will have been underestimated for the global whole.[30] The report indicated that the US remained the world's most polluting nation, having increased its emissions by 15.4 per cent between 1990 and 2004,

Global Warming

Global warming technically refers to the scientific observation that, especially since the nineteenth century, the average temperature of the Earth's atmosphere and oceans has risen and continues to rise, regardless of the cause. The term has become synonymous in most people's minds with greenhouse gases, especially CO_2, produced only by human activity, notably the burning of fossil fuels and deforestation. However, the emphasis placed on *carbon* emissions can detract from the contribution of other greenhouse gases, such as methane – whether naturally produced from marshes or from landfill sites – to global warming.

There has been conflict over the issue of global warming. Notably, representatives of industry, especially those related to oil production, have questioned climate models and whether the atmospheric rise in temperatures is human-induced. Yet global warming is already impacting the planet. Droughts and deserts are spreading, crops are failing, fresh water is diminishing and millions of people will be forced to migrate to survive. Water resource management and agricultural planning based on sound research on global warming will prove increasingly vital as climate change takes effect.

and the transport sector was given special focus since it had produced 23.9 per cent more emissions in 2004 than in 1990.[31]

Airlines are notably contributing to greenhouse gas-fuelled climate change. In the UK, the growth in aviation emissions is set to cancel out reductions in all other sectors if its development remains unchecked.[32] While the European Union is intent on incorporating the airline industry into its Emissions Trading Scheme (ETS) to counter its environmental impact, this policy reveals the limitations of many of the carbon control initiatives.

The ETS would enable airlines to buy their right to emit CO_2 from other industries. However, not all CO_2 emissions are created equal; aircraft emissions happen to be between two and four times more damaging to the climate than those from other industries. The altitude at which they are emitted makes them particularly damaging, and condensation trails and nitrogen oxide contribute too. Additionally the necessary high demand for emission permits would likely put pressure on the ETS from other industries to relax controls and the overall cap on emissions.[33] Airlines not only need to pay for their emissions, but reduce them year-on-year.

In September 2006, Sir Richard Branson, chairman of Virgin, who owns five airlines and is developing space tourism, pledged £1.6bn (US$3bn) to his own investment unit, Virgin Fuels, to research renewable energy, and in particular fund biofuel development from corn.[34] Yet on the same day, the US Department of Energy announced that, with alternative fuels only at a level of 2.5 per cent in the States, it would have to revise its target of 30 per cent of cars running on alternative fuels by 2010 to 2030.[35]

Massive biofuel production has its own environmental costs. It lowers the water table, and, as a monoculture, destroys biodiversity. Large-scale corn cultivation demands industrial levels of processing and transportation. It also requires large swathes of land, and so is likely to make vast inroads into the developing world's rainforests.

'There is new and stronger evidence that most of the warming observed over the last 50 years is attributable to human activities.'

INTERGOVERNMENTAL PANEL ON CLIMATE CHANGE

As with such apparently Green innovations as electric cars, nuclear power and carbon sequestering (where, for example, CO_2 is injected into sandstone) there is in reality a negative environmental impact. Electric cars are clean on the road but rely on power stations for their fuel; nuclear power depends on the limited supply of mined uranium; and carbon sequestering demands that carbon remain permanently isolated from the atmosphere and that it not be dislodged, say, by seismic activity.

Similarly, carbon offsetting also creates a false sense of security. Carbon offsetting is a method of compensating for carbon emissions in which an individual or organization's so-called 'carbon footprint' (the total carbon emissions expended in any given activity) is calculated and, for example, trees are planted to absorb that carbon, deeming the activity apparently 'carbon neutral'. However, it does not necessarily encourage a group or individual to be any less careful in how they live their life, and has been likened to giving money to an animal charity while continuing to kick one's dog.

An alternative would be to reduce industrialized nations' carbon emissions, while investing in the previously under-funded research and development of a combination of renewable energies such as solar, wave and wind power, and geo-thermal energy.

The Ozone Layer
Without the protective ozone layer in the stratosphere wrapping itself around the planet and acting as a sunlight filter, our nearest star's harmful UV rays would cause major damage to life on Earth. In fact, it is those very UV rays hitting the stratosphere at around 20 km (12.4 miles) from the planet that create the layer, splitting oxygen (O_2) molecules into two atoms. When either atom joins with another oxygen molecule, ozone (O_3) is created. Yet if O_3 joins with an oxygen atom, it will revert to two oxygen molecules.

There are two types of ozone depletion chemistry. Homogeneous depletion results from atmospheric gases mixing together and causes a reduction in global ozone levels. Heterogeneous depletion, on the other hand, is specifically that which occurs every spring over Antarctica owing to its meteorology.[36] According to the US Environmental Protection Agency (EPA), 'The ozone hole is the most obvious effect of the release of ozone-depleting substances into the atmosphere, and it is also the most extreme example of ozone depletion. However, the long-term downward trends in ozone levels over most of the globe also pose a serious threat. Although not as spectacular, homogeneous chemistry is a significant problem.'[37]

O_3 molecules are especially damaged by synthetic chlorofluorocarbon (CFC) pollutants containing chlorine and bromine. Initially believed to be safe and inert, these gases were put to widespread use in refrigeration systems, aerosols, air conditioners and solvents, but it was when they were released into the atmosphere that they were discovered to be a severe pollutant. In parts of the world, such as both Poles, where the ozone layer is at its thinnest because of the damage caused by CFCs, marine life suffers, and there is an increased risk of severe sunburn, skin cancer, damage to the immune system and cataracts.

Although the Montreal Protocol curtailed their worldwide use back in 1987, CFCs – and other chemicals such as nitrogen oxides and bromines – take a long time to break down so remain in the atmosphere; since the late 1990s, the amount of O_3 in the Earth's atmosphere has dropped by 0.3 per cent.[38] Signatories of the protocol agreed to reduce their emissions of CFCs to half of 1987 levels by 2000, and their usage was to a large extent effectively banned and successfully phased out. CFCs were to be phased out from signatory developing countries by 2010.[39] However, there was little incentive for non-signatory countries, and countless refrigeration and air conditioning systems containing CFCs needed to be disposed of correctly to avoid further ozone layer depletion.

Scientists at the British Antarctic Survey point out that without the Montreal Protocol, the state of the ozone hole would be far worse than at present. According to Jonathan Shanklin, one of the original discoverers of the ozone hole:

'This agreement shows us that global action by governments to stop the release of ozone depleting chemicals really can help society to successfully mitigate a global environmental problem. We are still experiencing large losses of Antarctic ozone each spring because CFCs and other chemicals live for a long time in our atmosphere. However, the ban ensures that we will see an improvement in the future. We now need to take similar actions to control greenhouse gases, otherwise we will bequeath future generations a significantly different climate from that of today.'[40]

Slowly, the ozone layer *is* recovering: it is expected to return to pre-1980 levels over all landmasses except Antarctica by 2049. Over Antarctica, it will take until 2065 to reach similar levels.[41] However, this does depend on the continuing effectiveness of both present and future regulations regarding CFCs and their replacements.

Additionally, the impact of climate change could jeopardize any environmental progress made; for example, ozone thinning would be exacerbated by long-term cooling of the stratosphere. While greenhouse gases warm the Earth's surface temperatures, they cool temperatures in the lower stratosphere, ultimately encouraging the formation of polar stratospheric clouds which promote ozone depletion.[42] Ironically, while not damaging the ozone level, hydrofluorocarbons (HFCs) – the CFC substitutes now widely used as propellants and refrigerants – are themselves potent greenhouse gases.[43]

Acid Rain

Although volcanoes are a significant source of acid rain, industrial pollution also contributes greatly to its occurrence. It is created by the burning of fossil fuels, and in particular from the gases produced from vehicle exhausts, but industrial processes such as the smelting of non-ferrous metals annually release an estimated six million tonnes of sulphur dioxide into the atmosphere. Pollutants such as sulphur dioxide (SO_2) and nitrogen oxide (NO) are absorbed and diluted to fall in rain, sleet or snow as nitric and sulphuric acid.

Acid rain corrodes buildings made from carbonate stone – but it has a far wider and decimating impact on natural habitats. It damages and kills trees and

Stripped bare: acid rain-ravaged pine trees provide evidence of atmospheric pollution over the Karkonosze National Park in Silesia, Poland.

plants, and lowers the pH level of the water it enters, killing life in streams and lakes. Although acid rain does not directly harm humans, the pollutant gases that cause it interact in the atmosphere to form sulphate and nitrate particles, which exacerbate lung conditions and heart disease.[44] In addition, acid rain, along with ozone depletion, drought and ultraviolet radiation, has been linked to the decline of North American songbirds,[45] and a worldwide reduction in amphibians;[46] both the waters where they spawn and grow into adulthood, and the surrounding damp land are damaged.

Neither is acid rain a respecter of national boundaries. As Japan, neighbour of China, is now discovering, the rain does not necessarily fall in the polluting country. During the 1980s, northern European countries suffered extensively from acid rain. In the United Kingdom, the Clean Air Act of 1968 – the successor to the 1956 act introduced in the wake of the smog crisis – resulted in the building of higher chimneys, which effectively exported the pollution to the Continent. The Scandinavian countries, Germany, Switzerland and Austria suffered greatly as their lakes became lifeless and forests dwindled. Blond hair was recorded to turn green when washed in the affected waters! Yet significant reductions were made in such pollution from 1990.[47]

Taking Action

1. Buy a telescope to enjoy space travel without polluting the atmosphere! Or join an astronomy club.

2. Make your own weather station. Access www.bbc.co.uk/weather/weatherwise/activities for guides to making your own equipment.

3. Contact the Royal Meteorological Society at www.royal-met-soc.org.uk to find out about international projects you can take part in, such as MetLink International.

4. For daily and dramatic images of ozone levels above both Poles, visit the National Oceanic and Atmospheric Association's (NOAA) 'Stratosphere: SBUV-2 Total Ozone' page at www.cpc.noaa.gov/products/stratosphere/sbuv2to/sbuv2to_latest.shtml .

5. For a useful overview of issues surrounding global warming and climate change, including a helpful introduction to relevant theories and climate models and a comprehensive bibliography, access http://dictionary.laborlawtalk.com/Global_warming . *Tiempo Climate Newswatch*, an authoritative weekly online magazine covering climate change and development, can be accessed at www.cru.uea.ac.uk/tiempo/newswatch .

6. Calculate your carbon footprint at www.carbonfootprint.com . Plant trees by all means, but do so via a reputable woodland organization or charity and remember that this will not offset your emissions. Instead, cut back on the energy you use in the first place.

The
Earth

'If we see the world as a superorganism of which we are a part – not the owner, nor the tenant, not even a passenger – we could have a long time ahead of us and our species might survive for its "alloted span". It all depends on you and me.'

JAMES LOVELOCK

CHAPTER 2

The Earth is the third planet from the sun, and is travelling at the speed of 108,000 km (67,000 miles) an hour.[1] Its total surface area amounts to 509 million sq km (almost 197 million sq miles), roughly 70 per cent of which is water and the remaining 30 per cent land.[2] Earth is the only planet in the solar system known unequivocally to harbour life.

Previous spread: Brooding presence: the Himalayan mountain range overshadows Indian, Nepali, and Tibetan lands.

Opposite: The rigid lithosphere beneath the Earth's crust is divided into massive floating tectonic plates on which the continents sit.

The Earth is shifting beneath our feet. The planet's outer crust to which we cling and depend for our very lives is in a constant state of flux. There are parts of the world, such as in Iceland, where you can watch the crust being newly created, although most takes place unseen on the ocean floor. Elsewhere the crust is dragged down in zones of subduction.

The motors driving such surface-level activity are the Earth's hub, a solid iron core heated to between 4,000 and 4,700°C (7,230 and 8,490°F) and its surrounding liquid outer core, the temperature of which ranges between 3,500 and 4,000°C (6,330 and 7,230°F). Such incredible heat is behind the movement of the Earth's mantle that lies beneath its crust. Cyclical convection currents flow upwards from the outer core through the mantle to beneath the crust, where they fall back towards the outer core.

The outer, rigid layer of mantle beneath the Earth's crust is the lithosphere, which is divided into massive tectonic plates on which the world's continents sit. The plates float atop the next layer of mantle, the semi-fluid asthenosphere. It is at the plate boundaries, as the broken lithosphere shifts and scrapes, where earthquakes occur and volcanoes have formed in specific regions around the planet. The 2004 Asian tsunami, for example, was caused by an earthquake in the Indian Ocean at a point beneath the sea where the African Plate grinds against the South Australian Plate.

Global warming only adds to the existing potential for global disaster. Rising sea levels, drought, lessened snow cover, melting glaciers and permafrost will have a dire effect on human populations and the very ecosystems on which they depend. Mass migration of species will occur; others will be endangered or become extinct, unable to adapt to the inevitable new conditions that will present themselves.

The poorer communities of the developing world are most at risk, since they do not have the resources to respond quickly and effectively to disaster. Relief agencies fear that any successes in development over previous decades will be completely undermined by climate change. It is estimated that by the end of this century, diseases such as malaria – their spread encouraged by global warming – could kill an extra 185 million people in sub-Saharan Africa. Additionally, the effects of climate change will cause tens of millions of people to go hungry as flooding, drought and unpredictable weather patterns take their toll on agricultural land, traditional pastures and communities.[3]

Disappearing off the Face of the Earth

Ours is a rich, vibrant, beautiful planet of deep variety. Yet as many as 37 per cent of terrestrial species could be facing extinction by 2050[4] – as well as habitats, landscapes and cultures, languages and people groups – much of it lost due to development. Already 80 per cent of the world's ancient forests have been destroyed or degraded.[5]

Hawaii holds the dubious distinction of being the extinction capital of the world. Over 75 per cent of the United States' extinctions have occurred there, and 25 per cent of its endangered species are located there – even though Hawaii takes up only 0.2 per cent of the nation's land area.[6] There are 282 endangered and ten threatened native plant species alone listed under the US Endangered Species Act.[7] Many of its flora and fauna species are unique to the island and so are especially vulnerable to dying out. As in the Galapagos Islands, it is alien species such as pigs, goats and weeds that prove the greatest threat since they can damage entire ecosystems. Conservation of large areas of ecosystem is the most effective means of protecting individual species.

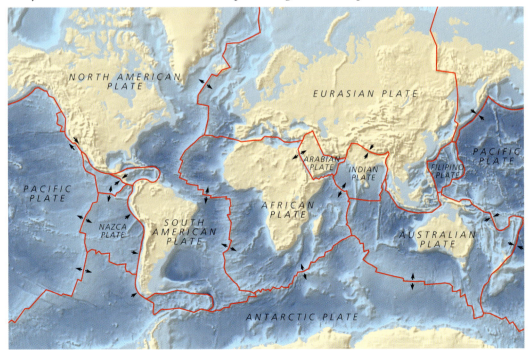

The loss of species and habitats is not simply a sad fact, nor is it secondary to our own species' survival. Quorum sensing is the phenomenon whereby a species dropping below a certain population size no longer is able to cooperate and repel attackers. There is effectively a loss of will to survive, and breeding no longer occurs. A species of fauna is therefore doomed long before the last pair remains.[8] Additionally, the knowledge of scarcity and, ultimately, extinction has a dampening effect on the human psyche: people invariably feel angry, powerless or disheartened, as Robert Trigger describes:

James Lovelock and the Gaia Theory

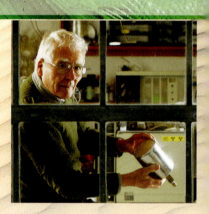

Born in 1919, James Lovelock studied Chemistry at Manchester University, and gained a PhD in Medicine at the London School of Hygiene and Tropical Medicine. Following research at Yale, Baylor and Harvard universities in the United States, he went on to develop scientific instruments for NASA's programme of planetary exploration. Among his inventions is the Electron Capture Detector, the development of which contributed to understanding CFCs and their role in ozone depletion.

While working with NASA in the 1960s, scientist Lovelock originated his Gaia hypothesis. Naming it after the Greek goddess of the Earth as suggested by novelist William Golding, Lovelock proposed that this planet, rather than being effectively a rock spinning in space, was in essence a living, self-regulating organism. With American microbiologist Lynn Margulis he co-authored a paper on the theory in 1973.[10] Not until an article referring to the Gaia hypothesis was published in *New Scientist* in 1975[11] did Lovelock's theory gain peer recognition. Lovelock's groundbreaking 1979 book explaining his theory, *Gaia – A New Look at Life on Earth*,[12] remains a classic in the field.

The Gaia Theory proposes that the Earth is a finely tuned superorganism consisting of the entire natural world. The planet's physical, chemical and biological processes interact with each other in order to maintain the optimum conditions for life. There is also a global control system consisting of surface temperature, atmosphere composition and ocean salinity. Lovelock deduced this from the constancy of the Earth's global surface temperature in spite of an increase in the sun's energy; the constancy of atmospheric composition when it should by right be unstable; and the constancy of ocean salinity.[13]

At the First Gaia Conference in 1988,[14] Lovelock took pains to stress that Gaia was no conscious force, as some had misinterpreted – and so it ensued that the

'It's possible to rationalise endlessly, but that doesn't deal with this issue: extinction gets us down. It diminishes us to know that living things are dying out, that diversity is being replaced by homogeneity. Perhaps in some grand scheme of things we are all connected, we are quorum sensitive to all of life, so that the disappearance of diversity makes us just that bit less intelligent, flexible, human.'[9]

The human delight in variety should be the spur to protect difference.

Gaia hypothesis was theoretically acceptable to the scientific community. The hypothesis developed into the Gaia Theory, and eventually Gaia Science, when it became clear that a range of approaches and modifications was emerging and needed to be clarified.

The Gaia Theory as a form of Earth system science that takes account of interactions between biota, oceans, the geosphere and the atmosphere has not been accepted uncritically by all scientists. Because natural selection acts on individual species, they argue, a planetary level of homeostasis is not possible. In 1983, Lovelock developed a model, the Daisyworld simulation,[15] to challenge this.

Lovelock's 2006 book, *The Revenge of Gaia*,[16] investigates how the planet-wide system has been forced out of kilter by both human overproduction of greenhouse gases and by human instigation of other environmental crises. In its attempt to regain equilibrium, Gaia is likely to threaten the survival of the human race: the global crisis will involve rising temperatures, a decline in available water, the dying of oceans, a decrease in food production and mass human migration.

Controversially, as an environmentalist Lovelock supports the development of nuclear energy as a clean, immediate alternative to the burning of fossil fuels if energy supplies are to be maintained. He also desires an end to the destruction of natural habitats that are key to planetary climate and chemistry in order that global warming might be halted. Otherwise, he contends, by the end of this century billions of people will have died, and those who remain will only survive in the Arctic's then-tolerable climate.[17]

'The self-regulation of climate and chemical composition is a process that emerges from the rightly coupled evolution of rocks, air and the ocean – in addition to that of organisms. Such interlocking self-regulation, while rarely optimal – consider the cold and hot places of the Earth, the wet and the dry – nevertheless keeps the Earth a place fit for life.'

JAMES LOVELOCK

Our Future World

Environmental degradation makes especial impact on the human race. According to Kofi Annan, former Secretary General of the United Nations:

'Climate change has profound implications for virtually all aspects of human well-being, from jobs and health to food security and peace within and among nations. Yet too often, climate change is seen as an environmental problem when it should be part of the broader development and economic agenda. Until we acknowledge the all-encompassing nature of the threat, our response will fall short.'[18]

Globally, an estimated 25 million environmental refugees are now fleeing storms, droughts and impending rising sea levels, including the Pacific population of Tegua, which is threatened by sea-level rise; Mexicans who are illegally entering the US due to the combined pressures of poverty and drought; and New Orleans' residents, who were forced to evacuate their homes due to Hurricane Katrina. It is difficult to calculate their numbers as they are not listed in official figures and in general are not covered by refugee conventions or agreements.[19]

> *'There will be millions more thirsty, hungry and ill poor people living in high-risk areas of the world by the end of the century. It makes sense politically, economically and morally, for governments to act with urgency now.'*
>
> TEARFUND'S 'FEELING THE HEAT' REPORT

As climate change continues to take hold, and, for example, coastal towns and countries across the world are swallowed by the sea, hundreds of millions of people will have to move or die. It is this human drama played out around the world that will prove to be one of the major knock-on effects of global warming.[20] The sheer logistics of dealing with all these desperate people, and the pressure their influx places on the states into which they pour, will urgently need to be addressed – concerns expressed in Tearfund's 2006 'Feeling the Heat' report.[21]

As well as the need for international action against global warming, financial billions must be committed to helping states adapt to its impending effects. Many of the states that are likely to be most affected by the problem are those suffering the effects of others' over-consumption: the world's poorest people living in the global South.

Hundreds of millions of people, especially those living in places where water is already limited, will face starvation and displacement as drought spreads across the globe as a result of climate change. Agriculture on poor soils, such as the small-scale farming reliant on rainfall that dominates the developing world, will be unsustainable, and the availability of fresh water will prove negligible to the extent that human and wildlife populations will have to migrate or die. At the end of the twentieth century, a quarter of the planet

Clinging to the edge: resourceful Chinese farmers will see their terraced rice crops decline as the atmosphere warms and mountain run-off evaporates more quickly.

experienced moderate drought. Temperature and rainfall projections of the UK's Meteorological Office Hadley Centre for Climate Prediction and Research indicate that half of the world's surface will suffer drought by 2100, and a third of the land above water could be desert, whereas currently it covers 3 per cent of the Earth's surface.[22] Yet the study still did not include the potential effects of drought made by global warming-induced changes to the Earth's carbon cycle.[23]

Already drought is affecting the world's wheat prices as harvests have declined in Australia, Argentina and Brazil; they soared 54 per cent in a year on the Chicago Board of Trade.[24] According to the United Nations' Food and Agriculture Organisation (FAO), forty countries faced food shortages in 2006, and extreme weather conditions cut the expected cereal harvest by 5 per cent. In South Asia dry weather raised concerns about the paddy crop. Projections that the global food harvest was down 8 million tonnes in six months caused the FAO to call for closer monitoring of the world food situation, and fears were expressed that stock levels would become even more precarious should weather problems prevent an increase in world cereal production in 2007.[25]

Seeking pastures new: valuable livestock and crops have been lost to long-term drought in the Horn of Africa, and have made millions of people dependent on food aid.

Such pressures on world harvests raise questions about any shift towards growing biofuels to replace fossil fuels in order to combat climate change and support increased economic growth, especially for the world's wealthier industrialized nations. Viable land is limited and will be increasingly scarce. The biofuel industry will be competing with migrating people for the same land.

Yet the need for fresh water will prove even more vital. Frighteningly, the amount of fresh water on the planet amounts to less than 1 per cent of all H_2O on Earth (the rest is either sea water or frozen as polar and glacial ice), and even that is declining due to pollution and run-off into the sea. Fresh water comes as rain; around 40,000–50,000 cu km (9,500–12,000 cu miles) fall per year, yet globally water consumption is doubling every twenty years; by 2025 the fresh water demand is predicted to rise 56 per cent *above* the amount currently available.[26]

Water scarcity will force water source ownership up the political agenda. Already, World Bank pressure on governments to privatize water and sanitation systems has priced the poor out of the treated water market. In Bolivia, when Cochabamba's supply and sanitation system was leased to private companies, water bills rose up to 300 per cent, with low income families spending a quarter of their money on water. Consequent civil unrest led the government to cancel contracts and renationalize the services.[27]

In a special report issued by the International Forum on Globalization (2001), Maude Barlow states:

> *'The wars of the next century will be about water.'*
>
> ISMAIL SERAGELDIN, VICE PRESIDENT OF THE WORLD BANK

'The time has come to take a clear and principled stand to stop the systematic devastation of the world's water systems. In the long term, nation-states have to be re-tooled in order to establish the regulations and protections necessary to save their water systems. International law must be developed that recognises and enforces the social obligations of global capital in the interests of the global "water commons". Most important, the citizens of planet Earth must move, and quickly, if we are to save it.'[28]

What in the World can be Done?

An international problem demands an international solution. Small, individual actions are the right thing to do, but the belief that they are making any major impact on a global phenomenon is misguided. In the UK, for example, carbon emissions amount to 2 per cent of the world's total;[29] an individual or small percentage of the 60 million population acting Greenly at home is only going to make a negligible difference to the planetary whole.

However, by uniting with others via conservation and environmental groups and campaigning for change at national and international levels, great strides can be made. Authors Mark Lynas[30] and James Lovelock[31] make considered proposals for national and international campaigns in their

Close to home:
developed
countries are not
immune to
flooding from
severe weather
patterns and sea-
level rise caused
by climate
change.

respective books on climate change. A country like Britain, for example, which is especially influential as a member of the G8 group of industrialized nations, can encourage development and innovation in alternative energies and technologies, and export that expertise to countries with fast-growing economies such as China and India, which are overproducing greenhouse gas emissions.

To slow climate change and eventually stabilize the climate, global emissions of greenhouse gases would have to be reduced to well below 1990 levels; that is, by at least 60–80 per cent over the next few decades. Environmental commentator George Monbiot has calculated that a 90 per cent cut in rich nations' emissions by 2030 is the only target that stands any chance of averting catastrophe.[32] This requires action on a global scale. The Kyoto Protocol was never designed to do that; a far more effective solution is needed.

So, it is important to remain vigilant. Representatives of 189 countries attended a November 2006 summit in Nairobi to determine post-Kyoto policy; Andrew Pendleton, climate change policy adviser for development agency Christian Aid, derided the meeting as 'a frighteningly timid response to a significant global problem'. He continued:

'The lack of vision and leadership has been staggering. Although the deal is no disaster and demonstrates that the UN Framework Convention on Climate Change is the place where climate negotiations can hold together, unless there is a seismic shift in ambition between now and 2007, we will have to conclude that our current crop of politicians is not up to the challenge. This must be the last of these talks at which there is no clear mandate for negotiating the level of cuts in emissions that the science now tells us are necessary.'[33]

That is not to say that at an international level environmental issues are not receiving due attention and action. The United Nations Environment Programme has, over the decades, drafted a range of conventions relating to environmental issues.[34] The Millennium Ecosystem Assessment[35] in 2001 drew together 1,300 experts from ninety-five countries to conduct an ongoing comprehensive evaluation of the world's major ecosystems. And 2007–08's International Polar Year[36] will bring into stark focus the severe impact of climate change on the Arctic and Antarctic – and what that means for the rest of the world.

Taking Action

1. What in your own life do you see threatened with extinction: a craft, a social activity, a local habitat or a favourite building? Consider what you might do to prevent its demise.

2. Spend a day identifying how much use you make of petrochemicals (substances produced from petroleum or natural gas) in the shape of fabrics, plastics, fuel and so on.

3. To develop an appreciation of all that farmed land has to offer – and the chain of labour involved from planting and harvesting to consuming – regularly cook a meal from basic ingredients. Grow your own too, even if it's only herbs on a windowsill.

4. If you can afford to, become a shareholder and press for a company's environmental and social accountability here and abroad.

5. Is your car journey really necessary? Reduce your car use and travel by public transport instead. For short journeys, try walking or cycling. Also, holiday in your own country and avoid flying, or savour the view from the window and travel overland by train.

6. Keep up to date with the Intergovernmental Panel on Climate Change's reports via their website at www.ipcc.ch/ .

The Oceans

'... the problems of ocean space
are closely interrelated and need
to be considered as a whole...'

PREAMBLE TO THE UNITED NATIONS
CONVENTION ON THE LAW OF THE SEA

CHAPTER 3

The World Ocean that spans the planet is divided into five interconnected oceans which, in descending order of size, are the Pacific, Atlantic, Indian, Southern (which completely surrounds Antarctica) and Arctic. (The Pacific and Atlantic, both being further divided into the North and South oceans, bring the total up to the poetic 'Seven Seas'.) Each of the oceans has its own seas, which are partly enclosed by land. The largest of these are the Caribbean, the Mediterranean and the South China seas.

Not for nothing has the Earth been called the 'blue planet'. Our human perception gives us the impression that we who live above water are in control. Yet a mere 29 per cent of the world is above sea level – and that area is set to shrink as the world continues to grow warmer, and thermal expansion of sea water and melting of polar ice caps cause sea levels to rise.

At the time of the earliest explorers, the so-called 'Seven Seas' that comprise the waters of the Earth referred to the then-charted and well-travelled bodies of water: the Indian Ocean, the Red Sea, the Persian Gulf, the Black Sea, the Sea of Azov, the Adriatic Sea and the Caspian Sea. Today, the oceans have been mapped, each separated by submarine ridges that limit the exchange of waters between an ocean and its neighbour. No doubt there are many discoveries yet to be made below the water, whether in unimagined new species able to exist at depths previously not believed possible,[1] microbial diversity[2] or sources of fuel and energy.

There are four types of motion by which the World Ocean circulates: surface and deep currents, which are powered by winds, solar radiation and the balance between evaporation and precipitation; tides, which are drawn by the gravitational attraction between the Earth and its moon; and tsunamis, which, powered by the planet's internal heat, force undersea earthquakes and landslips.[3] The Earth's rotation also plays a part in directing surface currents.

It is the ocean conveyer belt, known as thermohaline circulation, that is the prime force driving both the cold, salty deep currents and the warm shallow currents around the globe to sustain life below and above sea level. But global warming is threatening to bring the ocean conveyer belt to a grinding halt as the properties of the water are altered and the momentum for circulation is therefore lost. The Southern Hemisphere's oceans are projected

Previous spread: Paradise island: Huahine Island in French Polynesia is photogenically bordered by stunning lagoons and coral reefs.

Jacques Cousteau

Jacques Cousteau and his world-renowned ocean work were products of a modern, twentieth-century world. Born in France in 1910, he lived at a time when exploration of the world's watery denizens was in its infancy. As a member of the French Navy, he created underwater housing for a movie camera, and in 1943, with Emile Gagnon, co-invented a breathing regulator to be developed into the Aqualung or SCUBA (Self-Contained Underwater Breathing Apparatus). This proved instrumental in enabling the Allies to remove enemy mines from international waters after the war. Cousteau also developed a one-person, jet-propelled submarine, and the first underwater diving station.

In 1948, Cousteau purchased the minesweeper *Calypso* to convert into an ocean-going research vessel and yacht for the express purpose of marine exploration. Due to his award-winning documentaries about the sea, the ship almost became a personality in its own right. In 1956, he received an Academy Award for his documentary *The Silent World*, but it was in particular the television series *The Undersea World of Jacques Cousteau*, which ran from 1968 to 1976, that brought him worldwide recognition and acclaim. He also published many books about the oceans.

It was through the relatively young medium of television that he proved instrumental in opening up the undersea world to human study and appreciation for a worldwide audience otherwise unfamiliar with the treasures of the deep. The broadcast of the documentaries coincided with the burgeoning environmental awareness of the Sixties and Seventies. Cousteau's focus on the world of the deep drew people's attention to the particular threats faced by the marine environment and aquatic life forms, especially from human encroachment.

In 1973, he founded the Cousteau Society to raise finances for ocean exploration, research and conservation. Other ships, *Calypso II* and *Alysone* joined and eventually replaced the original *Calypso* to carry out further research voyages and encourage environmentalism.

Although Cousteau died in 1997, aged eighty-seven, his work continues through the Cousteau Society. It continues to produce the documentary series *The Discovery of the World*, which he launched in 1986. The society aims to help educate people about the environment so that they, in turn, might pressure governments to act positively. It also organizes voyages that provide marine research opportunities for conservation groups.

to become warmer. The Gulf Stream that edges Europe will weaken because of these changes, leading to a cooling of the landmass.

The fish and other creatures that depend on the sea are vulnerable to these changes in circulation patterns and water temperatures. Without thermohaline circulation, according to Professor Jack Matthews, former director of the Scottish Association for Marine Science, 'the oceans would become deserts, and there would be no replenishment of nutrients at the surface and no oxygen reaching the deep; there could be complete stagnation'.[4]

But marine life is also prey to human exploitation. Fisheries are being stripped bare by a combination of modern fishing techniques and an increasing demand for more exotic species. Additionally, the chemical composition of the oceans is changing and threatening ocean ecosystems.

'Jacques Cousteau may well have done more than anyone in history to educate mankind about the wonders of our underwater world, and to inspire entire generations with his never-ending quest to study and protect our planet's largest and most unexplored frontier.'

NATIONAL WILDLIFE FEDERATION
CONSERVATION HALL OF FAME

Low levels of dissolved oxygen, known as hypoxia, a phenomenon predominantly caused by nitrates from agricultural runoff and pollution, are leading to significant 'dead zones' throughout the world's oceans. Such areas lack sufficient oxygen to sustain most marine life. Those species that do survive are often weakened and more susceptible to predators. Embryonic fish are also affected by the nitrates and pollutants, changing sex and therefore resulting in more male fish; consequently, the species is unable to reproduce itself. According to UNEP, the number of such dead zones increased from 149 in 2004 to 200 in 2006.[5]

In addition, the world's oceans are becoming more acidic as atmospheric levels of carbon dioxide increase, much of which is absorbed by sea water to form a dilute carbonic acid. Carbon dioxide is naturally absorbed through photosynthesis by the phytoplankton that live on the water's surface. The phytoplankton in turn are eaten by zooplankton, the animal plankton, some of which (such as foraminifera) secrete shells. When the zooplankton die, their shells fall towards the sea floor, and the carbon that is locked in the shell in the form of calcium carbonate is then sequestered in the seabed sediment. However, if the ocean becomes more acidic the shell may actually dissolve on its way down or may not be secreted in the first place, so a very important carbon sink (disposing, we believe, of half the excess CO_2 emitted by man) will be completely lost. Apart from accelerating global warming, this will also cause disastrous changes to the marine ecology of the planet.[6] Coral, for example, is at extreme risk as sea water pH levels fall from the present pH of 8 to a predicted, more acidic pH of 7.4.[7]

Seas have risen 15 cm (6 in) in the past century, a rate ten times faster than the average of the last 2,000 years. Within this century, waters are predicted to rise by as much as 88 cm (35 in) as warmer temperatures cause the thermal expansion of oceans and melting glaciers release their pent-up water into the sea,[8] although the seas have been found to be rising faster than predicted.[9] With over a third of the world's population now living within 100 km (62 miles) of a shoreline, and thirteen of the world's twenty largest cities located on a coast, at some point they will need to take stock of rising sea levels.[10]

It is not merely the sheer *amount* of rising sea water that causes problems. Its salt water contaminates any freshwater habitats it encounters, destroying fragile ecosystems. It pollutes groundwater, destroying crops and the roots of coastal trees and grasses that bind vulnerable lands and prevent them from being washed away during seasonal storms. Human populations see their property and livelihoods wrecked as the encroaching water takes its toll, necessitating mass migration of communities to higher ground, which places further pressure on diminishing land area.

Ocean Circulation

The system of thermohaline circulation, also known as the ocean conveyer belt, draws oxygen down to the depths of the ocean and directs warm water from the Tropics towards both Poles.[11]

The surface-level stream of warm water is the world's longest river,

Thermohaline circulation – otherwise known as the ocean conveyer belt – directs warm water from the Tropics to both Poles and delivers oxygen to the ocean depths.

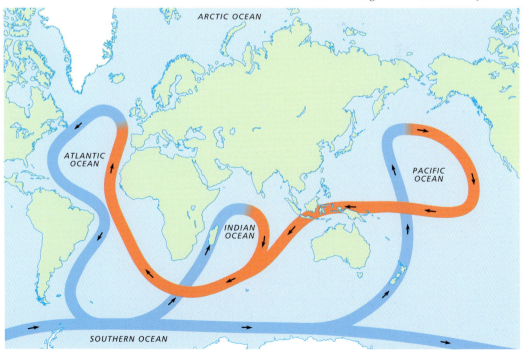

snaking its way from the Pacific Ocean, past northern Australia and around Africa's Cape of Good Hope towards the Atlantic, where it becomes the Gulf Stream. The warm water gradually evaporates on its journey and loses heat to the European landmass, and as it grows colder it becomes more salty and dense. North of Iceland, it sinks, propelling the global conveyer belt and flowing back toward the Pacific along the ocean floor until it rises to the surface again to repeat its global circulation.[12]

The flow of the North Atlantic Ocean's Gulf Stream around the edge of northern Europe perhaps best exemplifies the inherent value of the ocean's water circulation to species living on land. It is this current of warm water, heated at the Tropics by the sun, that pushes the winter temperature of countries – including the United Kingdom – between 9 and 18° higher than that of comparable latitudes elsewhere. (The UK, for example, shares its latitude with Canada's very chilly Labrador peninsula.) Averaged over a year, the Gulf Stream provides Western Europe with a third as much warmth as the sun does,[13] or the equivalent of one million power stations' worth of energy.[14]

Contrary to many people's understanding that global warming will increase atmospheric temperatures – though initially this appears to be the case with evidence of species from warmer climates moving northwards – for those states dependent on such warming currents, the complete opposite could occur. As the northern polar ice melts, fresh water will be discharged into the salty North Atlantic seas. Since fresh water is less dense than salt water, this dilution of the Gulf Stream could effectively still the system; a reduced amount of its heavy cooled water would sink downwards as it passes Iceland to propel ocean circulation. The knock-on effect could have a potentially cooling impact on Europe's temperatures since it would no longer benefit from the warming waters of the Gulf Stream passing by its shores.

Already the Gulf Stream has begun to slow. Measurements taken in the Greenland Sea in early 2005 indicated that once-giant 'chimneys' of cold, dense water sinking from the icy surface to the seabed 2,500 m (1.6 miles) below had virtually disappeared. As the water sank, it was replaced by warm water flowing from the south, so fuelling circulation. This mechanism that drives the Gulf Stream has weakened to less than a quarter of its former strength.[15]

Furthermore, measurement of the strength of the Gulf Stream's current between the continent of Africa and North America's east coast in 2005 showed circulation had slowed by 30 per cent – the equivalent of 6 million tonnes of water a second – since 1992. Previous expeditions in 1957, 1981 and 1992 had recorded minimal change. Should the weakening continue, temperatures in Britain, for example, would likely drop by an average 1°C within a decade.[16]

Climate modellers claim that it is unlikely the Gulf Stream will grind to a complete halt within the twenty-first century, or as suddenly as depicted in the Hollywood film *The Day After Tomorrow*. But the impact of any drop in temperature in northern Europe remains unclear. Winters would likely turn

The Pacific Ocean

The Pacific Ocean is the Earth's largest single geographical feature. At 155 million sq km (60 million sq miles), it is comprised of enough water to swallow every one of the world's landmasses – and still have enough space left to contain another continent the size of Asia. It has the highest global ratio of ocean to land: 1 sq m of land per 10 sq km of water (about 11 sq ft of land per 4 sq miles of water). It is also the deepest ocean on the planet at 10,924 m (35,837 ft), incorporating as it does the Marianas Trench – the world's deepest marine trench. It is half as deep again as Mount Everest is high. This is not simply a fascinating fact from *The Guinness Book of Records*. For oceanographers, geologists and biologists the trench provides vital information about life beneath the sea. The water is also home to an estimated half of the planet's remaining fish.[17]

Such statistical dominance, plus the ocean's sheer richness and diversity, demands its environmental state be maintained; there is too much for the rest of the Earth to lose.

more severe and summers cooler. Yet ironically, it might be that the very global warming that is slowing the Gulf Stream could effectively neutralize the effects of the current's absence, and vice versa. Heightened atmospheric warming elsewhere across the globe would be dampened by the chill of northern Europe.[18]

Every two to seven years, a current of warm water emerging out of the Southern Ocean flows for around a year through the eastern Pacific, off South America's west coast. Sailors first noted its appearance after Christmas, so named the phenomenon El Niño, 'the Christ-child'. Its impact is far from Christ-like, however; in its wake come storms, floods, drought and famine across the globe.

El Niño has a sister, La Niña, which brings cooler waters, and whose effects are less pronounced. Both phenomena alter air pressure above the Pacific Ocean; this cycle is known as the El Niño Southern Oscillation (ENSO).

El Niño weakens Pacific winds and consequently alters rainfall patterns. Inevitably, this promotes a band of dry weather across southern Africa, South-East Asia and northern Australia; a weakened Asian monsoon; and heavy rainfall and flooding in Peru and Ecuador. While these are not new phenomena, population growth and concentration in cities and in coastal areas have led to a vast increase in the number of people exceedingly vulnerable to El Niño's disaster cycle.

The 1991–92 El Niño caused southern Africa's worst drought that century and affected nearly 100 million people. The following cycle in 1997 brought droughts to Malaysia, Indonesia and Brazil, and encouraged forest fires, the smoke from which posed a major public health problem. Increased incidences of diseases transmitted by mosquitoes, including malaria and dengue fever, have been linked to El Niño too. Before the advent of DDT for malaria control in 1944–45, the chances of contracting malaria in Asia's Punjab region increased five times following an El Niño.[19]

El Niño disrupts wildlife too. Around the Galapagos Islands, the consequent heating of surface waters has propelled local fish further afield.

The Atlantic Ocean

The Atlantic Ocean is an 82.2 million sq km (31.7 million sq miles) body of water with an average depth of 3,660 m (12,000 ft). It extends in an 'S' shape from the Arctic Ocean across to the east coast of both North and South America, where it meets the South Pacific Ocean, and also down towards the Southern Ocean via the western shores of Europe and Africa, where it edges the Indian Ocean.

The equator further divides the ocean into the North Atlantic and South Atlantic oceans, each of which has a distinct circulation system: the North Atlantic's currents move clockwise, the South's anti-clockwise, and both are separated by the Equatorial Counter Current. Each current has its own characteristics in terms of water temperature, levels of salinity and the marine life that exists there. Off the coast of Newfoundland, a bank of fog makes it visibly clear where the cold Labrador current meets the warm waters of the Gulf Stream.[22]

The Mid-Atlantic Ridge runs along the ocean floor from Iceland, south through the middle of the Atlantic basin, to near the Antarctic Circle. Its average height is 3,050 m (10,000 ft), while its deepest level is at Milwaukee Deep, 8,605 m (28,230 ft) below sea level at the bottom of the Puerto Rico Trench. The ridge is a literal hotbed of volcanic activity and earthquakes, its seafloor spreading and filling with molten rock from the Earth's interior and consequently widening the ocean.[23]

The Atlantic Ocean incorporates the Caribbean, Baltic, Black, North, Mediterranean and Weddell seas. More large rivers, including the Mississippi, the Congo and the Amazon, drain into the Atlantic than into any other ocean.[24]

The Atlantic's rich resources of crude oil and natural gas in the Gulf of Mexico, Caribbean Sea, North Sea and Gulf of Guinea, and its marine life of fish and mammals, including seals and whales, have made it vulnerable to over-exploitation. Many of the larger species such as manatee, turtles and whales are endangered, and municipal sludge and oil pollution occurs off the North and South American, and European, coastlines. It is the Atlantic's coasts that worldwide have been most damaged by oil spills.[25] Fog and icebergs prove a hazard to shipping at the further extremes of the ocean.

This, in turn, has affected the Galapagos' fur seal population that feed on them, virtually wiping out seals aged between one and four years old. Coastal birds abandoned their traditional nest sites in the absence of the fish.[20]

The ENSO observation system of satellites and buoys tracks the current. The UN Inter-Agency Task Force on El Niño[21] is developing disaster preparedness measures to minimize any negative impact. It is feared that global warming may exacerbate the El Niño phenomenon. Yet El Niño enables scientists to gauge how climate variability affects human health.

Eye of the storm: the fierceness of the world's hurricanes is directly related to the temperature of the ocean waters below them.

Winds and Waves over the Oceans

The ocean waters and the air above them are inextricably linked in the formation of weather patterns. Indeed, 60 per cent of the North Atlantic's tropical storms and 85 per cent of the world's major hurricanes – including 2005's Hurricane Katrina – grow from low-pressure wavefronts and belts of thunderstorms moving westward from Africa's coast every three days or so. Separated by 200–300 km (124–186 miles), the wavefronts create the hurricanes that batter the Gulf of Mexico and Caribbean between May and December.[26]

Measuring barometric pressure is the most accurate means of determining hurricane intensity. A low pressure reading usually signals an impending hurricane; anything less than 28.00 in (949 mb) is rare. During Hurricane Camille, the lowest sea level pressure in a land-falling hurricane along the Gulf coast was recorded. Taken at Bay St Louis, Mississippi, it measured 26.84 in (909 mb).

When wind speeds are given they are based on sustained winds; that is, the average of one minute of wind. But peak winds can gust at a strength of as

The Indian Ocean

The Indian Ocean stretches 73.6 million sq km (28.4 million sq miles) between the landmasses of Africa, Asia, Australia and Antarctica, and includes the oil-rich Middle East's Persian Gulf, Gulf of Oman and Arabian Sea, as well as the Bay of Bengal and Red Sea, among others.

The Indian Ocean is characterized by monsoons and tropical cyclones sweeping across it, fuelled by both the low atmospheric pressure of south-west Asia's hot summer air, and the high pressure of northern Asia's cold winter air. A broad, circular system of currents – or counter-clockwise gyre – dominates the south Indian Ocean's surface waters. These are reversed in the north Indian Ocean. At its southernmost extremities, ships must contend with icebergs from May to October.

The Indian Ocean is where the Indian, Antarctic and African tectonic plates converge. The Mid-Indian Ocean Ridge and its branches of South-East Indian Ocean Ridge, South-West Indian Ocean Ridge and Ninety East Ridge mark their boundaries. The deepest point of the Indian Ocean is the Java Trench at 7.26 km (4.5 miles).

An estimated 40 per cent of the world's offshore oil production occurs in the Indian Ocean, its waters especially vulnerable to oil pollution from the heavy traffic of petroleum products from the Persian Gulf and Indonesian oil fields. Vast shrimp and tuna stocks attract fishing fleets from Russia, Japan, Korea and Taiwan. Beach sands are heavily excavated too. Endangered species include turtles, dugongs, seals and whales.[27]

much as an extra 25 per cent speed. For example, October 2005's Hurricane Wilma, the most intense tropical cyclone ever observed in the Atlantic basin, had sustained winds of 185 mph (about 300 km/h), but gusts of over 215 mph (346 km/h) were also measured.[28]

Human population growth has contributed to the devastation wreaked by the regular onslaught of hurricanes in the region. Houston, Tampa and New Orleans, all situated along the Gulf coast, are three of the largest metropolitan areas in the United States, with a combined population of over seven million people. The subtropical climate has attracted the development of holiday homes along the edge of the Florida panhandle and in southern Louisiana, despite these regions being highly vulnerable to seasonal storms.

This all takes place in the shadow of climate change. Rising sea levels result in higher storm surges and consequent coastal erosion and flooding along the Gulf coast shoreline and Mississippi Delta area. Yet a direct link has also been made between stronger, longer-lasting hurricanes and global warming.

For a hurricane to occur in the first place, the surface ocean temperatures must be over 80°F (about 27°C).[29] When local air pressure drops at sea level as a result of seasonal changes in ocean wind patterns, air is forced to rise over warm waters. The moist, warm air rising lowers air pressure at sea level, drawing further surrounding air inward to repeat the upward pattern – and thus creates a vortex. The increase in the temperature of the ocean heightens the sea's thermal energy, which powers a storm.

On 26 December 2004, a tsunami ripped as much as 5,000 km (3,000 miles) across the Indian Ocean to Africa, devastating any coastal community in its path, and in particular Indonesia's Banda Aceh, which was closest to the seafloor rupture. Hundreds of thousands of people perished.

Yet the death toll would likely have been far lower had there been any warning system in the Indian Ocean. There was none. Although the Asian

In the line of fire: the Asian tsunami of 2004 devastated ocean communities, including idyllic tourist resorts, and killed hundreds of thousands of local people.

earthquake was recorded elsewhere, US seismologists considered an initial measurement of 8.1 too low to create a giant tsunami. It was only revised to 9.0 after the giant waves had already struck land.[30]

Yet tsunamis are far more likely to develop in the Pacific Ocean than in the Indian Ocean. The subduction zones that produce the powerful earthquakes beneath the sea, which give rise to the massive tsunami wave train, are far more numerous across the Pacific. A tsunami does not emerge from an earthquake's epicentre, but in fact originates out of the entire length of the split in the Earth's surface. The Cascadia subduction zone, which runs from British

The Southern Ocean

Only in 2000 was the ocean around Antarctica officially designated the Southern Ocean following a decision by the International Hydrographic Organization. It had previously been labelled the Antarctic Ocean, though there was confusion over delineation from the southern regions of the Atlantic, Indian and Pacific oceans. The Southern Ocean is a 360° ring of deep water of an area about twice the size of the United States which encircles, and stretches outwards from Antarctica to latitude 60°S, the boundary of the Antarctic Treaty system that governs Antarctica. It incorporates, among others, the Ross Sea, Weddell Sea, Amundsen Sea, Bellinghausen Sea and part of the Drake Passage.

Antarctica is also ringed by the 21,000 km (about 13,000 miles) long Antarctic Circumpolar Current. The world's largest ocean current, it transports 130 million cu m (4.6 billion cu ft) of water per second, and moves perpetually eastward, helping drive the ocean conveyer belt. It incorporates the Polar Front or Antarctic Convergence at its middle, separating southern cold polar surface waters from warmer northern waters. The Front is effectively the northern extent of the Southern Ocean.

The Southern Ocean is a deep ocean. Its lowest point is -7,235 m (-23,700 ft) at the southern end of the South Sandwich Trench, and between -4,000 and -5,000 m (-13,000 and -16,400 ft) in general. Whereas the global mean depth of the continental shelf is 133 m (436 ft), the edge of the narrow Antarctic continental ice shelf lies between 400 and 800 m (1,300 and 2,600 ft) down.

Sea temperatures range from 10°C to -2°C (50°F to 28°F). The Antarctic ice pack surges from an average minimum of 2.6 million sq km (1.0 million sq miles) in March to about 18.8 million sq km (7.3 million sq miles) in September and as far outward as 65°S towards the Pacific. The contrast between the temperature of the open waters and the 0.5–1 m (1.6–3.1 ft) thick sea ice that can fall below 0°C (32°F), creates cyclonic storms – and the strongest average winds – on the planet.[32]

The Southern Ocean contains a wealth of marine life, its waters turning to a veritable soup when the microscopic phytoplankton plants bloom during the spring and early summer months and float over thousands of square kilometres of sea. Phytoplankton blooms can vary by up to 25 per cent from year to year, so it is

Columbia to California, is regarded as presenting the biggest tsunami threat to North America's Pacific coast.[31] Landslides and volcanic eruptions can also trigger bands of enormous waves, but more frequently it is the shifting of the tectonic plates either below or above each other that displaces a tremendous amount of sea water, raises the sea level and sets the tsunami in motion.

The race is on to develop warning systems against future tsunamis around the planet. Since the 1960s, the United States' National Oceanic and Atmospheric Administration (NOAA) has managed a federal tsunami-monitoring system; elsewhere, however, monitoring remains patchy. A global

difficult to tell whether levels are being affected by changes in the atmosphere such as higher levels of UV light pouring through the thinned ozone layer.

At the bottom of the Southern Ocean's food chain, phytoplankton are eaten by zooplankton such as copecods and krill – the Norwegian term for 'small fry'. Krill especially feeds the fish, seals, birds and baleen whales, including the majestic blue whale – the world's largest mammal – which literally sieve the krill out of the sea through the baleen plate in their mouths. Yet Antarctic krill populations have fallen by 80 per cent since the 1970s, a drop attributed to warmer temperatures;[33] water temperature has increased by 2°C in the last fifteen years.[34]

The twelve species of Southern Ocean whale that migrate from warmer tropical waters to benefit from the marine life-rich waters of the Antarctic summer also include toothed whales such as the orca and southern bottlenose, which eat fish and squid. Of the approximately 120 species of fish that live in the Southern Ocean, 90 per cent belong to the group *Notothenioidea*, which have acclimatized to the extremely cold water in which they swim. The Antarctic cod, notably, produces a kind of 'antifreeze' to lower its blood's freezing point to -2°C (28°F).

Although the Antarctic Treaty's 1980 Convention on the Conservation of Antarctic Marine Living Resources (CCAMR) was designed to regulate fishing, illegal over-fishing has nevertheless dealt a blow to Patagonian toothfish.[35] Additionally, the hooked long-line method used has been so decimating the albatross population that the species is now endangered. The fur seal population was over-exploited during the eighteenth and nineteenth centuries but today is protected under the Convention on the Conservation of Antarctic Seals. Similarly, the International Whaling Commission prohibits commercial whaling in the Southern Ocean.[36]

earthquake satellite system using an InSAR radar will enable scientists to detect deformations in the Earth's crust as a means of predicting where earthquakes might occur, although the two are not necessarily connected. In the meantime, Global Positioning System (GPS) networks monitor the Earth's crust.[37]

The World's Fisheries

A virtual global free-for-all for ocean resources, including oil, gas and especially fish, during the middle of the twentieth century was brought to heel through a plethora of international conventions during the 1950s, culminating in the 1958 Geneva Convention on Fishing and Conservation of the Living Resources of the High Seas.[38]

Further fine-tuning over the years established the United Nations Convention on the Law of the Sea in 1982. This maintained the measured freedoms of the high seas for all nations, while recognizing a coastal state's sovereignty over the sea up to 12 nautical miles out, alongside rights to any natural resources within a 200 nautical mile Exclusive Economic Zone (EEZ), and control of the local continental shelf. Landlocked states have rights of access to and through these seas.

Although 90 per cent of the world's fisheries lie within these EEZs, as fisheries decline, stocks are being plundered further afield from open waters. Deals are also being struck. In July 2006, in an agreement worth 516 million

Net value: fish stocks must be caught sustainably if fisheries are not to collapse through sheer loss of numbers.

euros (£350m/US$690m) to the Mauritanian government, the European Union bought the right to allow about 200 European vessels to fish sustainably for shrimp, tuna, hake and other species off the African state's coast. The money was to be invested in Mauritania's own fishing industry, yet there were fears that African stocks too would soon suffer from over-fishing.[39]

Modern technology is enabling further prospecting for minerals and energy sources. Like vultures, oil companies are circling the ice-free waters of the Arctic Ocean for beneath-the-sea oil reserves.[40]

Fish are one of the few remaining food sources to be caught in the wild, but over-fishing and environmental degradation are decimating stocks. Indeed, a four-year study of records of fish catches dating from 1950 to the present day concluded that the world's fish stocks would be totally eradicated by 2048 if current over-fishing trends continued. It also discovered that, in losing species, the loss of entire marine ecosystems followed; biodiversity – that is, the richness of marine life – proved vital to survival.[41]

Wild seafood must be caught from sustainable fisheries by sustainable methods if fish species are not to die out. The Marine Stewardship Council (MSC) goes some way to enabling the fishing industry to do so. In 1996, global environmental organization the World Wildlife Fund (WWF) joined forces with Unilever, one of the world's largest consumers of fish, to found the MSC. The aim was to set standards of sustainability in the fishing industry to secure future stocks and supplies, and to administer accreditation. Since 1999, the MSC has been an independent, non-governmental charitable organization, and there are now hundreds of fish products carrying its logo: the MSC standard 'is the only internationally recognised set of environmental principles for measuring fisheries to assess if they are well managed and sustainable'.[42]

> '... a legal order for the seas and oceans which will facilitate international communication, and will promote the peaceful uses of the seas and oceans, the equitable and efficient utilization of their resources, the conservation of their living resources, and the study, protection and preservation of the marine environment...'
>
> FROM THE PREAMBLE TO THE UNITED NATIONS CONVENTION ON THE LAW OF THE SEA

The MSC logo helps to guide consumers, but environmentalists have criticized the MSC for failing to ensure accredited fisheries maintained fish stocks at healthy levels,[43] further emphasizing the constant need for environmental vigilance. Indeed, a study using fifty years of data that compared commercially important fish stocks with fish populations *not* targeted by ocean-going fish vessels found that measures aimed at conserving fish were, in fact, making stocks more vulnerable to depletion.[44]

Taking only the biggest fish alters the age structure of remaining populations, and the immature fish left are less able to withstand environmental change, whether caused by global warming, industrial pollution, or natural phenomena such as El Niño, or the brutal onslaught of a tsunami. Heavily fished populations are likely to contain few older fish so are dependent on the successful growth of fish larvae and baby fish – recruits – to maintain numbers. A population can collapse if these juveniles face environmental devastation. Imposing maximum size limits for fish caught and establishing marine reserves are ways that larger fish could be protected.[45]

Intensive fishing methods are detrimental not only to fish stocks but also to marine habitats. A 2006 WWF report on European fisheries claimed:

'Over-fishing does more than deplete valuable fish populations and put livelihoods at risk. Fishing gear, particularly bottom trawls, can be extremely damaging to fragile marine habitats. Vast quantities of unwanted juvenile fish and other marine life are hauled up by unselective nets and hooks, only to be thrown away dead or dying. This destruction and waste threatens endangered marine species, hampers the recovery of depleted fish populations, and reverberates throughout entire marine ecosystems.'[46]

Arctic Ocean

The Arctic Ocean, which lies at the top of the world within the Arctic Circle at 66°30'N latitude, is the smallest of the world's oceans at 14 million sq km (5.4 million sq miles). Yet its relative size belies the attention it is attracting as climate change takes hold and distinctly alters the ocean's properties.

The permanent layer of drifting pack ice that covers most of the ocean's waters is fast diminishing. Until recently, the ice reflected most of the solar radiation back out into the atmosphere, and the sea beneath was untouched by solar heat. The vertical stability of the ocean prevented inorganic salts such as phosphates, nitrates and silicates from welling upward, which in other oceans supports life in the sunlit region beneath the water's surface. Without its icy covering, the open sea will instead absorb the sun's heat. While this will encourage a northern movement of marine life, the Earth's atmosphere will also heat up with the extra amount of solar power.

The decline in the thickness of the Arctic sea ice has been recorded over half a century. In 1958 it stood at 3 m (10 ft) deep; by 1999, it had all but halved to 1.7 m (5.5 ft).[48] By 2006, NASA studies reported a surge in the loss of sea cover. Arctic perennial sea ice shrunk by 14 per cent in just twelve months between 2004 and 2005. The overall decrease in the ice cover was 720,000 sq km (280,000 sq miles); in other words, an area almost equivalent to the size of Turkey.[49]

Ironically, the effect of the climate change exacerbated by fossil fuel burning is acting like a magnet to those who wish to continue burning fossil fuels. The melting of the sea ice, which could see the polar ocean ice-free by 2060,[50] is drawing the attention of oil and gas companies to the previously untapped resources beneath the Arctic ice cap. It also gives the lie to the pretence that any such companies

The endangered Atlantic salmon is a case in point, with populations across the ocean at their lowest in recorded history. Between 1994 and 1999, the number of adult fish returning to North American rivers was estimated to have declined from around 200,000 to 80,000.[47] Additionally, poorly managed salmon fish farms – a method of food cultivation known as aquaculture – can spread disease and parasites that pass via escaped farmed fish into wild salmon populations. The wild fish gene pool is also diminished this way.

Rising Temperatures at Sea

Coral reefs across the world are largely doomed to die out before the end of this century if average water temperatures continue to rise in line with UN projected CO_2 emissions. Such decimation will deeply affect the economies and cultures of the largely island peoples who depend on them for their livelihood. It will also have a devastating effect on the ecosystems that have developed around these skeletal forms. Fish feed on the algae, shrimp and coral that house them, so they would be lost too.

might be 'beyond petroleum' and instead are looking to invest greatly in alternative, cleaner energy sources.

Conflict flared up in the spring of 2006 between British and American polar scientists over the collaboration of the US Geological Survey (USGS) and oil companies BP and Statoil. Oil and gas prospecting was to be undertaken under the auspices of International Polar Year (IPY), a scientific initiative running from 2007 to 2008 involving sixty countries responding particularly to climate change affecting the polar regions.[51] British scientists strongly objected to the oil companies' involvement. Professor Chris Rapley, the director of the British Antarctic Survey, said:

'I would be very uncomfortable with a project that simply was out to log the hydrocarbon reserves of the Arctic as a geological activity. I don't think that fits very comfortably within either the scientific guidelines or the ethical underpinning of the IPY.'[52]

Oil companies such as Exxon, Amoco, Texaco, Conoco and Petrocanada are already involved in Arctic Energy Assessment, part of USGS's World Energy Project – a global attempt to map untapped hydrocarbon fuel reserves.[53] The opening up of the North West Passage and Bering Sea will make possible the exploitation of the oil and gas reserves of Sakhalin Island, off Russia's eastern coastline, which is believed to contain some of the world's largest untapped deposits.[54] Yet increased ship exhausts along new Arctic Ocean routes could triple low-lying ozone levels and seriously damage plant life.[55]

An embarrassment of riches: healthy coral provides the foundation for a rich and multi-coloured biodiversity, but warmer ocean temperatures threaten the entire ecosystem.

Coral bleaching is the whitening of coral that results when the sea temperature rises and the colourful algae that live on the skeleton are expelled, possibly to make way for the colonization of hardier species. *Zooxanthellae* are algae that feed the coral tissues via photosynthesis, the same way plants convert light from the sun into food. Without this colourful coating, coral cannot survive and build the limestone foundations it needs for its skeleton.

The more frequent such incidences of 'whitening', the more difficult it is for coral to have time enough to recover. If it occurs as many as three times in a decade, then the coral is likely to die out. Bleaching is happening on a more intense and wider geographic scale due to a widespread rise in sea temperature, which, like the average global rise in temperature, is fuelled largely by the widespread burning of fossil fuels.

Corals can only live in water of between 18° and 30°C (64° and 86°F). A 1°C increase in temperature above the summer maximum will set off most bleaching events. Tropical sea temperatures have crept up by 1° in the past 100 years, and are currently rising at a rate of 1–2° per century. Coral is unable to adapt fast enough to survive the change in its environment. Coral bleaching, when combined with the effects of industry and tourism, rising sea levels, more frequent cyclones and decreased alkalinity, will result within the next half-century in coral reefs being unlikely to replenish themselves.

In 1998, the worst known incidence of coral bleaching was recorded. Every reef system in the planet's tropical oceans was affected, and in some regions of the Indian Ocean, entire reef systems died. Those coral reefs that survived did so with a reduced reproductive capacity and ability to grow in warmer waters.

It is a critical time for coral reefs. They are vital ecosystems that are very sensitive to changes in water temperature, as well as those of atmospheric CO_2 and rising sea levels – and this could seal their fate. Current estimates of CO_2 levels by the mid-twenty-first century will inhibit the ability of coral to lay down its limestone skeleton by 30 per cent. Since high rates of ongoing skeletal construction are necessary for coral to simply maintain its current extent and distribution, there will be a worldwide loss of reefs.

> *'Coral reefs may be dysfunctional within the near future. The current understanding of coral bleaching suggests that corals may be the single largest casualty of "business-as-usual" greenhouse policies.'*
>
> GREENPEACE

Taking Action

1. The United Nations designated 1998 the Year of the Ocean (YOTO). The US Government's National Oceanic and Atmospheric Administration (NOAA) maintains the archived YOTO website at www.yoto98.noaa.gov/facts/gen.htm . Access it for an overview of ocean issues.

2. 'An abrupt climate change meta-directory', listing articles and books, websites and internet forums concerning the Gulf Stream, is available at www.gulfstreamshutdown.com . Current velocities of the Gulf Stream are recorded at http://rads.tudelft.nl/gulfstream .

3. For an overview of the El Niño and La Niña phenomena, and for more information on the El Niño/Southern Oscillation (ENSO), visit the NOAA Climate Prediction Center's site at www.cpc.ncep.noaa.gov and click on 'El Niño/La Niña' on the sidebar.

4. Full texts of marine-orientated international laws can be found at www.oceanlaw.net/texts .

5. The British government's Meteorological Office provides a range of brochures for download detailing the effects of climate change, including the impact of rising sea levels and future trends. Visit www.met-office.gov.uk/research/hadleycentre/pubs/brochures .

Bird's Head Seascape, Papua

Over fifty new species of marine life were discovered among over 1,200 species of fish and almost 600 coral species recorded by Conservation International (CI) scientists at the Bird's Head Seascape reef in 2006. With three-quarters of the world's total marine species represented, the seascape off the coast of Papua New Guinea is possibly the richest marine environment in the world, even more so than Australia's Great Barrier Reef.[56] Scientists broke world records for the number of species found at single sites: at an area called Fak-Fak 330 types of reef fish were identified. Such is the reef's richness that scientists have termed it a species factory; new species identified include shark, fish, coral and shrimp. Further examination is expected to reveal dozens more previously unknown species. Nesting Pacific leatherback turtles and migratory populations of whales and dolphins have also been found in the region.[57]

The area faces increasing pressure from commercial fisheries, and bomb and cyanide fishing. Local coastal mining and timber operations can also introduce harmful sediments into the sea. Only a tenth of the area is protected, and CI is pressing for further conservation. Coral bleaching occurring at other ocean reefs is likely to be avoided due to a favourable combination of strong currents and cool water. In 2005, scientists discovered a 'lost world' including new species of birds, butterflies and frogs in Papua's isolated Foja Mountains.[58]

6. When ordering seafood, take heed of WWF's 'Fish "Yes" List', which names the species with currently healthy populations:

- Halibut – Alaska/Canada
- Striped bass – Atlantic
- Squid – Pacific 'market'
- Albacore – Pacific
- Mahi-mahi
- Rock lobster – West Australian
- Spot prawn- west coast US
- Dungeness crab
- Caviar – farmed US
- Salmon – wild Alaskan

7. Additionally, request that fish bought at fish shops, supermarkets and restaurants is certified by the Marine Stewardship Council. For all information regarding fisheries in the MSC programme, visit www.msc.org/html/content_463.htm . To keep abreast of issues regarding MSC accredited stocks, visit the European Cetacean Bycatch Campaign at www.eurobc.org .

8. Take care what you flush into the water systems and pour down drains. Untreated waste and engine oil can devastate marine habitats, while chemical pollutants enter the food chain.

9. Protect marine life. Do not dispose of fishing lines, nets or plastics in or near water.

10. Be considerate of sea life habitats. Do not feed seabirds, mammals and turtles or disturb their nesting grounds.

11. If you live by the coast, mobilize or get involved in regular beach clean-ups.

12. To give practical support to marine life scientific research, join an Earthwatch ocean expedition. Access www.Earthwatch.org for information regarding projects around the world.

Ankara
TURKEY

SYRIA

IRAQ

SAUDI
ARABIA
Kuwait

Riyadh

YEMEN   OMAN

'*You must be the change you
want to see in the world.*'

MAHATMA GANDHI

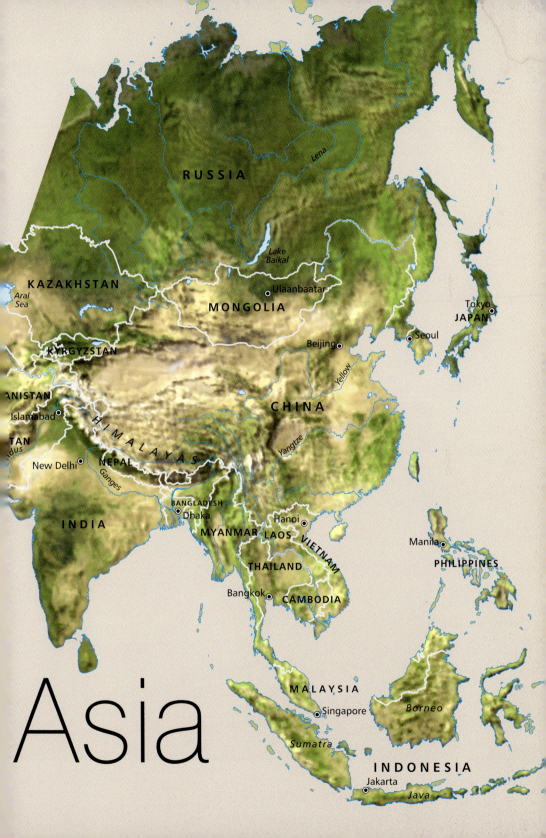

Asia is the world's largest continent. It is hemmed in by the Arctic Ocean to Russia's north, the Pacific Ocean around South-East Asia, and the Indian Ocean. Two of its countries, Turkey and Russia, are also part European; the geographical demarcation points of both continents run along the sixtieth meridian through the Ural and Caucasus mountain ranges, both the Bosphorus and Caspian seas and across the lowland region of Russia's Caspian Depression, and end at the Black Sea. Indonesia is a multi-island state belonging to both Asia and Oceania. Asia is separated from Africa by the Israel/Egypt border.

Previous spread: Mountain home: cultures and villages dependent on their neighbouring mountains face decline along with the glaciers and snowfall.

Asia's very size, coupled with a human population that accounts for three-fifths of the world's people, ensures that the nations within the continent form specific and significant political and racial groupings. The region is divided into the Middle East, the Commonwealth of Independent States that emerged out of the break-up of the Soviet Union, the Central Asian Republics, including the Indian subcontinent, East Asia (China, Japan and Korea) and South-East Asia.

The continent includes dramatic geographical features, such as the Gobi Desert of the Mongolian plateau, the sacred Ganges River, the world's highest peak, Mount Everest in the Himalayan mountain range, and the shore of the Dead Sea, which, at 395 m (1,296 ft) below sea level, is the lowest land-based point on Earth. However, heavy industrialization and environmental destruction have caused profound changes to many of the continent's prominent features. The Yangtze River, once the continent's longest river, which flowed 6,100 km (3,800 miles) from Tibet to the East China Sea, had its course dammed up in 2006 to provide hydroelectric power.[1] Mountain ranges too are having their tops sliced off like boiled eggs to give up their coal. The consequence of such unbridled development is that waterways such as Siberia's Lake Baikal, the world's deepest lake, holding a fifth of the planet's fresh water reserves, are threatened by gross pollution.[2]

Below:
Top of the world: the majestic pinnacle of the Himalayan mountain range that the Tibetans call Qomolangma, the Nepalese call Sagarmaths, and that is known worldwide as Mount Everest.

The development and industrialization of the emerging economic powerhouses of China and India are proving a growing threat to any attempts to curb global greenhouse emissions. The countries' dependency on fossil fuels to power their runaway growth is undermining any international bids to stem climate change. While their per capita carbon emissions are relatively small – in 2001, India's stood at 0.25 metric tonnes; that is, twenty-two times less than that of the United States – *national* carbon emissions are increasing at an alarming rate. Between 1990 and 2001, India's carbon emissions soared by 61 per cent, second only to the phenomenal 111 per cent rise of those of China over the same period.[3] Rapid industrialization and mass urbanization contribute to devastating levels of air pollution; vehicle emissions and

Sunita Narain and Rainwater Harvesting

In 1982, after short spells researching Gujarat's wildlife and ecology, and employment with the Bombay Natural History Society, Sunita Narain began work at New Delhi's Centre for Science and Environment (CSE) – where she still remains. Her focus has been on researching the relationship between India's environment and development, communicating her findings, and advocating policy promoting sustainable development. In 1992, she began publishing the fortnightly *Down to Earth* magazine, and in the same year also became director of the Society for Environmental Communications. In 2001 she was made CSE's director.

In 2002, she was awarded the Dr B.C. Deb Memorial Award for Popularisation of Science by the Indian Science Congress Association. She has co-written papers on environmental issues including water harvesting (the collecting of monsoon rains) and the state of India's environment, especially in the context of rural development.[5] She has co-edited the books *Dying Wisdom: Rise, Fall and Potential of India's Water Harvesting Systems* (1997), *State of India's Environment, The Citizens' Fifth Report* (1999), and *Making Water Everybody's Business: The Practice and Policy of Water Harvesting* (2001).

Her experience and expertise are in demand at international conferences, especially in the role of spokesperson on behalf of Asia and its environment in the context of her wider research interests concerning global democracy and climate change. Narain won the Media Foundation's 2004 Chameli Devi Award for Outstanding Woman Mediaperson, and in 2005 CSE was awarded the Stockholm Water Prize for its work in promoting effective water management along with improved human rights. She was also awarded the Padma Shri by the government of India, the highest civilian honour, for her commitment to protecting the environment. She said:

untreated industrial smoke are major contributors to some of the world's worst levels of urban air quality.[4]

The environmental cost of habitat destruction and full-scale pollution looks set ultimately to kill the goose that laid the golden egg. If the fish in the rivers and sea are dead because they have been poisoned, the farmers have fled their desert-encroached fields for the city, and the skies are so filled with smog that it is difficult to breathe and respiratory diseases become rife, then people cannot be fed, and the quality of life is too poor to maintain the one-time burgeoning economy.

Yet it is not simply heavy industry that is threatening Asia's future. A relatively small improvement in the standard of living of many small-scale

'This award in 2005 rewards the growth of the environmental movement, which shows that to bring in change, it is sometimes necessary to push the system to demand more. This award is for all of us in the environmental movement and for all the protests and fights that need to be won.'[6]

Water harvesting resurrects the *tanka* method of irrigation that was common across India until the early nineteenth century, and involves collecting the monsoon rain in specially dug ponds. Rather than evaporate or flow away in flash floods, the water is able to percolate down through the soil to revitalize the water table and, in turn, refill village wells.

Retired police officer Haradevsingh Hadeja's development of the drainage system in his village of Rajsamadhiya proved so successful that for over a decade the community has not needed the service of the government water tankers on which other local villages depend for drinking water. It also means that newly irrigated crops are flourishing, and ponds and wells are full. Where once the water table was 30 m (98 ft) down, today it is only 7 m (23 ft) down.[7]

It is believed that around 20,000 Indian villages are active rainwater harvesters, but the burgeoning social movement is as relevant to India's cities, including New Delhi and Bangalore, as it is to its rural districts. Tanks and ponds long fallen into disrepair and full of waste are being rehabilitated to collect water again; the water tables are consequently rising. Sunita Narain believes New Delhi could obtain a third of its water from such harvesting.[8]

The practice is relatively cheap and does not require a large infrastructure. It gives control of water back to villages and strengthens their communities since it must be a communal project to work. Water harvesting is particularly ecological since it can only make use of the rainwater that falls; it simply uses it more efficiently. Similar schemes are being developed in Peru, China and Tanzania.

farmers across the continent, and especially in India, is that of the 'low-cost', mass-produced water pump. It is revolutionizing farm work, but draining the water table to unsustainably low levels. This low-water situation will be exacerbated by the loss of the Himalayas' glaciers, which directly feed many of the continent's great rivers – and ultimately its population.

The environmental impact of industrial development, whether that be pollution or a drain on water resources, occurs in the context of a continent especially beset by natural disasters, including storms, tornadoes, earthquakes and tsunamis. While climate change has increased the severity of these weather conditions, the resultant high death tolls are invariably due to poor preparation and infrastructure.

Asia has a striking collection of wildlife. The giant panda is an iconic symbol of environmental concern both as the long-term logo of the World Wildlife Fund, and because its demise has long been prophesied. Yet here is a success story: the Chinese government has recognized the species' worth, and programmes have been established to maintain its habitat and protect the animal. However, a black market trade in species including endangered rhino, tigers and orang-utans is decimating populations, even as their habitats face degradation from development.

Seventy per cent of China's energy needs are met by coal, and China is the second-largest consumer of oil after the United States.[9] Yet Asia's booming economic sector must transfer to alternative energies if its growth is not to have a negative global impact.

Asia's Natural Disasters

From 1991 to 2000, natural disasters across the world, including floods, landslides, volcanoes, storms, cyclones, earthquakes and fires, killed nearly 700,000 people, 83 per cent of them in Asia.[10] While such catastrophes have always occurred throughout history, their severity has increased dramatically because of climate change: weather events such as storms and tornadoes have become more violent. Nevertheless, the impact of major disasters is invariably exacerbated by poor human preparation or response. Deaths attributed to 'Acts of God' such as earthquakes often have more prosaic causes. Structures are poorly built and so easily collapse when the ground shakes. The 2004 Asian tsunami death toll would have been lower had a warning system been in place. Geophysicist Dr Stuart Weinstein and colleagues of the Pacific Tsunami Warning Center spent hours trying to phone to warn the countries that would be affected – but terrifyingly, they had no direct way of reaching them.[11]

The Kashmir earthquake of October 2005 killed 80,000 people, yet in the provision of emergency relief to the survivors, it became clear that poorly structured buildings located in a known earthquake belt had been largely responsible for the massive loss of life. Additionally, poor communication among remote mountain communities made it difficult to locate victims and supply aid to them. While earthquake prediction itself is a young and inexact science,[12] various measures can be taken to minimize the risk. A year after the Kashmir quake, for example, UK development agency Tearfund remained in the region, developing a programme of disaster risk reduction among villages to reduce their future vulnerability.[13]

Forests act as barriers against rainfall, and deforestation leads to flood damage. The draining of coastal mangrove forests and building on floodplains – Bangladesh is effectively one huge floodplain – threatens lives. The growth of mega-cities invites disaster as populations swap rural lives for urban sprawl, many packing into homes constructed without permits in areas susceptible to earthquakes or flooding. By 2015, a Global Earth Observation System of Systems (GEOSS), which links already developed satellites that help to estimate crop yields, detect earthquakes, forecast droughts, predict floods, and monitor air and water quality, is to be used to warn of and respond to natural disasters.[14]

Bangladesh's very position at the delta where both the Brahmaputra and Ganges rivers flow into the Bay of Bengal make the state highly susceptible to flooding. Indeed, approximately 70 per cent of the country consists of floodplains, and most of the land is less than 6 m (20 ft) above sea level.[15] However, the country has developed a strong disaster preparedness and management programme that incorporates all levels of society, and saves lives when the waters rise during the wet season. The Flood Forecasting and Warning Centre of the Bangladesh Water Development Board has, since 1972, been responsible for river flood forecasts and flood warnings during the wet season. The Bangladesh Meteorological Department gives forecasts and warnings of tropical cyclones and storm surges from the Bay of Bengal. At ministerial level, a national guideline, known as the Emergency Standing Order for Flood, details the flood preparedness measures to be carried out before, during and after floods. The Ministry of Disaster Management and Relief's Disaster Management Bureau carries out action programmes at the grassroots level; for example, 21,000 Bangladesh Red Crescent Society volunteers have been trained to respond in the flood-prone coastal regions. And, while since 1993 the Bangladesh National Building Code stipulates planning procedure in a Flood Prone Area, homesteads are traditionally flood-proofed in rural settlements by raising them on mounds above maximum flood levels.[16]

Problems develop, however, when the waters become permanently raised by sea-level rise. Already, mangrove swamps, which act as barriers to the river waters, are dying from salt water poisoning, and people are being displaced too. The latter is a particularly pertinent issue; Bangladesh's

'If there is a 1 per cent increase in average global temperature, we will lose about 10 per cent of our land. That is a huge problem for Bangladesh.'

SABIHUDDIN AHMED, HIGH COMMISSIONER FOR BANGLADESH AND FORMER PERMANENT SECRETARY AT THE BANGLADESHI ENVIRONMENT MINISTRY

population numbers 150 million people squashed onto 144,000 sq km (55,600 sq miles) of land. According to Bangladesh's High Commissioner, Sabihuddin Ahmed, 30–40 million people will be threatened by climate change caused by the world's rich nations, their crops and homes permanently flooded, their drinking water contaminated – and there will be nowhere for them to go.[17]

Deluge and Drought

The melting of the Himalayan mountain range's glaciers, numbering almost 50,000, is set to force water shortages across South-East Asia. Some of the world's major rivers, including Pakistan's Indus, India's Ganges and those that originate on the Qinghai–Tibet plateau – Tibet's Brahmaputra and Salween, and China's Mekong, Yellow and Yangtze rivers – are at least partly fed by the Himalayan ice fields.

The source of these world-class rivers will dwindle, and the water reduction will have catastrophic results on communities downstream too. Increased glacial run-off from the Qinghai–Tibet plateau worsens soil erosion, spreading deserts, drought and sandstorms further across China. Irrigation systems and hydropower will also suffer.

The Taklamakan Desert in north-west China could first be flooded before drying out. Yet, often any water from melting glaciers has evaporated before it reaches downstream, where it might have had some short-lived agricultural use. The 100 million farmers already suffering from the overuse and pollution of China's water supplies and an already dry climate will face further water shortages which could destroy crops.[18] The major cities at the foot of the Himalayan mountain range, including Delhi, Kathmandu, Calcutta and Dhaka, will simply lack enough water to sustain their huge populations.[19]

The melting of the glaciers has been recognized and recorded for some time. In the past forty years, glaciers across the Tibetan plateau have shrunk by 6,800 sq km (2,625 sq miles) – particularly since the 1980s. They now cover about 105,000 sq km (40,540 sq miles) of the 2.5 million sq km (965,000 sq miles) plateau, the rest of which is frozen tundra.[20] Nevertheless, rising temperatures caused by global warming are causing the ice to diminish faster than previously expected, at a rate of 7 per cent a year. Over 80 per cent of the ice on the plateau has been affected.[21] It is projected that Tibet's glaciers will have vanished within 100 years.[22]

The study of 5,000 glaciers in the region by researchers from the Chinese Academy of Sciences recorded that, while temperatures had risen by 0.2°C every decade over a fifty-year period, around 82 per cent of the glaciers had receded by 4.5 per cent during the same time. Only a handful of glaciers were found to be expanding. However, for the Himalayas' dense ice packs to melt could take centuries.[23]

Across northern China, drought and the accompanying sandstorms are already taking their toll. There have always been deserts in the region but they are expanding rapidly; the capital, Beijing, is regularly swathed in the choking red dust from sandstorms hundreds of miles wide blown in from Inner Mongolia. While millions of trees have been planted in Beijing to hold back the Gobi Desert, it is creeping up to the city's edge.[24] The dust clouds blow as far as South Korea, causing severe air pollution in Seoul, and are laced with toxins, a by-product of China's industrialization.[25] Productive agricultural land

Clinging to life: as Bangladesh's seasonal flooding becomes permanent owing to sea-level rise, there will be nowhere for its population to flee.

has been lost to the Gobi Desert as crops have dried up and valuable topsoil has been blown away. Villages have been abandoned. A black windstorm in northern China in 1993 killed eighty-three people and over 100,000 farm animals, and destroyed crops.[26] Rivers, including the great Yellow River, are also dwindling.

Such devastating drought and desertification have been linked to gradual climate change and rising temperatures as the continental interior heats up and rainfall levels decline. Yet over-grazing and deforestation, along with rapid industrialization and economic development, are exacerbating the problem. Every year, 2,500 sq km (965 sq miles) of China turns to desert, and the process is accelerating: the rate has almost doubled since the 1950s and large sectors of the country are becoming uninhabitable.[27]

Pump-action Dehydration

A revolution in the acquisition of relatively cheap electric water pumps by millions of farmers across the developing world – 21 million in the course of a decade in India alone[29] – is transforming agriculture. However, the mass increase in the drawing up of irrigation water from deep under ground is drinking the water table dry. Since there is not enough annual rain to replenish it, mass global starvation looms.

According to Fred Pearce, environmental correspondent for *New Scientist*:

'Today, the world grows twice as much food as it did a generation ago but it uses 3 times as much water to grow it. Two-thirds of all the water abstracted from the environment goes to irrigate crops. This use of water is massively unsustainable.'[30]

This amounts to hydrological anarchy; there are no controls on tapping the previously untouched underground reserves, yet they are fast running out. Farmers are using the apparently unlimited supply of water for thirsty crops like rice, sugar cane, alfalfa and cotton. The International Water Management Institute (IWMI) is monitoring the phenomenon but sees no means of regulating pump use.[31]

Already, millions of traditional hand-dug wells and deeper-sunk tube wells have dried up across such states as Gujarat and Tamil Nadu as the water table has plummeted out of reach. People are fleeing arid districts, and suicides among farmers are common. The 'food bubble' – the Earth Policy Institute president Lester Brown's term for the record output of such unsustainable farming practices[32] – has spread across Asia, South America and the US; it is set to burst, leaving a world unable to feed itself.

Asia's Economic Boom

For all of its supposed benefits, Asia's rash industrial development, especially in China and India, is having a detrimental impact on the environment and the well-being of many people. More than 70 per cent of the water in the Yellow, Huai and Hai rivers, which between them supply half of China's population, is too polluted for human use.[28]

China's major economic and maritime hub, the Bohai Sea, will be dead by 2020 unless industrial pollution of its waters is quelled. One of only twelve internal seas in the world, and the largest in China, it is known both as the 'fish storehouse' for the richness of its spawning grounds, and as one of the country's environmental blackspots for the belching cities and factories that line its shores. Its marine life is facing extinction.

About 2.8 billion tonnes of contaminated water is dumped into the 50,000 sq km (31,200 sq mile) body of water every year. Barely any of the forty rivers

Killing the golden goose: China's unregulated industrial development threatens to destroy the very environment on which the country's economic growth – and its human population – depend.

flowing into the Bohai Sea are clean, and more than a third of Bohai's water falls short of even basic clean-water standards. 'Red tides' of lethally toxic seaborne algae blooms have forced beaches to close, and are decimating the Bohai's famed stocks of shellfish.[33]

Acid rain, once the scourge of Scandinavia's forests, is now severely affecting any developing country where industrialization is underway. India's world famous Taj Mahal monument is slowly being eroded by the pollution,[34] and China, as the world's leading burner of coal, is seeing its own forests start to die. Neither is acid rain respectful of borders; Japan is suffering transboundary pollution due to the untrammelled industrial excesses of its Chinese neighbour.[35]

A global rise in man-made methane in the atmosphere is directly related to China's soaring economic growth rate since 1999. In under a decade, the country's economy more than doubled, and the burning of fossil fuels at vast power plants to power this industrialization has channelled huge amounts of the gas into the skies above Asia.[36] Additionally, the industrial production of toxic substances, including herbicides and pesticides, accumulates as diffuse pollution, contaminating water, air and soil. In 2002, an international convention aimed to curb such poisons worldwide by banning Persistent Organic Pollutants (POPs).[37]

Ordinary household and business waste levels are reaching a crisis point: by 2020 China's annual levels of rubbish are predicted to reach 400m tonnes, equivalent to 1997 figures for the entire planet. The China Council for International Cooperation and Development warns that inadequate waste management could lead to methane explosions, the release of toxic gases and pollution of water supplies.[38] The economic and environmental costs of containing pollution and its corresponding damage to health, agriculture, local habitats and water sources could outweigh any advantages of industrialization. It could cost China as much as 10 per cent of its GDP.[39]

For India, the 1984 Bhopal disaster remains a stark warning. The town's Union Carbide factory released 27 tonnes of the poison gas methyl isocyanate into the night air; half a million people were exposed to the gas and 20,000 have since died. The site remains polluted by organochlorines and heavy metals, and children born to gas-affected women are prone to be born with debilitating conditions.[40]

Mindful of China's dependency on ever-more-expensive oil, and the potential for political instability as both urbanites and farmers grow restless over the increasing levels of largely coal-fired industrial pollution, the Chinese government is keen to invest in alternative, cleaner, cheaper energies. China accounts for nearly 60 per cent of global solar capacity – that is, worldwide levels of already installed solar electricity systems; it has 30 million solar households. By 2020, renewable sources are targeted to account for 15 per cent of China's energy needs.[41] Additionally, Beijing is set to hold what is being billed as the first 'Green' Olympics in 2008,[42] which will prove a test case for the viability of alternative energy.

However, alternative power is not always benign. The Three Gorges Dam, the world's biggest, will produce 22.4 million kw of hydroelectric power when fully operational in 2009.[43] But it will also damage the Yangtze River. By creating a 640 km (400 mile) long lake, the dam will drown the lower part of the Three Gorges, considered one of the most beautiful landscapes in the world, bury thirteen cities, 140 towns and 1,300 villages as well as ancient archaeological sites, and threaten the survival of river dolphins and sturgeon, and various endemic floras, ferns and palms.[44] In India, a protest movement by indigenous tribespeople has emerged in the wake of plans to flood their lands to make way for hydroelectric projects such as the Tipaimukh Dam in Manipur state,[45] and the Narmada Dam, which has especially garnered controversy.[46]

Asian economic development is not confined to urban districts. Even the age-old subsistence lifestyle of Tibet's nomads herding yaks and goats across plateau grasslands is threatened by new technology. A move towards ranch-style farming could see a single helicopter replace the tribal knowledge of land management passed down through generations – and make redundant an entire people group.[47]

The Middle East, Oil and War

The Middle East has a high profile within the Asian continent. It features some of the world's richest countries such as Saudi Arabia, the United Arab Emirates and Oman alongside the politically unstable regions of Iraq, Iran, Syria, Lebanon and Israel. What unites all these countries is the issue of oil – and who owns it. The Middle East accounts for a staggering 57 per cent of the world's reserves.[48]

It is such oil riches that have brought money into the region, and have transformed the standard of living of a number of countries. Yet it is only through the artificial and high carbon emission-producing means of air conditioning that such success has been bought, since around 80 per cent of the Gulf's desert climate is too hot to sustain human life. The average life expectancy of someone living in Oman has increased by thirty years in four decades,[49] and its per capita carbon emissions almost tripled between 1980 and 2003.[50]

> *'Wars, ethnic conflict and terrorism are part of a huge industry entailing the destruction of human, economic and environmental resources.'*
>
> DR ANNE-MARIE SACQUET, DIRECTOR OF THE FRENCH COMMITTEE FOR THE ENVIRONMENT AND SUSTAINABLE DEVELOPMENT

The presence of large oil reserves in the Middle East, however, makes them a military target. In 1991, during the Gulf War, Iraq deliberately released 800,000 tonnes of oil off the coast of Kuwait.[51] The Israeli bombing of the

Jiyyeh power station in Lebanon in 2006 released an oil slick that stretched at least 80 km (50 miles) along the Mediterranean coast, threatening both wildlife and people's livelihoods.[52]

The world's military conflicts have a devastating impact on the environment that is seldom acknowledged. While the commercial aviation industry faces close scrutiny over its contribution to greenhouse gas emissions, air force manoeuvres are not subject to any controls regarding their impact on global warming or the air and noise pollution they cause. Military flying is specifically excluded from the Kyoto Protocol. If military operations *were* included, then any country would be able to reduce emissions simply by cutting its military activities. The world would thus benefit twice over. Military and training exercises alone represent 10 per cent of total fossil fuel consumption, and the military sector is a major producer of chemical and nuclear waste.[53]

Yet, when the war is over, the environment remains scarred and potentially lethal for up to decades later. Although wild cedar is the national symbol of Lebanon and is legally protected, the remaining rare cedar forests, which only also exist in Syria and Turkey, have not escaped damage by military activity.[54] During the Vietnam War, the herbicide Agent Orange was used to obliterate vegetation; over thirty years later the country's flora has not fully recovered.[55] When soil is polluted and mines remain in the ground, this prevents full habitat restoration and cultivation.

The impact of war, regardless of the reason for which it was originally fought, is destructive to life forms, habitats and the environment. Government money devoted to defence expenditure represents finances stripped from more cooperative ventures such as healthcare, education and the environment.[56]

Asia's Endangered Wildlife

Asia's striking mammals suffer greatly from the illegal wildlife trade. Indeed, WWF used a Halloween mailshot to underline the threat to the continent's tiger, rhino and orang-utan species. Having declined 95 per cent in the last century to only 5,000–7,000 left in the wild today, the tiger population faces a resurgence of a black market trade in their skins. Only five breeds of rhino remain after tens of thousands were killed for their horns for medicines and as dagger handles in the Middle East. The WWF supports breeding populations in protected areas in India, Bhutan and Nepal to ensure the species' future survival. Similarly, it is working to conserve Asia's only great ape, the

War of the world: oil wells ablaze blacken out the sun during the Gulf War.

orang-utan, from the illegal wildlife trade by establishing well-managed, secure, protected areas.[57]

Certainly, habitat destruction and fragmentation has had severe implications for Asia's wildlife, including its giant pandas. But it is the wilful theft and smuggling of many of these creatures that has been most responsible in recent years for the dramatic decline in Asia's mammals. The black market generates about £5bn (nearly US$10bn) a year, behind only gun-running and drug-smuggling as a profit-maker in the region.[58]

Zoos, conservation parks and private collectors across the world especially desire baby orang-utans, so hunters obtain them by killing their parents and snatching the young apes from the islands of Sumatra and Borneo, the only places they are found in the wild. Additionally, a craze for pet orang-utans in Indonesia is further contributing to the species' annihilation. The very forests on which the orang-utans depend for tree bark, flowers, insects and fruit are also being wiped out to make space for oil palm plantations, a hugely lucrative crop. In the West, palm oil is an ingredient used in around 10 per cent of products found on supermarket shelves. Additionally, palm oil is a key ingredient of the growing biofuel market, and its cultivation indicates how a misdirected response to climate change can have its own disastrous consequences.

Of a world population of 60,000 orang-utans, about 5,000 die each year. It is a slow-growing species, the young apes nursed until they are six years old, and the females able to bear only four or five offspring on average during their forty-year lifetime. Orang-utans are thus being killed off faster than they can replenish their numbers.[59] Many conservationists fear that they could be extinct in the wild within ten years.[60]

Michael Morpurgo, author of *Kensuke's Kingdom*, a children's novel about orang-utans living on an island in the Coral Sea,[61] points out:

'This is a relatively small problem. The plight of the Orang-Utan is a microcosm of why conservation is important. If we can't say to the market we don't want palm oil, if we can't put pressure on the UN and government to curtail deforestation, we certainly can't handle the big problems. We are in danger of wiping out a fellow species, not because it is dangerous but because we are greedy. It's not just a shame or a pity – it's about whether there will be a planet at all in 300 or 500 yrs. If the market continues to dominate the world, there won't be. We need to protest to governments about it – as we did very successfully with the panda. If you pick off those endangered one by one and try to conserve them, we are acknowledging our responsibility to conserve the richness of the planet we all inherit. If we don't, it's simply self-destruction.'[62]

Conservation icon: the continued survival of China's giant panda is a symbol of hope and effective conservation policy.

The giant panda was expected to have been wiped out by now, but tales of its imminent extinction proved premature. Indeed, 2005–06 was a bumper year in terms of cubs born in captivity in China, and they were lined up like human sextuplets for their photo-shoot.[63] More significantly, however, a 2000–04 study of China's giant pandas – including two years of intense fieldwork – unexpectedly revealed that there were almost 1,600 still living in the wild, 40 per cent more than were previously thought to exist.

Conducted by China's State Forestry Administration and WWF, the Third National Survey revealed there to be as many as 500 more of the animals than there were between 1985 and 1988 when the last panda survey took place.[64] In 1989, satellite imagery revealed a halving of occupied habitat since 1974.[65] The 2004 research combined fieldwork and GPS technology stretching over 23,000 sq km (8,900 sq miles) in a bid to count every one of the country's giant pandas, rather than extrapolate numbers across China from the panda count in a specific region as was done previously. Additionally, researchers took account of the condition of natural resources, and how people lived within the habitats studied.

Although giant pandas were newly discovered to be living in areas such as Liuba and Ningqiang counties, the higher numbers detected suggest improvements in research methods rather than an improvement in habitat. Deforestation, illegal logging, and poaching are notable threats, though the Natural Forest Protection Programme banning logging in natural forests, and the Grain-to-Green policy designed to convert hillside agricultural land back into forest are making some impact.

The survey identified the Sichuan's Minshan mountain ranges and Shaanxi's Qinling mountain range as areas requiring essential conservation work including reforestation, anti-poaching action and continued wildlife monitoring.

In the Shaanxi province, the survey supplemented an existing partnership between the local government and WWF that had been established the previous year. Benefiting directly from the Chinese state's establishment of the

'Before, my job was to prevent forest fires and to stop the illegal use of land, but I didn't know anything about wildlife. But now I view pandas as a national treasure. I feel it's an honour to manage an area where giant pandas live.'

ZHU DONG FENG, HEAD OF THE NEW THIRTY-STRONG CONSERVATION TEAM AT HOUZHENZI FOREST PLANTATION

National Conservation Management Plan for the Giant Panda and Its Habitat in 1992, the pair worked to create five new panda reserves and five forested corridors re-linking important panda habitats across the region to curb inbreeding among isolated panda communities, some numbering fewer than fifty animals. In twenty years, the number of panda reserves has all but quadrupled to forty and over 16,000 sq km (6,200 sq miles) of forest habitat has been protected.

The Chinese government has been concerned about the nation's panda population for over forty years. Its then Ministry of Forestry carried out the First National Panda Survey from 1974 to 1977, and WWF, the first international conservation organization invited to work in China, became involved in giant panda work in 1980. The third and latest survey introduced nature reserve staff to valuable technology and training to support their conservation work. Technicians were even able to identify individual pandas by the length of bamboo shards found in droppings, as each animal has a different bite.[66] The very success of the Third National Survey could make a fourth one unnecessary; nature reserve staff are now regularly patrolling and monitoring their patches and networking with other reserves. By 2012, WWF's Giant Panda Programme aims to have increased panda populations and habitats by a minimum of 10 per cent in selected priority areas and to stabilize them elsewhere.

While China's ongoing work conserving giant pandas is commendable, neighbour Japan has faced criticism for its long-term commitment to overturning the International Whaling Commission's (IWC) 1986 ban on commercial whaling.[67] Japan argues that whaling is central to its culture, and that increasing whale populations are depleting fish stocks, though scientific evidence refutes this.[68] Japan already hunts minke whales within the Southern Ocean Whale Sanctuary.

Although a majority of nations voted in favour of legalizing commercial whaling at the 2006 Commission in St Kitts, there was not enough of a majority for the ban to be lifted.[69] Nevertheless, the voting pattern represents a shift away from conservation towards management of hunting whales; led by Japan, the pro-whaling nations such as Iceland can now set the agenda of the IWC.[70]

South-East Asia's Biodiversity Hotspots

The South-East Asian nations of Vietnam, Cambodia, Thailand, Myanmar and Laos are united with Bhutan and Nepal, as well as neighbouring coastal islands, by their designation as the Indo-Burma hotspot. Encompassing both lowlands and mountainous regions, this area boasts a rich range of flora and fauna; as many as half of the plants in any habitat are endemic. Similarly, 41 per cent of reptiles, 56 per cent of amphibians and 22 per cent of mammals are endemic to the region.[71] Owing to its unique geology and geography, Indonesia is one of the most biologically diverse countries in the world, and incorporates both the Sundaland and Wallacea hotspots. While its 13,000 plus islands cover only 1.3 per cent of the planet's land surface, the country contains 10 per cent of the world's flowering plant species, 12 per cent of the world's mammal species, 17 per cent of the world's bird species and over 25 per cent of all fish species.[72]

Yet growing industrialization of agriculture across South-East Asia is encouraging deforestation and threatening wildlife, including the Asian

Asian Vultures

The loss of Asia's vultures is especially a crisis for India's Parsi population, 60,000 of whom live around Mumbai. Their Zoroastrian faith demands that their dead be placed on slabs of marble to be devoured by the birds so that the body does not contaminate the sacred elements of Earth, fire and water.[73] Vultures play a vital role in India. Without them, disease and pollution from unclean carcasses can spread, and the growing population of wild dogs that feed on what was once the bird's food heightens the risk of rabies.

Yet the birds have been dying out because their regular diet of cattle carcasses was contaminated with the widely used anti-inflammatory drug Diclofenac. Once one of the most common birds of prey, the Indian vulture population plummeted by 97 per cent in the fifteen-year period up to 2006.[74] The white-rumped and slender-billed vultures, the latter the rarest of the three species, have also been designated as 'critically endangered' because of this threat.

In 2005, the Indian government announced a phasing out of Diclofenac;[75] a safe alternative, Meloxicam, is now available. Captive breeding has also been encouraged to sustain the vulture population. BirdLife International has collected good numbers of each of the species and taken them into care until the environment proves safe enough for them to return.

elephant and tiger. Hunting both for food and for the exotic species market also decimates these already-threatened species. Coastal ecosystems including coral reefs are prey to destructive fishing methods. In poorer regions, age-old slash-and-burn methods of subsistence farming lead to loss of forests through uncontrolled fires. Many South-East Asian countries have expressed a commitment to controlling deforestation and protecting wildlife, but economic development is contributing to environmental stress in the region.

Taking Action

1. Be aware of the amount of water required to grow the crops on which you depend for everyday necessities, such as food and clothing. According to Fred Pearce:

'By some calculations, as much as a tenth of the world's food is being grown using underground water that is not being replaced by the rains. Without our knowing it, much of the rich world is importing crops grown using over-pumped

underground water reserves – cotton from Pakistan, rice from Thailand, tomatoes from Israel, coffee from Ethiopia and even Spanish oranges and Australian sugar.

Looked at another way, every teaspoonful of sugar in your coffee requires 50 cups of water to grow it. Growing the coffee itself requires 140 litres of water, or 1,120 cups. In ways such as this, a typical meat-eating, milk-guzzling westerner consumes as much as a hundred times their own weight in water every day. Clothing only adds to the hydrological pain. You could fill 25 bathtubs with the water that grows the 250 grams of cotton needed to make a single T-shirt.[76]

This is water that developing countries cannot afford to lose. As Mahatma Gandhi once said, 'Live more simply so that others can simply live.'[77]

2. If the water from your taps is drinkable, value this source; fill a jug and keep it in your fridge and it will taste better than bottled water. Fill up a reusable bottle to carry with you rather than buy a new one.

3. Palm oil is often listed simply as vegetable oil so it is not possible to simply stop buying products made of it. And boycotting it would not help communities struggling out of poverty. According to Friends of the Earth, 'Ethical shopping alone won't change the behaviour of the palm oil companies. New rules are needed to hold companies accountable for the damage they do.'[78] Contact your local Friends of the Earth to support their campaigns.

4. The World Commission on Dams (WCD) was established in May 1998 to address controversial issues associated with large dams and the difficulties with reconciling economic growth, social equality, environmental conservation and political participation. Its final report was published in November 2000. It was followed by the UNEP's Dam and Development Project. Visit www.unep-dams.org for information about follow-up initiatives around the world, reactions to the WCD's final report, and submissions on good practice.

5. The Friends of River Narmada is an international coalition of individuals and organizations (primarily of Indian descent) who act as a support and solidarity network for the Narmada Bachao Andolan ('Save the Narmada movement'), which has been fighting for the democratic rights of the citizens of the Narmada Valley. Access their website at www.narmada.org/about-us.html to keep abreast of the campaign.

6. To financially support the Bhopal Medical Appeal for the provision of free medical care and treatment to Bhopal survivors, contact www.bhopal.org/donations/index.html .

7. Volunteer to work at Bhopal's Sambhavna Trust Medical Clinic. Access www.bhopal.org/volunteer.html for further information.

8. Adopt-A-Minefield is a campaign of the United Nations Association of the USA that helps save lives by raising funds for mine clearance and survivor assistance and by raising awareness about the problem of landmines. For details of how to support its work, and of partner campaigns, contact www.landmines.org/about .

9. In 2003, outbreaks of avian flu in South-East Asia led to the slaughter of over 150 million poultry. Visit the World Health Organisation's webpage on the issue at www.who.int/csr/disease/avian_influenza/en and the US Government Department of Health and Human Services website at www.pandemicflu.gov to keep up to date with developments.

10. For further information on China's giant pandas, the Third National Panda Survey, and WWF's Giant Panda Programme, visit www.wwfchina.org/english/pandacentral and www.panda.org/species/panda .

11. The annual International Union for Conservation of Nature and Natural Resources (IUCN) Red List is an ongoing database of the world's threatened species. Access it at www.iucnredlist.org, select a species and support those organizations working to save it.

12. Paved-over land prevents rainwater from percolating through the soil and bolstering water table levels, and increases the chances of flooding since water cannot drain away. Provide land space in your driveway and garden to allow nature to literally take its course.

'... *God is the spirit that unites all life, everything that is on this planet. It must be this voice that is telling me to do something, and I am sure it's the same voice that is speaking to everybody on this planet – at least everybody who seems to be concerned about the fate of the world, the fate of this planet.*'

Wangari Maathai

Africa

CHAPTER 5

The continent of Africa covers 30,300,000 sq km (11,700,000 sq miles) and is made up of approximately fifty-four countries (some are disputed) plus Madagascar and other islands. Sudan, at 2,505,816 sq km (967,500 sq miles) is the largest country. Africa is bounded by the Atlantic Ocean on the west, the Indian Ocean on the east, the Mediterranean Sea to the north and the Red Sea to the north-east.

The geographical make-up of the world's second largest continent has had a profound influence on the developmental and environmental state of modern Africa. That it is home to both the Sahara, the planet's largest desert, and the Nile, the world's longest terrestrial river, is symbolic of the extremes found within its borders.

Africa is the only continent to span both north and south temperate zones, sandwiching a thick tropical core. Although grasslands cover much of Africa, while rainforests flourished in central Africa close to the equator, its landscapes are more diverse than those of any other continent. In fact, according to the WWF, it can be divided into 104 terrestrial ecosystems – including the rich Karoo in western South Africa and Namibia; the Western Congolian swamp forests and the Angolan Miombo woodlands; and the Sahara – 'each unique in its physical and climatic features and harbouring a distinct plant and animal community'.[1]

However, throughout Africa's history, such diversity has not proved beneficial to its human population, which now totals 900 million people. The continent's very north-south orientation hindered the development of agriculture, the domestication of wild animals and plants, and the consequent human settlement in permanent villages that was occurring east-west with relative ease elsewhere around 10,000 years ago. For example, it took 5,000 years for domesticated sheep and cattle to spread from the Mediterranean to the southern tip of Africa. Its different latitudes required adaptation to a range of climates, seasonal shifts, day lengths and diseases.

The continent's native plant species such as sorghum, oil palm, coffee, millets and yams were only domesticated thousands of years *after* Asia and Europe had developed their own agriculture. In addition, the crops of equatorial Africa could not spread into Africa's temperate zone.

Today, while South Africa has the richest agricultural lands of the continent, its successful wheat and grape crops are northern temperate crops

Previous spread: Standing tall: Mount Kilimanjaro in Tanzania towers over the striking landscape and wildlife its threatened meltwaters support.

Wangari Maathai and the Green Belt Movement

In 2004, Wangari Maathai was awarded a Nobel Peace Prize Laureate in international recognition for her inspirational environmental work across Kenya. In 1977, she founded the Green Belt Movement, a tree-planting campaign, in a bid to reforest her homeland and create employment. Once regarded a dissident, she was eventually made Kenya's Assistant Minister for the Environment because of her valuable work.

It was while she was a professor in the University of Nairobi's Faculty of Veterinary Medicine in the 1970s, visiting rural areas, that she first began to make connections between local people's unfulfilled basic needs such as firewood, clean water and nutritious food, and the conversion of Kenya's indigenous forests into plantations for cash crops. She noted that without adequate vegetation knitting it together, topsoil was being washed away in the rains, leading to widespread land degradation.

Via a National Council of the Women of Kenya forum, Maathai suggested that women engage in tree-planting not only to combat soil erosion but also to provide wood and a food source. She was thus regarded as rebellious, not for the actual tree-planting, but because its very organization emphasized the mismanagement of the environment by other interests.

Today, Wangari Maathai's work is deeply respected in her homeland and across the world. She promotes the need for education about the environment and the government to encourage citizens' active involvement in positively shaping their nation. But she sees it as a two-way process: without those in power – whether at a local or national level – respecting the people's rights and wishes, then the environment will gradually be destroyed by the privatization of public lands.

She recognizes that establishing the value of the environment will secure development. Natural resources, managed responsibly and shared equitably, reduce conflicts between peoples. At a local, rural level it also discourages migration to Kenya's cities in search of employment.

Her environmental work goes hand in hand with her belief in the importance of women contributing as much as men to Kenya's development. She wants to see a world where women of all ages are honoured and rewarded for their contribution to society. In particular, she wants girls and young women across the world to be inspired and grow committed to pursuing and achieving worthwhile goals.

In the rural communities of the developing world, women's voices and experiences are often disregarded in spite of their rich and vital contribution to society. Maathai's tree-planting initiative is a parable in itself: out of little seedlings, women have gained confidence in what they have to offer and how they can change their world for good.

that were brought on ships by European colonists in the seventeenth century. Africa's thick tropical core otherwise forms a distinct barrier, particularly to agriculture and animal husbandry. Similarly, only guinea fowl, possibly donkeys and one breed of cattle proved amenable to domestication, so not only farming but also training native animals for military purposes was not possible.[2]

Additionally, approximately a third of Africa's mainland countries are landlocked, and the only river navigable from the ocean for long distances inland is the Nile. Such lack of waterways to transport cumbersome goods has further limited Africa's progress.

> 'Along with the human struggles come human impacts. Although some areas of landscape are less heavily inhabited than they might be, others are overburdened, eroded, blighted by the presence and demands of too many people.'
>
> CONSERVATIONIST AND AWARD-WINNING SCIENCE, NATURE AND TRAVEL WRITER DAVID QUAMMEN, IN AN ARTICLE FOR A NATIONAL GEOGRAPHIC SPECIAL ISSUE ON AFRICA

That the human race emerged in Africa before its expansion into Europe and Asia may be part of the reason why, for now, large mammals still survive on the African continent. They gained a healthy fear of people in tune with humans' gradual development of hunting skills. In contrast, the Americas and Australia were settled a mere tens of thousands of years ago by homo sapiens with more developed brains and better hunting skills. The woolly mammoths, sabre-toothed cats and Australia's rhino-sized marsupials were therefore unsuspecting, easy prey and quickly died out.[3]

However, as the long-ago 'cradle of humanity', Africa proved ripe for the cross-species spread of disease, including malaria, yellow fever, sleeping sickness and AIDS. Disease-causing microbes in animals need a long time to evolve into human diseases, and Africa provided that. And vice versa. The microbes required relatively little evolutionary adaptation to jump from humans to the continent's great apes and monkeys.

Today, climate change is damaging the inroads made into fighting poverty and promoting sustainable development across the continent. Indeed, of all the world, Africa will be worst hit by a destructive combination of rising sea levels, low crop yields and stricken habitats.[4] Since 2004, the Horn of Africa has been suffering tremendous drought, which is cutting a swathe through both human and animal populations. Should the rains continue to fail, then potentially an entire quarter of the landmass will become uninhabitable for none but the most hardy, desert-based species.

Development and the Environment

As in other developing regions of the world, in Africa there is potential conflict between encouraging human communities to improve their standard of living by improved access to education, healthcare and employment opportunities, and protecting the environment. However, the development of new technologies is already offering an alternative, less exploitative means of improving people's lifestyles.

It has always been difficult to establish the necessary wiring for full-scale electricity provision and landline phone maintenance across Africa. Fewer than one in five Africans have direct access to reliable sources of electricity, and in some rural parts of the continent, fewer than one in fifty people do so. In addition to the cost of communication provision and maintenance, a lack of roads and unreliable energy sources, as well as political instability and corruption, all serve to put a spanner in the works.

New technologies, however, are allowing people in many places to bypass such poor infrastructures and so access modern conveniences. It is easier and cheaper, for example, to set up mobile phone towers in remote regions such as southern Sudan than to string wire overland. Previously, the closest landline phone was a week's trek away in Uganda. Between 1999 and 2004 there was a tenfold increase in mobile phone users in Africa – from 7.5 million to 76.98 million – a growth rate faster than that of anywhere else on the planet.[5] Today, 70 per cent of Africa's phone subscribers are connected by cellular phones, served mostly in regions that previously never had phone access at all.[6]

It is not simply the professional classes in burgeoning urban districts – such as bank customers in Nairobi keeping track of their accounts via text messaging – who benefit. Vital information can also be shared across rural districts using accessible new technology too. Shepherds in the drought-ridden Sahel region are directing each other to scarce grazing pastures on handheld GPS units and cell phones. In Ethiopia, teachers use solar-powered satellite radios to receive lessons to broadcast to their classes.

The man behind the mobile boom, Celtel owner Mohammed Ibrahim, has since used his business acumen and finances to establish the Mo Ibrahim Foundation Prize for Achievement in African Leadership, which encourages good governance in African states, and consequently promotes development.[7]

Others are homing in on the continent's business potential too. The northern Arab states and English-speaking sub-Saharan African states are being touted as growth markets for call centres and data and telecommunications outsourcing to rival India.[8] China is now Africa's third most important trading partner after the US and France, with oil the main commodity. Africa represents a source of raw materials and a market for China's rapid economic growth; while it has invested in African infrastructure and cancelled $1bn of the continent's debt, it has also pumped money into dubious regimes, such as Robert Mugabe's in Zimbabwe, and supplied arms to warring states. The international community is putting pressure on China to modify its policies for Africa's benefit.[9]

However, development does not have to be destructive. People can be raised out of poverty and not be mired in conflict. The continent's rich resources can benefit local communities rather than be snatched from them. Environmentally, abundant resources such as the central African rivers can be used to generate hydroelectric power, which, although bringing its own problems such as the flooding of valleys and wildlife habitats behind high dams, does not produce greenhouse gases that contribute to global warming. Ecotourism, too, has proved a major source of revenue in eastern and southern Africa as visitors come to see the continent's large mammals in the wild. Additionally, the world's second largest rainforest could be better managed; instead of being farmed out illegally to timber companies by the Congalese government,[10] it could be logged in a sustainable manner as a lucrative and renewable source of income.

The Impact of Climate Change

The world's poorest communities are proving the least able to adapt to and cope with the already pressing impact of climate change. They are also the least responsible for the greenhouse gas emissions predominantly responsible for it. The average Briton, for example, produces the same amount of carbon dioxide in ten days that the average Kenyan citizen does in a year,[11] but it is the latter who is watching their land turn to dust. Indeed, as atmospheric temperatures rise, huge swathes of the continent look set to ultimately become uninhabitable, leading either to mass starvation or the enforcement of wholesale migration.

The semi-arid Sahel region south of the Sahara Desert is spreading and encroaching on previously fertile land, forcing nomadic tribes such as the Masai further south in search of pasture for their cattle.[12] Already, in the Horn of Africa the loss of crops and valuable cows and goats (for many families, their only source of wealth) to long-term drought is devastating pastoralists' livelihoods, and forcing millions of people to depend increasingly on food aid. In addition, malaria-carrying mosquitoes are spreading into highland areas historically free from malaria, and water-borne diseases are on the increase.[13]

Unfortunately, the international aid system tends to *respond* to emergencies with food aid, rather than be involved earlier in disaster preparedness, which could help to protect people from the worst effects, such as loss of livestock – a symbol of wealth and status and the bedrock of pastoral communities. UN estimates in 2006 suggested eleven million people in Somalia, Kenya, Ethiopia, Eritrea and Burundi would need food airlifts to survive the drought.[14] In Rwanda, which has a predominantly agriculture-based economy, the shrivelled crops and evaporated water supplies proved disastrous for a country still recovering from the 1994 civil war in which almost one million of its people were killed. An estimated thirty-five million people across the continent's central sub-Saharan region, which stretches from Niger in the west to the eastern tip of the Horn of Africa, were threatened with starvation in 2006.[15]

In addition to increasing temperatures, annual dry seasons are extending in some African regions from a once-standard four months of the year to more than half of the year. Such conditions not only lead to crop failure but also drain food stocks and confuse farmers over the correct planting times. Wisdom and hard-gleaned knowledge about the weather and seasons that has been passed down through generations is proving useless in the face of these new climate patterns.

Conflict has developed between local communities as well as between people and wildlife as they compete for dwindling resources. Against the wishes of Kenya's wildlife rangers, the country's familiar Masai herdsmen have begun to encroach on nature reserves in search of pastureland for their own hungry livestock. In northern Kenya – where more than 70 per cent of domestic animals died from thirst or starvation in 2006, their abandoned carcasses scarring the landscape – and also northern Uganda and southern Somalia, violence has increased as warring tribes raid each other's remaining livestock to survive. Tragically, more men have died in such conflicts over grasslands and water sources than have died from Kenya's actual drought.[16] When heavy rains did eventually come, they caused severe flooding and threatened an already fragile food situation by washing away vital roads used to provide humanitarian relief, and making 3,000 people homeless.[17]

'Climate change threatens to undo decades of development work.'

TEARFUND

Yet the problems of climate change besetting Africa cannot be seen in isolation. Political unrest such as that in Darfur, Sudan or Zimbabwe, plus the huge impact of AIDS and the potential vast consequences of bird flu across the continent, indicate the interconnectedness of Africa's environmental, political and social conditions.

The Spreading Desert

Around a third of the Earth's land area is harsh, barren desert with northern Africa's Sahara Desert the largest of them all. Indeed, the same dry region effectively spreads eastward along the planet's meridian line into the Middle East, where it is known as the Arabian and Iranian deserts. The southern region of Africa incorporates the Kalahari and Namib deserts.

The most arid of deserts experience an average rainfall of less than 100 mm (4 in) per year. However, it is also low humidity levels and consequent lack of cloud cover that expose the land surface to direct sunlight and drive the evaporation of water faster than the rain can replenish it. It is this lack of water, rather than the high temperatures of most desert regions, that is their most significant characteristic, especially in relation to life forms trying to exist within such a severe environment.

The Sahara Desert extends from the Atlantic Ocean in the west to the Red Sea in the east, and covers an area of over 9 million sq km (3.5 million sq miles); the equivalent size of the United States and a third of Africa. In parts of Libya, temperatures higher than 55°C (131°F) have been recorded,[18] whereas in other areas, frost has been seen during winter. Its landscape crosses all desert types, from classic shifting sand dunes (*ergs*) to vast rock-strewn plains (*reg*).

The Melting Snows of Kilimanjaro

Tanzania's Mount Kilimanjaro is an iconic geological feature that rises up out of the East African plateau and draws tourists from around the world set on mastering its snowy peak. But the increasing retreat of the extinct volcano's ice fields and their predicted disappearance between 2015 and 2020 – due in part to global warming – will do more than just disrupt a local economy that has grown dependent on the tourist industry.

Around 20,000 tourists visit the world-famous mountain every year, making Kilimanjaro the highest foreign currency earner throughout the whole of Tanzania. Mount Kilimanjaro's breathtaking aesthetic appeal, however, masks the necessity of its seasonal melting waters for the human communities and wildlife that live close to the mountain.

Without these waters, they die of thirst. Already, with the average temperature in the area having risen by about 1°C, water volume in some of the Tanzanian rivers that feed local villages and hospitals has declined. Drinking water supplies, crop irrigation and hydroelectric production are all threatened.[19]

The mountaintop's plight therefore starkly represents our planet's dependence on the viability of the environment, whether locally or further afield. For the tourists who visit in their thousands to perceive the beauty of the snow-covered peaks, and for scientists who record the gradual melting, the loss of the snows is a cause for concern. However, the real problem lies not in the mere disappearance of snow, but in its wider implications for the human populations who will be affected: Mount Kilimanjaro shows how they cannot be so simply disconnected. One – quite literally – feeds into the other.

Geophysics experts from the United States' Ohio State University have surveyed the decaying ice fields via expeditions and aerial recording, calculating that over 82 per cent of the fields were lost between 1912 (when they were first mapped) and 2000.[20] Yet the speed of current glacial retreat is such that scientists are not convinced that it is due to human-induced global warming alone. Kilimanjaro has been iceless before, when the Earth's Tropics experienced severe droughts 8,300, 5,200 and 4,000 years ago and civilizations across the globe collapsed as a result. Whatever caused such climate change could occur again – a recurring cyclical event.

Global warming is making an impact on even the world's hardy desert environments. The spread of any desert into neighbouring regions – known as desertification – is a notable result. Globally, useful land lost each year exceeds 6 million hectares (15 million acres), and the Sahara has spread southwards by an extra 65 million hectares (161 million acres) in the last half a century.[21]

As atmospheric temperatures become warmer and drier, plants and animals on the periphery of any desert cannot be supported by the decline in available water. Yet local human activity has also contributed significantly to the loss of land. Intensive agriculture that does not allow soil to remain fallow for any length of time to renew itself, overgrazing of livestock, and felling of trees and shrubs for fuel all contribute to desertification. Without cover, the fragile soil is prey to erosion from the region's harsh winds, rain and sun.

Over centuries, farmers have developed efficient and relatively environmentally harmless methods of harnessing the water from the desert's limited supply of springs, oases and underground sources. However, in more recent times, human population growth has intensified pressure to increase food production and has encouraged unsustainable irrigation practices that further suck the land dry.

Because of the limited rain and the high levels of sunshine across most of the Sahara, the desert as a potential site for solar energy production has been postulated in certain quarters. Some have argued that a mere 1 per cent of the entire Sahara could provide Africa's populous developing nations with cheap, clean electricity and in fact all of the Earth's inhabitants with as much renewable energy as they need and desire.[22]

However, storms and strong winds also are erratic and unpredictable features of the world's desert weather systems. As with rain showers, the winds can be highly localized, or alternatively they can blow for extended periods, and the dust and sand they inevitably carry can reduce visibility to nil. Whirlwinds – or 'dust devils' – can prove extremely disruptive and dangerous to anything that might be in their path. Strategically placed solar panels or solar chimneys[23] would no doubt prove to be in the line of fire of such natural phenomena.

The Nile River

As the longest terrestrial river in the world, what is happening environmentally to Africa's Nile River can be extrapolated to the world's other great rivers too. Historically, the land surrounding the Nile has been highly fertile and productive with access to a proven water supply. But, like other rivers worldwide, the water levels are declining, leading ultimately to civil war among the populations dependent on them. For example, the lower reaches of the Nile used to carry 32 billion cubic metres of water a year, now they are down to a mere 2 billion.[24]

The Aswan Dam, like dams elsewhere, alters the course of the river and much of the huge collection of water in the reservoir behind it evaporates into

Earth's Biggest Wildlife Cavalcade

Every year, around a million wildebeest (gnu), along with approximately 200,000 zebras and 300,000 Thomson's gazelles, plus their hangers-on (and given the wealth of free-range meat available there are a lot of carnivorous hangers-on) migrate. These two million-plus mammals embark on a nearly 1,300 km (800 mile) cyclical journey across East Africa from Tanzania's Serengeti plains in autumn/winter to begin their calving season in the normally lush volcanic open plains below the Ngorongoro Crater, and then 'thunder north towards Kenya in one of the greatest natural spectacles on Earth'.[25]

The ungulates, or hoofed mammals, leave the dry season behind them to follow the rains and feed off the potassium- and calcium-rich grass that sprouts afterwards, so that they might produce healthy calves. From strategic vantage points provided by the rocks and trees that edge the route, predatory lions, leopards and hyenas observe the steady migratory stream, preparing to pounce on any stragglers or weaker members of the herd. Crocodiles also take advantage of the mass crossings of as many as tens of thousands of ungulates across rivers that traverse their transnational route.

The wildebeest migration is the biggest movement of wildlife on Earth; nowhere else can such a range of species and sheer number of animals be witnessed together. It also makes a vital contribution to the maintenance of East Africa's savannah and grasslands. The annual storm-through of creatures provides a yearly cropping-back of the grasses. But this mind-blowing spectacle is threatened by drought.

In 2006, the rains did not come. It was the worst local drought in more than three decades. The animals, driven to search for water beyond their natural pastures to survive, became confused as to where to go in search of better grazing. There were no rains to draw them, and the bone-dry pastures disguised the route through once well-worn migratory corridors. The reduced numbers of calves born had not enough food or water to survive, and that year's birth rate proved dangerously low.

The migration has occurred for thousands of years, having experienced periodic slumps in number from disease and drought, or from hunting and poaching by local people. Too much rain or erratic storms can also cause confusion among the animals and lead to disruption of the migration as they scatter to scavenge the new fresh and juicy grass. Additionally, human settlements have begun to encroach on the northern migration routes. Heavy rains recorded in the entire Masai Mara in September 2005 'so confused the wildebeests and zebras that they did not know which direction to follow'.[26] A month earlier, herds had been observed crossing the Mara River more than

Opposite:
The longest journey: clouds of dust thrown up by the thundering of wildebeest hooves follow the annual migration across East Africa's plains and rivers.

once, the sated crocodiles merely watching, because of the disorientation caused by the rains.[27]

The 2006 decline could therefore be an inevitable seasonal dip. Yet if the drought that stalked both humans and wildlife in East Africa in the early years of the twenty-first century was a symptom of global warming, then the cycle of migration can only thin out more.

the atmosphere. Additionally, the damming has led to a building up of silt, which reduces the amount of fertile land, damages fish supplies and causes soil erosion.

Ironically, the very use to which the Nile's waters have been put for millennia – that of irrigating crops – is killing the river. As populations have increased so too has pressure on resources; today, irrigation siphons off 70 per cent of the river's water supply.[28]

But the population increase does not only impact agricultural needs. Due to an influx of sewage, pesticides, fertilizers and industrial waste from increased development, the Nile is one of the world's most polluted rivers. However, because the Nile snakes its way through a range of countries, it is difficult to monitor their adherence to treaties.

Africa's Wildlife

Africa's wildlife faces a precarious future, not simply because of the impact of climate change and localized threats such as bush meat production, poaching and political corruption. In the face of large-scale human suffering, particularly that due to drought or rising sea levels, the fate of wildlife, especially how humans can help it survive an increasingly harsh environment, comes a poor second.

When hungry wildlife – such as more than half of the elephant population of Kenya's Tsavo National Park[29] – leaves its reserves in search of food and starts encroaching on human habitation, it is humans (themselves facing famine) who inevitably receive the greater sympathy. With limited compensation available for damage caused by wildlife, it is also understandable, although regretful, when people take the law into their own hands and hunt animals down in order to protect their property.

Yet these much-loved creatures represent the diversity and richness of the continent, and without them the whole world becomes a poorer place. Yes, they attract much-needed tourist money, but these species also have their own value and integrity whether or not they are viewed by human visitors.

The fauna of East Africa and its Rift Valley in particular are under threat, and it is arguable that humans alone can protect the Serengeti and Masai Mara ecosystems. Already, hippopotamuses dependent on mud to keep them cool are dying with the disappearing rivers. The impact of different species being forced to share the same fast-diminishing habitats is exemplified by the case of endangered Grevy's zebras, which have been killed by anthrax believed to have been contracted from cattle grazing on neighbouring pasture.[30]

Madagascar's endangered lemur population – which are only found in this country – face extinction because of their reliance on water during their reproductive cycle. Since it is only recently that three new species of lemur have been discovered, there is a fear that others might die out before they are ever known.[31] Even a small reduction in rainfall affects the quantity of milk female lemurs can produce to feed their young.[32] Although lemurs live within the damp rainforest, such a habitat is highly susceptible to changes in climate, which threaten the species that thrive there.

Today, a more direct human activity is having a detrimental effect on Africa's wildlife. The billion-dollar 'bush meat' industry is decimating numbers. As much as five million tonnes of 'bush meat' – from wild animals including antelope, primates, crocodiles, and even elephants and hippos – are taken, much of it illegally, from central Africa's rainforests every year.[33]

For forest tribespeople for whom bush meat has always been their only source of protein, the widespread poaching and consequent loss of these animals is leading to malnutrition and, ultimately, starvation. For those who live outside the forest, bush meat represents a cheap alternative when fish is scarce or too expensive. Besides being a valuable source of protein, however, bush meat is also linked to the spread of Ebola and AIDS. Urbanites, too, continue to eat it to remind them of their heritage and also because it carries with it a certain social cache.

To reduce hunting in Ghana, fish farming, the rearing of grasscutters (a domesticated native rodent),[34] and the cultivation of low-cost protein sources like beans are being encouraged as alternatives. Employment programmes have been developed to reduce the desperate need for bush meat, and hunting regulations are also being enforced.

The threat to Africa's wildlife and its environment is very real, yet countless vital conservation projects across Africa often have scant resources. Since 2000, the African Conservation Foundation's (ACF) website has brought together these widespread initiatives to share information and experiences and so develop a continent-wide network of support. The ACF is also involved directly in wildlife and habitat protection projects, and trains, equips and funds research and communication technologies for those in the field. Its overall goal is 'to change the approach of the management and utilization of natural resources to one in which the needs of human development in the region are reconciled with natural resource conservation'.[35]

Similarly, WWF has developed programmes supporting local projects and the continent's network of national parks and reserves; endangered species, including African hunting dogs, goliath frogs and the iconic black and white rhinos, have been given some protection, though their existence remains precarious. For example, the WWF-backed Rwanda Mountain Gorilla Project unites the government and local people in increasing conservation awareness. It also raises funds for scientific study and environmental protection through controlled tourist visits to the gorillas' mountain habitat on the borders of the Democratic Republic of Congo, Rwanda and Uganda. By the early 1980s fewer than 500 remained in the wild, their numbers depleted by hunting, capture for the zoo trade and loss of habitat.[36] Today, the biggest threats to the species are disease and regional armed conflict.

Africa's Valuable Mineral Resources

Africa is a continent rich in resources, including oil, gas, gold and diamonds. Their exploitation and ownership has been at the heart of most of the conflict across the landmass over at least the past half-century. Interests of foreign investors, national governments, the local population and those concerned with the impact on the natural environment often compete over the issue of resource exploitation. While on the surface such resources would appear to bring much-needed revenue into a region, the money is often siphoned away from the local economy and the people who depend on it.

Money from the mining and trade of Africa's diamonds is notorious for funding armed conflicts in countries such as the Democratic Republic of Congo. The United Nations imposed an embargo against diamonds from rebel-controlled areas of Angola and Sierra Leone because links between the diamond industry and the gross abuse of the civilian population were so

Ken Saro-Wiwa and Nigeria's Oil

On 10 November 1995, Ken Saro-Wiwa, the Nigerian environmental activist, recipient of the Goldman Environmental Prize, Nobel Prize-nominated writer, and spokesperson of the Ogoni people, was executed – with eight of his compatriot activists – by the Nigerian government for protesting about the despoilation of their homeland in the fertile Niger River Delta by the Royal Dutch Shell Corporation. But their protest was not simply about the destruction of the environment. The non-violent Movement for the Survival of the Ogoni People (MOSOP) campaigned for social and ecological justice for Saro-Wiwa's homeland and its inhabitants.

They also exposed a devastating conspiracy: that a corrupt military regime led by General Sani Abacha was financed by and colluding with Shell Oil, a giant multinational corporation, in a bid to exploit a community's resources, in this case its oil. As the land became sodden and poisoned with oil, MOSOP accused both parties of waging an ecological war – and precipitating Ogoni genocide too.

MOSOP's David and Goliath struggle gained worldwide attention. The oil companies eventually pulled out in 1993, but not before Ken Saro-Wiwa and his MOSOP teammates lost their lives; they were arrested, imprisoned and, having been denied a fair trial, were hanged. Their execution sent shockwaves around the world. In 1996, Ken Saro-Wiwa was posthumously awarded the United Nations Environment Programme Award and thereby elected to the Global 500 Roll of Honour.

strong. The international diamond trade has also attempted to introduce a system of 'rough controls' – a chain of warranties guaranteeing that diamonds are mined in countries that have a legal diamond industry of economic benefit to the nation. The diamond industry hopes that such controls will work, in part, to protect the jewel's image as a symbol of love and commitment, and help to disassociate diamonds with wholly negative connotations of war and conflict.

Some aid agencies, including Oxfam, suggest that Africa's rich gold reserves could be sold to finance debt relief. But other bodies, such as Cafod, argue that gold mining is one of the world's dirtiest industries, polluting water and displacing poor communities.[37] Sodium cyanide used to extract gold from ore can leak into water systems, upsetting species balance and contaminating fish stocks. The development of Tanzania's Gelta Gold Mine on Lake Victoria was criticized by environmentalists, including Professor Wangari Maathai, for the risks to East African communities.[38] On the island of Madagascar, mining for gold and semi-precious stones threatens the habitat of the golden-crowned sifaka lemur – and therefore the species' very future.[39]

> *'My father's story is the story of Africa.'*
>
> KEN WIWA

Taking Action

1. Access the African Conservation Foundation's website at www.africanconservation.org to keep abreast of continent-wide action.

2. Join with others worldwide to campaign for trade justice and debt relief. Find further information at www.makepovertyhistory.org and www.oxfam.org .

3. Western big game hunters are paying thousands of dollars to 'bag' Africa's wildlife – including lions, leopards and elephants – and bring home a trophy. Write to your government to outlaw 'caged hunting' (which makes these animals a drugged and easy target), and the import of dead or alive endangered species.

4. Adopt an African animal! The African Wildlife Foundation (AWF) enables sponsorship of named individuals or groups of animals to support AWF's Africa-wide conservation work. Visit the AWF site at www.awf.org for more information.

5. Avoid buying exotic meats abroad to bring home; as well as reducing animal populations, bush meat can also spread disease, and in some countries, such as the UK, importing it is already illegal.

6. When buying jewellery, avoid 'conflict diamonds' that fund military action across Africa. Visit the Global Policy Forum site at www.globalpolicy.org/security/issues/diamonds for more information.

lost and found

Ethiopian Wolves

Ethiopian wolves could be plucked from the brink of extinction by a rabies vaccine designed to prevent a repeat of the 2003 outbreak that decimated numbers by three-quarters. The rarest carnivores in the world, no more than about 500 Ethiopian wolves exist, so another outbreak could wipe them out completely.[40] Vaccination followed the 2003 epidemic, and computer models by Oxford University's Ethiopian Wolf Conservation Programme[41] suggest that it worked, and that at least the short-term future of the species is secure.

The wolves live only in the Ethiopian highlands in six breeding populations, and depend on a specialist diet of alpine rodents. However, domestic dogs belonging to local shepherds have introduced diseases such as distemper and rabies into the wolf population. Owing to the remoteness of the packs, it was feared impossible to vaccinate all of their members. The solution was instead to vaccinate only the 30 per cent of animals most likely to come into contact with the dogs. While there remains a risk of some of the wolves contracting rabies, the chance of another full-scale outbreak of disease that would prove fatal to the species is substantially reduced. In future, it is hoped that oral vaccinations might be developed to be given in food for the more remote wolf populations.

However, the Ethiopian wolf is not completely out of the woods. Climate change and habitat loss are driving the beasts to higher altitudes; ultimately, they will simply run out of space in which to thrive.

Howling success: a rabies vaccine developed specifically for endangered Ethiopian wolves has secured their short-term future.

7. The Democratic Republic of Congo's (DRC) Grauer gorillas have already faced slaughter from an influx of people fleeing Rwanda in 1994, and disruption of their mountain habitat. Now the cell phone looks set to finish them off, since a basic component is made from coltan, a metallic ore found principally in DRC and Australia. Prices have soared, and coltan prospecting is rife in the Rwanda-governed Kahuzi-Biega World Heritage Site, where Grauer gorillas and their habitat are supposed to be under UN protection.[42] Contact the Rwandan Ambassador to the UN and the DRC Ambassador to the UN at 134 East 39th Street, New York, NY 10016 to request that they ensure they are.

8. Avoid buying exotic pets. Madagascar's large angonoka or ploughshare tortoise is on the brink of extinction because of its attraction for domestic collections.

9. If buying an African woodcarving, select one made from fast-regenerating species such as gyenegyene, as opposed to African mahogany, to help preserve forests.

10. Africa's cut-flower market sells predominantly to the West and has huge social and environmental costs in its extensive use of water and pesticides, and in its substandard working conditions. Supermarkets are now stocking fair trade flowers from companies in which employees are treated better and less intensive methods of using water are utilized. Either pick your own flowers from your garden, or look for the Fair Trade logo.

11. Ideally, buy local food in season that has not travelled far. Find out where the food you do buy comes from – and consider whether you are helping or hindering development; when South Africa was an apartheid regime, for instance, campaigners chose *not* to buy the country's produce. When buying food from developing nations, opt for fairly traded produce when you can.

12. To view Africa's annual wildebeest migration and support conservation, access www.wildwatch.com .

'Only after the last tree has been cut down, only after the last river has been poisoned, only after the last fish has been caught, only then will you find money cannot be eaten.'

CREE PROPHECY

North

Greenland
(Denmark)

R O C K Y   M T S

CANADA

Vancouver

Missouri

Ottawa

New York

Chicago

Washington

UNITED
STATES

Colorado

Los Angeles

Mississippi

Rio Grande

BAHAMAS

Havana

CUBA

JAMAICA

MEXICO

Mexico
City

GUATEMALA

HONDURAS

NICARAGUA

COSTA
RICA

PANAMA

America

CHAPTER 6

The continent of North America is comprised of four distinct entities. It is dominated by the North American landmass, which is made up of the United States of America, Canada and Mexico. To the north-east is the isolated country of Greenland. South of Mexico is the isthmus of Central America, which consists of Guatemala, El Salvador, Nicaragua, Costa Rica, Belize, Honduras and Panama. Alongside the isthmus are the twenty-six countries and territories of the Caribbean. North America is edged by the Pacific Ocean on its western coastline and the Atlantic Ocean on its eastern coastline.

The world's most powerful country, the United States of America dominates North America both politically and geographically. Because of the refusal of the government under President George W. Bush to sign the 1997 Kyoto Protocol, the USA has gained a reputation for a reluctance to address global climate change and recognize human culpability.

However, in July 2005 the United States announced its collaboration with fellow non-signatory Australia, along with China, India and South Korea, in the Asia-Pacific Partnership on Clean Development and Climate, with the aim of cutting greenhouse gas emissions.[1] The US has traditionally emphasized its determination to tackle global warming by developing new technologies, as opposed to placing any limits on its economic growth. Given the dependence of China and India – as the fastest-growing industrialized nations – on fossil fuels, the involvement of the US and Australia has been interpreted by some as a means of opening the growing Asian market to Western companies selling renewable energy and carbon dioxide-cutting technologies.

The United States is sandwiched by the developed nation of Canada – the second largest country in the world – in the north and the developing nation of Mexico to the south, reflecting the economically top-heavy make-up of the continent. The US state of Alaska at the north-west tip of the North American landmass, Canada's colder northern latitudes and Greenland to the north-east are sparsely populated frozen regions of the continent. Yet the rapid climate change that is being recorded in this part of the world – most notably reflected in Greenland's melting ice cap – is increasingly recognized as indicative of the worldwide scale of global warming. Additionally, it is what is

Previous spread: Blue lake and rocky shore: North America's mountain-edged national parks are wildlife havens.

Rachel Carson and *Silent Spring*

Born and brought up on a Pennsylvania farm, Rachel Carson dreamed of becoming a writer. She thus enrolled at the Pennsylvania College for Women to study English but switched to Biology, and went on to complete an MA in Zoology at Johns Hopkins University. She worked at Massachusetts' Woods Hole Marine Biological Laboratory, and taught at the University of Maryland and Johns Hopkins before securing a writing post with the US Bureau of Fisheries (which later became the Fish and Wildlife Service). She was promoted to staff biologist and, in 1949, she was made chief editor there.

Carson's first book, *Under the Seawind*, based on her scientific writings about the oceans, was published in 1941. After World War II, she was able to take advantage of access to formerly classified data about the oceans for her 1951 book, *The Sea Around Us*, which was her first bestseller; it won the John Burroughs Medal and the National Book Award and sold more than 200,000 copies in hardcover. A year later, she left government employment to concentrate on her writing.

Following four years of research, *Silent Spring* was first serialized in *The New Yorker* in 1962. Focusing on the effect of pesticides and herbicides, including DDT, and its threat to wildlife, the book took its evocative title from the potential loss of the songbird. As early as 1946, she had become alarmed by the US government's control of predators and pests by using new chemical pesticides without regard for the welfare of other species, but could not obtain interest in publishing her concerns. It was widespread wildlife mortality in the wake of mosquito, gypsy moth and fire ant eradication programmes in the late 1950s that galvanized Carson to write what was to become her seminal work.[2]

Silent Spring made a dramatic impact almost immediately. President John F. Kennedy initiated the President's Science Advisory Committee, which, in 1963, backed Carson's findings, to the chagrin of the critical agricultural chemical industry. In 1970, the Environmental Protection Agency (EPA) was founded, and in 1972 DDT was banned.

Rachel Carson died of cancer in 1964 aged fifty-six, so barely saw the huge influence her book made in inspiring the environmental movement. It remains a classic. Shortly before she died, she was elected to the American Academy of Arts and Sciences.

happening in this polar region that is challenging previously accepted projections and computer models of the rate of glacial decline and consequent sea-level rise. This is occurring much faster than was originally calculated.

In his 2006 State of the Union address, President George W. Bush declared that the United States is 'addicted to oil'.[3] Rather than see his statement as a call to restrict energy use, environmentalists largely interpreted it as a signal for oil production to shift from the precarious Middle East to the offshore Alaskan oil fields. However, the Bush government's reticence over the impact of climate change and global warming could be tempered by the shift of many of America's evangelical Christians – many of them traditionally Republican voters – towards demanding environmentally positive action in the wake of the devastation wrought by Hurricane Katrina in New Orleans and the drought witnessed in East Africa by America's Christian missionaries.[4]

> '*The beauty of the living world I was trying to save has always been uppermost in my mind – that, and anger at the senseless, brutish things that were being done. I have felt bound by a solemn obligation to do what I could – if I didn't at least try I could never be happy again in nature. But now I can believe that I have at least helped a little. It would be unrealistic to believe one book could bring a complete change.*'
>
> RACHEL CARSON

At the south of North America is the isthmus comprised of a chain of tiny Latin American states that joins North America to the South American landmass. Storms and hurricanes have always been a recognized weather pattern in the Gulf of Mexico, but global warming – resulting in sea-level rise and an increase in water temperature – is arguably fuelling much stronger and more frequent hurricanes.

To the east of the isthmus is the Caribbean, comprised of the Caribbean Sea, its islands and countries, and dominated by Cuba, Jamaica, Haiti and the Dominican Republic. Tourism provides a major contribution to the Caribbean economy, but it remains important to strike a balance between inviting visitors to the relatively unspoilt palm-edged beaches and maintaining this seeming island paradise in the wake of so much tourist traffic. The development of ecotourism is one alternative.

The United States' energy consumption threatens both developed countries and the poorer southern states. Already the effects of such human-induced climate change can be seen: water levels in Canada's Great Lakes have dropped, wildlife has been displaced and treelines have shifted. Drought throughout the United States' own national parks, the melting permafrost to the north, and hurricanes devastating east-coast cities prove the damage has come home to roost too.

The Melting Northern Latitudes

The higher latitudes of North America, which incorporate northern Canada, Alaska and Greenland, are proving particularly vulnerable to climate change. As the atmosphere warms, the ice that undergirds the region, from the permafrost to the glaciers that comprise the Greenland ice cap, is threatened with disintegration.

Much emphasis has been understandably focused on the resulting worldwide sea-level rise as the frozen water becomes liquid. But the traditional, millennia-old lifestyles of the Inuit people of the North are also likely to be lost. In addition, the Arctic's iconic and much-loved mammal, the polar bear, tragically will become extinct as the ice floes from which they hunt for seals disappear.

Yet the more urban and industrialized communities of the North are not immune from the effects of melting ice. Melting permafrost is destroying the foundations of buildings as they begin to sink into the waterlogged mud beneath them. Roads and railway tracks are concertinaing and manmade harbours collapsing into the sea as the ground beneath shifts. But permafrost is also estimated to hold up to 30 per cent of the world's carbon; its disintegration could release more greenhouse gases into the atmosphere than are produced by the burning of fossil fuels.[5]

Of all North America's circumpolar regions, Greenland is most occupying the minds of climate scientists. Satellite studies of the Greenland ice cap by NASA in 2006 showed that it is melting at twice the rate it was five years earlier, and its ice is slipping into the sea, fuelling sea-level rise.[6] Over the past twenty years, the air temperature of Greenland has risen by 3°C; the summer of 2005 broke all previous records for the ice sheet's melting rate. Some of its glaciers are moving three times faster than they were in the mid-1990s.[7]

Climate models, including those cited by the UN's Intergovernmental Panel on Climate Change,[8] have been based on the assumption that the ice sheet would slowly disintegrate as a melting single block over a period of a thousand years. Yet what is actually happening is that melting ice on the ice sheet is accumulating in lakes, which percolate down any crevasses to its base to form rivers. The rivers cause the ice above to slide towards the ocean at a much faster rate than was previously calculated. It is icebergs breaking off from these fast-moving glaciers, rather than meltwater, that are responsible for around two-thirds of the sea-level rise caused by the Greenland ice sheet.[9]

NASA climate scientists, including Jim Hansen, director of the NASA Goddard Institute for Space Studies and President George W. Bush's top climate modeller, have dismissed what they regard as the now-useless computer models, and are instead investigating previous ice ages to calculate the Greenland ice sheet's projected destruction. What they have found is that when the world *was* 3°C warmer than it is now – the temperature projected for later this century – sea levels were 25 m (82 ft) higher.[10]

Inuit and Polar Bears: Disappearing with the Ice

The 155,000 Inuit who live within the Arctic Circle have carved their existence out of the ice. They are direct descendants of the Thule people, who arrived in Alaska around AD 500 and reached Canada about AD 1000, where they encamped across its icy wastes.[11] But their ancient culture's days are numbered. Polar bears are also at risk. The future of the large, striking white polar bears, which exist only in the planet's north polar region, is as flimsy as the sea ice on which they depend for their survival.

Thousands of years of adaptation by the nomadic Inuit to a particular climatic environment are today proving useless. Indeed, they have come to use the word 'uggianaqtuq' to refer to the climate wrought by global warming; it means 'a friend acting strangely'.[12] They simply can no longer predict the weather as they used to, and, as a result, are uncertain as to how to alter their lifestyle accordingly.

The Inuit's traditional dome homes built from snowblocks represent the human race's ingenuity and resourcefulness, and its awesome ability to live in extreme, inhospitable parts of the Earth for which our relatively puny, furless bodies are not designed. However, the Canadian government is pressuring the Inuit, most of whom live on Baffin Island, to adopt more settled lifestyles rather than migrate in search of food as they have always done. As life on the ice becomes less sustainable, it seems inevitable that the Inuit will succumb, and the survival wisdom and knowledge that has proved so valuable to them for millennia will soon be lost forever.

In February 2006, temperatures on Baffin Island – which sits across the Arctic Circle – reached 9°C (48°F) when they should have been -30°C (-22°F). Air conditioning had to be introduced into local buildings, which, having been tightly constructed to keep out the cold, were now acting as heat traps.[13]

Living in settled communities is no guarantee of permanence. In Shishmaref, an Eskimo village (Alaska's aborigines prefer not to be called 'Inuit'[14]) at North America's north-western extremity, the thawing permafrost has tipped coastline and homes into the sea; within decades it will have fallen off the map.[15] Creatures once hunted, such as the walrus, have grown scarce, migrating from a warming sea.[16]

Unfamiliar wildlife for which the Eskimos have no names, such as salmon, barn owls and robins, are migrating north with the warmth. This ancient people's whole world is changing. Simon Kohlmeister, a hunter from Labrador whose snowmobile fell through the fast-melting ice, said, 'Some day we won't have any snow. We will no longer be Eskimos.'[17]

Polar bears are land mammals that must migrate annually across sea ice for nutritious seals. As the Arctic waters have, in

recent years, frozen later – in 2005, Hudson Bay on Baffin Island froze a month late[18] – it has provoked a corresponding delay for the bears' migration. For each day they are forced to wait, they lose 1 kg (2.2 lb) in body weight, leading to eventual starvation. In desperation, they might forage among the rubbish tips of local towns, such as Churchill, where they have been known to attack humans. More startlingly, between January and April 2004, three incidences of polar bear cannibalism – including that of a female in her den – were recorded in the southern Beaufort Sea.[19]

Even when the water does eventually ice over, its fast diminishment due to global warming has led to an increasing number of polar bears drowning. There are far fewer ice floes to climb onto after they have dived for seals. Of the reduced numbers that survive, their weight and litter sizes are down. As the ice further retreats due to the Arctic Ocean's warming, these magnificent, iconic beasts of the North could well be the first significant victims of its absence.

Melting away: a family of polar bears traverse ever-diminishing ice floes in search of food.

Between a rock and a hard place: the splendour of the rich flora and fauna that make their home in North America's northern mountain ranges will be squeezed out as atmospheric temperatures rise.

Describing the significance of these findings, Hansen said:

'So that is what we can look forward to if we don't act soon. None of the current climate and ice models predict this. But I prefer the evidence from the Earth's history and my own eyes. I think sea-level rise is going to be the big issue soon, more even than warming itself.'[20]

His prophecy is a terrifying prospect. Greenland's ice sheet measures approximately the size of Mexico, covering an area of 1.7 million sq km (656,000 sq miles). At some points it is up to 3 km (1.8 miles) thick. If it melted it would raise global sea levels by approximately 7 m (21 ft), flooding low-level countries and cities worldwide.[21] To prevent such devastation, a reduction in greenhouse gases is imperative. Were atmospheric temperatures to rise by merely 1°C, the planet would be hotter than it has been for half a million years – and the destructive process would become unstoppable.[22]

In 2006 Hansen calculated that carbon dioxide emissions had to be stabilized within a decade; however, it is now clear that it is too late to wait for new technologies – such as capturing emissions from burning coal – to be developed. Instead, the *immediate* emphasis has to be on promoting and developing energy efficient practices, and investing in renewable sources of energy that do not burn carbon. The all-but-silent dripping away of the

Greenland ice sheet is a sobering reminder of how environmental concern cannot simply be an add-on to a 'business-as-usual' mentality. Our entire mindset has to change.

Great Lakes and National Parks

North America boasts a rich natural heritage exemplified by its national parks and Great Lakes. Yet their majesty and very character is under attack from climate change; the Canadian government's Parks Canada Agency claims that climate change is 'one of the biggest threats to the ecological integrity of the national parks system'.[23]

Forest fires, melting glaciers, a rising snow line and declining species of wildlife are threats facing twelve national parks in the western United States. Average temperatures here have risen twice as much as elsewhere in the country.[24] In the US's Glacier Park the sixty-eight glaciers recorded in 1968 had shrunk to only twenty-seven by 2006; they are expected to have vanished altogether by 2030.[25]

Each national park acts as a protected microcosm of a wider ecosystem. Because of global warming, however, biomes will be forced northward. In mountainous regions, species will shift to higher altitudes until there is nowhere left for them to go. Parks Canada is establishing how climate change might affect each of the nation's regions as well as its network of national parks and Great Lakes. Wetlands will be altered as water levels of the Great

Alaska: North to the Future?

On 24 March 1989, one of the worst environmental disasters ever to affect US waters occurred when the Exxon Valdez tanker ran aground in Prince William Sound, Alaska, and disgorged 50 million litres (11 million gallons) of crude oil into the sea, which led to a 12.8 km (8 mile) slick that devastated the local environment. Approximately 2,080 km (1,300 miles) of coastline were contaminated; 250,000 seabirds were killed as well as 3,000 sea otters and up to 22 killer whales.[29] (Coincidentally, it occurred exactly eleven years to the day that the Amoco Cadiz oil tanker split in two off the French coast, the world's worst spill at the time.)

In 2003, the United States' National Marine Fisheries Service was still identifying sea otters and harlequin ducks harmed by toxins from oil patches remaining from the 1989 disaster[30] – a clear sign of the potential long-term impact of oil pollution in the region. It is this consideration that fuelled much of the opposition to oil exploitation in Alaska.

Indeed, many of the environmentalists' worst fears were realized in March 2006, when a leak in the Alyeska or Trans-Alaska Oil Pipeline spewed over 11 million litres (250,000 gallons) of crude oil onto the Arctic tundra, affecting land used by caribou herds and leading to a criminal inquiry by federal authorities.[31] In August 2006, BP had to shut half of the Alaska field after government inspections discovered widespread corrosion of pipelines at Prudhoe Bay; top executives of BP's US operations were later accused of gross neglect, and the company's 'notorious track record' was denounced at a congressional committee meeting.[32] Prudhoe Bay had previously accounted for 8 per cent of US oil production; after the shutdown, output was cut from 400,000 barrels a day to 250,000 and oil prices hit an all-time high.[33]

Lakes drop, and the wildlife particular to Canada's Arctic parks – and the people dependent on it – is at special risk from an increase in atmospheric temperatures and a consequent loss of vegetation.[26]

In recent years, North America's Appalachian mountain range and its largely forest ecosystems have faced widespread destruction from mountaintop mining. Explosives and heavy equipment are used to literally remove mountaintops to extract the seams of coal beneath. The 'overburden' – the millions of tonnes of former mountainside – is dumped as waste into neighbouring valleys. By such means, coal companies have buried over 1,900 km (1,200 miles) of headwater streams.[27] 'Fly rock' rains down on local communities, building foundations are dislodged, and floods and landslides are common. Dangerous amounts of slurry from coal washing are collected behind dams; breaches contaminate local water systems and pour through villages. It is essential that the campaign to limit, or even eliminate, mountaintop mining continues for the sake of both the fragile ecosystems at risk and the local inhabitants of the region.[28]

Opposite: Morning mist: wildlife abound in Yellowstone National Park – the world's first national park – which stretches across the states of Wyoming, Montana and Idaho.

The State of Alaska Department of Environmental Conservation aims 'to conserve, improve, and protect its natural resources and environment and control water, land, and air pollution'[34] and indeed includes a Division of Spill Prevention and Response.[35] But Alaska's uninhabited vastness, including earthquake-prone regions and increasingly unstable permafrost across which the pipeline runs to join the Prudhoe Bay oil fields to the ice-free port of Valdez, makes the region increasingly vulnerable.

Alaska's population of just over 626,000 people resides in a state 'about the size of California, Montana and Texas combined together';[36] the relatively small human impact on wildlife and the state's geographical isolation have helped to retain most of Alaska's native species. In addition, the establishment of conservation laws and policies, including 1998's Species of Special Concern,[37] plus a valuable network of national parks, has effectively served to encourage wildlife that is endangered or threatened elsewhere throughout the United States. Approximately 31,000 grizzly bears, 7,500 wolves, 80 per cent of the US's 50,000 bald eagles, 150,000 sea otters and one million caribou[38] are testament to Alaska's environmental value to the entire country, as well as to the world.

Careful management combined with habitat protection is vital to ensure the continuance of the nation's biodiversity. But even Alaska, in its relative isolation, is not immune from the ravages of climate change.

America's Addiction to Oil

US President George W. Bush's 2006 State of the Union address will be remembered for his admission that 'America is addicted to oil'. In his address he admitted that affordable energy could not continue to be imported from unstable parts of the world; the goal was to replace more than 75 per cent of US oil imports from the Middle East by 2025.[39]

Mr Bush also announced a 22 per cent increase in federal research spending on alternative sources of energy, including solar, wind and nuclear power, and encouraged a greater take-up of hybrid vehicles. But his apparently 'Green' manifesto was met with scepticism by environmental commentators. Writing for *The Independent*, Rupert Cornwell commented:

Car trouble: over a quarter of US carbon emissions are produced by its road traffic.

'Not once did he mention global warming. The words "conservation" and "Kyoto" did not once pass his lips. There was no reference to higher fuel efficiency standards for vehicles, which consumes roughly half the oil used by the US.'[40]

Indeed, over a quarter of US carbon emissions are produced by cars and trucks, while electricity generation is the premier source, contributing to a third of the United States' carbon emissions.[41]

Instead of promoting a per capita reduction in energy consumption, the president reiterated that the solution to the United States' energy problems – and indeed to global climate change – lay in developing appropriate technology that took advantage of new energy sources, and did nothing to curtail economic growth. Mr Bush notably did not mention further exploiting domestic US oil reserves – and specifically drilling within the Arctic National Wildlife Refuge. With less than a fifth of America's oil imported from the Middle East (Venezuela, Canada and Nigeria remain the US's biggest suppliers), it seems that the nation's addiction will barely be tempered at all.

However, a political sea-change occurred in 2006 in the United States that began to give environmentalists worldwide a little hope. Arnold Schwarzenegger, Republican Governor of California, backed the Democrat-dominated state legislature in signing the landmark Global Warming Solutions Act; greenhouse gas emissions were to be cut by a quarter by 2020. California, the richest and most populous US state and one of the global top ten economies, now had the most rigorous legislation on reducing emissions anywhere in the world.[42] Policies proved to be changing from the bottom up, beginning at the local and state levels. Mayors of more than 300 cities across the USA also signed a Climate Protection Agreement, each pledging to meet the Kyoto Protocol emissions-cutting timetable, never mind their president not having signed it.[43]

Storm Havoc in the Gulf of Mexico

In 1900, 6,000 people were killed in America's worst human disaster when a hurricane levelled the city of Galveston, Texas. Since 1900, there have been forty major hurricanes (Category 3 or higher, of 111 mph or more) entering the Gulf of Mexico; that is, on average one every thirty months. Between September 2004 and September 2005, however, *four* hurricanes of windspeeds between 115 and 125 mph battered the Florida Panhandle and Louisiana regions, breaking all records for the number of hurricanes in one cyclone season and also the most intense ever measured.[44]

The local human communities were hit hard by the onslaught of wind and the havoc it wreaked. Yet the devastation of ecological habitats and the swathes cut through the Maya rainforest of the Central American isthmus made it an environmental disaster too. When watersheds, mangrove forests, swamps, coral reefs and coastal wetlands are destroyed, the local human population goes unprotected from the absorbent properties these natural resources once provided.

When the levees broke: the historic city of New Orleans was devastated when a storm surge caused by Hurricane Katrina broke through its water defences.

The United States' worst natural disaster took place on the morning of 29 August 2005, when the 300-year-old city of New Orleans was devastated by the tail-end of the whirling 175 mph winds of Hurricane Katrina, which first struck the city at 6.10 a.m. It was to cost $75 billion in damages, kill more than 1,300 people and leave half a million people homeless.

It was the breaching of the low-lying city's network of levees by a storm surge of water rolling towards New Orleans that caused the most damage, rather than the winds. Millions of tonnes of water poured into New Orleans and flooded 50 per cent of the city within twenty-four hours. In total, water would cover approximately 388 sq km (150 sq miles) – 80 per cent of New Orleans.

Built 8 m (26 ft) below sea level within the great Mississippi River's floodplain, with the Gulf of Mexico to its south, the historic city is surrounded by water in one of the most hurricane-prone regions of the world. Since the disaster, urban planners have questioned whether it would be better to relocate the flooded areas to higher ground.

Chillingly, research after the flood suggested that New Orleans had effectively been playing Russian roulette for years. Measuring the city-wide tide mark left behind after the waters receded, and establishing a time map by collecting stopped clocks from among the debris, scientists calculated that the levee breach took place before the storm surge peaked at 20 m (66 ft) high and shot through, washing away homes in the frontline, and even before Katrina hit (a Category 3 hurricane by the time it reached the metropolis). Yet the single-line defence of 560 km (350 miles) of levees and ten pumping stations, which had cost billions to construct, had been designed to withstand and so protect the city from the force of a Category 3 strength storm. These findings proved, however, that the levees would not have held out for even a Category 1 storm.[45]

The Lower Ninth ward, a poor district of the city bordered by the levees, was especially badly hit. Although there had been warnings to flee the city beforehand, those without their own transport were left behind and had to survive without basic provisions, including food and clean water, and face vicious lawlessness. Fires also broke out, and floodwater turned toxic within days. Many people of the United States – one of the wealthiest and most developed countries in the world – were horrified to see how slowly their government responded; it took at least four days before aid began to trickle in. Fortunately, the historic French Quarter virtually escaped damage. As an established and continuing tourist attraction it brings much-needed dollars into the area, helping to revive the storm-damaged community. Still, a year later, the population of the 'Big Easy' had fallen from pre-Katrina levels of 460,000 people to about 171,000 – 1880 levels – and it is questionable how many of the remainder will ever return.[46]

> '*Nature has told us that we should not be living here.*'
>
> LARRY SCHMIDT, LOUISIANA'S DIRECTOR OF THE TRUST FOR PUBLIC LAND

After Hurricane Katrina struck, heads of conservation bodies working in the region wrote to President Bush demanding that the immediate restoration of the natural hurricane buffer system of wetlands and barrier islands be a central component of the plan to rebuild the region's shattered coastal communities.[47] In 2006, a new governmental body – the Coastal Protection and Restoration Authority (CPRA) – proposed shifting the course of the lower Mississippi so that silt washed out into the Gulf would build into a barrier island with a renewed delta of wetland, which had been lost over the past eighty years.[48]

In 2006, a predicted harsh hurricane season in the Gulf of Mexico turned out to be mild after atmospheric pressure over the Atlantic kept storms away from land, and a new El Niño climate pattern prevented winds from developing into hurricanes. Canada, however, experienced an above average onslaught. Debate continues among scientists as to whether or not global warming exacerbates the severity and frequency of hurricanes.[49]

The Caribbean Islands

Tourism is a major economic force across the Caribbean. But the paradisal vistas of white sands, deep blue seas and palm trees that draw mostly Western visitors are arguably the very attractions that could seal the region's over-exploitation.

One way of balancing tourism's negative impact is to encourage ecotourism, in which the protection and conservation of native species, habitats and heritage sites remain paramount to any economic development. Indeed, there is a strong conservation impetus across the Caribbean Islands, with the America-based international environmental body, the Nature Conservancy, BirdLife International – which established the Important Bird

Area Program (IBA) in the Americas[50] – and the Caribbean Conservation Association, among others, seeking to protect the islands' wildlife.

Since 2002, the annual Caribbean Endemic Bird Festival has sought to celebrate the region's rich birdlife and encourage people to value and protect birds and their habitats. Coordinated by the Society for the Conservation and Study of Caribbean Birds (SCSCB), the month-long festival runs from 22 April ('Earth Day') to 22 May ('International Biodiversity Day') and emphasizes the Caribbean Islands' status as one of the top three areas on the planet for biodiversity conservation.[51]

In October 2004, an agreement signed by the governments of Jamaica and the United States, along with the Nature Conservancy, instigated a US$16 million debt-for-nature swap programme aimed at preserving Jamaica's natural flora and fauna in return for the cancelling of its US debt. The agreement came in the wake of 2004's Hurricane Ivan, where almost 800 hectares (nearly 2,000 acres) of the island's virgin forests suffered severe wind damage.[52] The mechanism for the transaction is provided for under the 1998 Tropical Forest Conservation Act – also known as the Portman Act – which allows developing countries to relieve debt owed to the US while generating funds to support local tropical forest activities.

One of the most biologically diverse islands in the Caribbean, nearly a third of Jamaica's interior remains forested. Running partly along the island's mountainous spine, the rainforest houses most of Jamaica's wildlife, 'as well as 3,582 plant species, of which 912 are unique to the island. The slopes of the so-called Spinal Forest are some of the most significant migratory bird habitats in the Caribbean. Jamaica also supports more than 30 bird species, 26 of which are exclusive to the country.'[53]

It is such richness as this throughout the Caribbean Islands – 40 per cent of its plant life is found nowhere else on Earth[54] – that the world cannot afford to lose. In 2000, Caribbean countries established the protocol for Specially Protected Areas and Wildlife (SPAW) to ensure the quality and harmony of conservation practices across the region. Conservation is also being promoted via partnerships between businesses (including tourism), the government and environmental bodies. Although habitats remain threatened by deforestation and human encroachment, the depth and variety of conservation measures throughout the Caribbean serve as a valuable example to the rest of the world.

Taking Action

1. Access www.greatdreams.com/wisdom.htm and read the collection of Native American quotes about their perception of the world they inhabit.

2. Consider the resources you use as you go about your daily life. Be thankful for them, and seek to use them with respect and care. According to Brooke Medicine Eagle:

lost and found

Canada's Great Bear Rainforest

Five million acres (around a third) of the ancient temperate Great Bear rainforest, which runs 400 km (250 miles) along Canada's Pacific coast and which was previously threatened by logging, have been designated a protected sanctuary for wildlife. Based on recommendations from the British Columbia government, local governments and communities – including indigenous peoples, environmental groups and major logging companies – the Great Bear Rainforest Agreement was signed in February 2006. Under this agreement, logging companies would be allowed to work the rest of the forest, but only under strict rules designed to safeguard the region's ecosystems. Key valleys, animal breeding areas and fish-rich rivers – even in non-sanctuary sections of the forest – are not to be touched.[55]

Species including grizzly, black and rare white 'spirit' bears, wolves and wolverines, and birds of prey are given sanctuary, along with the river spawning ground for 20 per cent of the world's wild salmon. Notably, local native groups, known as 'First Nation' people, have been awarded an extended role in managing land integral to their history and culture.

In the last decade, pressure on the Great Bear rainforest from the timber industry initiated a huge environmental campaign to protect a region that includes some of the world's tallest and oldest trees, including cedars up to 1,000 years old. During the late 1990s, more than eighty US, European and Japanese hardware and furniture companies were involved in a boycott of Great Bear products.[56] It is hoped that the 2006 agreement will prove a model for the Amazon and other endangered forests. 'Diverse interests have come together in a unique partnership that will support economic opportunity while preserving some of B.C.'s most spectacular wilderness areas and protecting habitat for a number of species, including the rare Spirit Bear,' said Gordon Campbell, Premier of British Columbia.[57]

'The ancient people of the land understood that to be in harmony with all things was not only the highest and finest way to live, but also the most practical, useful, beneficial and abundant. Their practice was one of being in harmony. To be on the path of sacred ecology today means to take our spiritual work back into the realms of daily practice. This means becoming conscious of the kind of houses we live in, the ways that we use water, the ways we use energy and electricity.'[58]

3. If you have a religious faith or spirituality, identify what stand it and its followers are making on behalf of the environment. View the National Religious Partnership for the Environment's website at www.nrpe.org .

4. Access the website of the Union of Concerned Scientists – '[American] citizens and scientists for environmental solutions' – at www.ucsaction.org and sign up for its Action Network, Greentips newsletter, FEED (Food and Environment Electronic Digest) and/or EnergyNet for information and news on clean energy issues.

5. Students at American universities can apply to the Nissan-WWF Environmental Leadership Program, which aims to empower young leaders on US college campuses to become effective advocates for the environment via research projects in the US and overseas. For further details see www.worldwildlife.org/nissanleaders .

6. For an account of the human impact on the Caribbean Islands' biodiversity and information on the conservation action taking place here and elsewhere, read Conservation International's 'Biodiversity Hotspots' page at www.biodiversityhotspots.org/xp/Hotspots . For a helpful introduction to the Caribbean environment, access the Nature Conservancy's pages on the Bahamas, the Dominican Republic, the Eastern Caribbean and Jamaica at www.nature.org/wherewework/Caribbean .

7. For information about conservation work in the Caribbean, access the Caribbean Conservation Association's (CCA) website at www.ccanet.net for links to member organizations across the islands.

8. The hurricane season in the Gulf of Mexico and its environs is an annual occurrence. Support the work of the Nature Conservancy, National Wildlife Federation, Environmental Defense and National Audubon Society to protect natural buffer systems including wetlands and islands.

9. The National Wildlife Federation (NWF) aims to inspire 'Americans to protect wildlife for our children's future'. Look at its website at www.nwf.org and identify what you could do to protect wildlife.

10. What is your favourite animal, bird or part of the world? Use your local library and the internet to find what you can do to help protect such natural resources and species.

11. Access information about Parks Canada at www.pc.gc.ca to learn about work being done to protect Canada's valuable open wild spaces. Visit such places in your own country to view native species of plants and animals in their natural habitat.

12. The United States' National Resources Defense Council (NRDC) reports 'assess and provide solutions to today's environmental problems'. Visit www.nrdc.org/publications/reports.asp for information especially pertinent to US concerns.

South America

Galapagos
(ECUADO

'At first I thought I was fighting to save rubber trees, then I thought I was fighting to save the Amazon rainforest. Now I realise I am fighting for humanity.'

CHICO MENDES

CHAPTER 7

The landmass of South America begins at the southern tip of the Panama isthmus and extends far south beyond the Earth's equator and Tropic of Capricorn to Chile's Cape Horn. It incorporates the twelve countries of Argentina, Bolivia, Brazil, Chile (the longest country in the world), Colombia, Ecuador, Guyana, Paraguay, Peru, Surinam, Uruguay and Venezuela, plus territories including French Guiana, the Galapagos Islands and the Falkland Islands. The continent is surrounded by the Caribbean Sea to its north, the Atlantic Ocean to its east and the Pacific Ocean to its west.

Brazil is by far the largest South American country, but its size is dwarfed by the magnitude of the continent's geographical features. The Amazon River and its basin dominate the north of the landmass and a significant proportion of Brazil, and this area is home to the largest tropical rainforest in the world – arguably the richest ecological region on our planet.

Running along the Pacific coast is the Andes mountain chain, appearing like the spine of the continent and featuring volcanoes, glaciers and snow-capped mountains. At over 8,000 km (5,000 miles) long, it stretches from Venezuela through Colombia, Ecuador, Peru, Bolivia, Chile and Argentina, to the continent's southernmost tip at Tierra del Fuego, emerging from the sea as the Falkland Islands.

South America is home to a surprising number of world-class geographical features beyond the great Amazon and the Andes. Ecuador governs the ecologically rich Galapagos Islands. And the Manu Biosphere Reserve in Peru attracts the greatest concentration of bird species on the planet.[1] Peru also houses the architectural remains of the Inca empire, drawing tourists from across the world.

Venezuela, through which the Orinoco River runs, is also home to the world's highest waterfall and South America's biggest lake, as well as the largely unexplored sandstone table-top Tepuis Mountains, the sheer rock walls of which rise 1,000 m (0.6 miles) from the forest floor. According to William Miliken, a botanist at London's Kew Gardens: 'The flora of these mountains is diverse, partly due to the range of environmental conditions and habitats they support, and partly due to their bio-geographical isolation. About a third

Previous spread: A river runs through it: the Amazon rainforest's verdancy is fed by the river that gives it its name.

120

of all the plant species so far discovered in these mountains occur nowhere else on Earth.'²

Politically, geographically and culturally, it is important to differentiate between South America and Latin America. The first documented use of the name 'America' was on a 1507 map,³ and a distinction later emerged between North America and *Latin* America. While Latin America and South America overlap, they are not the same thing. Latin American culture, for example, encompasses all of the Spanish and Portuguese speaking cultures of *both* North and South America. In fact, the majority of American people live in Latin America. For Latin America *is* a place: it consists of all the countries south of the United States of America, including Central America and the entire South American continent.

Latin America is a particularly politically motivated region. Individual countries have had to fight against the United States' intervention in their affairs. In recent years the pro-US governments across Latin America have begun to fall like dominoes, as if there has been a continent-wide change of will and renewed confidence in the Latin American identity.

This movement towards establishing new political models is transforming Latin American politics, and arguably giving voice to the previously neglected, poor majority of these nations who desire improved conditions. The Bolivian government, for example, has nationalized both its oil and water industries. Already the Southern Common Market – known as Mercosur – which represents 45 per cent of the population, and the Andean Community are seeking to establish beneficial trading patterns across South America, and increasingly with other nations. The challenge for the continent is to benefit from resulting economic growth without despoiling the environment that enables it to grow – via tourism and natural resources – in the first place.

South American Birdlife

Peru's Manu Biosphere Reserve boasts the greatest concentration of bird species on the planet. While over 3,100 species – a third of the world's birds – are either resident or migrant across the continent of South America, 925 species of bird have been recorded in Manu alone. Given that there are just under 9,000 species of birds in the world, this means that Manu holds a staggering one in ten of all known bird species. No other protected area on Earth contains so many birds.⁴

Manu's reserve owes its attraction for birdlife to its striking variety of altitudinal zones and habitat types. Altitudes range from over 4,000 metres (13,000 ft) above sea level in the high Andes down to the lowland Amazon rainforest at 350 metres (1,150 ft). For every 1 kilometre up or down, the make-up of the bird communities differs.⁵ As well as the difference in altitude, the reserve has a distinct range of habitat, from the various forest types to grasslands and lakes. Additionally, so-called 'micro-habitats' of bamboo stands, reed-beds and treefalls encourage further diversity of birdlife.

High-flyers: Amazonian parrots find a safe haven in Peru's Manu Biosphere Reserve.

The altitudinal zone between 1,500 m (about 5,000 ft) down to 900 m (about 3,000 ft), which is the humid upper tropical forest, is particularly important in the context of the Manu refuge. Elsewhere in Peru, forests at the same altitude are readily cut to provide land for growing cash crops of tea, coffee and cocoa; there is nowhere for birds to nest high up.

At the lower echelons of Manu River, the white sand beaches along its banks, which edge the tropical forest of the Amazon basin, create valuable nesting opportunities for visiting birds where they will not be disturbed. Where the river flows slowly, high banks develop on river bends, providing a suitable habitat for brilliantly coloured macaws and parrots, which eat the clay to aid their digestion.

Yet while the Manu Biosphere Reserve is an especial place for attracting the world's birdlife, thousands of species can be seen across South America. Prime bird-watching areas include the Galapagos and Falkland Islands, and the Netherlands Antilles.

Many of South America's native bird species are particularly iconic, including the scarlet ibis, the Andean condor – which flies along the Andes from Venezuela and Colombia to Tierra del Fuego and southern Chile and Argentina – the harpy eagles, and Chilean flamingos. But the continent's birds are also some of its most endangered species. While many of them have few natural predators because they thrive in inhospitable places, it is the human impact of habitat exploitation and destruction that is threatening the birds' very existence. The large green macaw of the lowlands, Buffon's macaw in Ecuador, the sunbittern, toucan, jacamar, antbird and cotinga all face such human pressures.

South America's Rainforests

Tropical rainforests cover less than 6 per cent of the Earth's surface but contain over half of the world's plant and animal species.[6] The Amazon rainforest contains the largest collection of living plant and animal species in the world; one in five of the world's birds live there, and a single hectare (2.47 acres) of land contains an estimated 900 tonnes of living plants, including more than 750 types of trees and 1,500 other plants.[7]

However, in Brazil alone, levels of deforestation remain high despite having slowed under President Luis Inacio Lula da Silva's government; over half the trees of the Brazil/Bolivia border region have already been cut down.[8] The enforcement agency of Brazil's Ministry of Environment, IBAMA, allows selective logging where seedlings are planted to replace those limited number of trees which are taken; legal documentation is required to cut down trees in this region. Considering the difficulty in policing such a vast area of land, there is much criminality in the logging and timber industry. Local ranchers and farmers also obtain their land by clearing forests.

In the Chilean Andes, the 70-million-year-old landscape of monkey puzzle forests backed by snow-capped mountains has all but been wiped out in the conflict surrounding the continent's trees. Though the monkey puzzle trees do have protected status, this could not prevent almost 10,000 hectares (nearly 25,000 acres) – a staggering 71 per cent of the total population – from being destroyed by fires in 2001–02, which were believed to have been started deliberately by local landowners angry at being denied logging rights.[9]

The fervent clearing of rainforests – approximately 20 per cent of the Amazon has already been destroyed[10] – also jeopardizes the use and further discovery of materials that could benefit humanity. In addition to timber, fruit, oils, latex, fibre and drugs are already sourced there. But for all the wonders therein that might help *us*, rainforests and their rich ecosystems have their own value and integrity without our intervention.

Yet there is an economic alternative to deforestation: agro-forestry, the growing of trees and crops in livestock areas. In the Amazon, for example, the same land used to grow bananas and limes can be used as pasture land for cattle. The environmentally friendly cultivation of Brazil nuts helps protect the rainforest, as does a project such as Ecuador's La Selva Butterfly Farm, where butterflies are bred for sale around the world.[11]

Deforestation is not just a local concern. Without South America's tree cover, the whole world suffers; the rainforest effectively acts as the lungs of the Earth, both producing oxygen and absorbing carbon dioxide from the atmosphere, which it needs for its own growth, and therefore helping to dampen the impact of global warming. Without these trees, the carbon released into the atmosphere by the burning of fossil fuels, exacerbated by 250 years of industrialization around the globe, can only build up, thereby raising the temperatures. The South American nations, therefore, have understandably begun to demand support and financial assistance from the rest of the world in the battle to protect the rainforest, and to offer a real economic reason for these nations not to despoil their environment. Yet suggestions to establish an international trust from which shares could be purchased – effectively rainforest privatization – challenge national sovereignty and encourage profiteering from carbon trading at the expense of the local population. Selling off swathes of the rainforest therefore is not a straightforward solution.[12]

Threats to Amazonia

Amazonia, or the Amazon River Basin, is colossal, covering approximately 2,500,000 sq km (475,000 sq miles) – around 35 per cent of South America – and spanning nine countries. Formed where the Ucayali and Maranon headstreams meet in the Andes Mountains of north Peru, the Amazon River traverses the entire width of northern Brazil before reaching the Atlantic Ocean close to the port of Belem, where it pours over 174 million litres (about 46 million gallons) of water per second into the sea.[13]

At around 6,280 km (3,900 miles), the Amazon River is the second longest in the world, but carries more water than any other river in the world. However, in 2006, its water levels fell by 10 metres (around 33 ft) when it succumbed to the worst drought on record.[14] Since the Amazon is the very lifeblood of the rainforest to which it gives its name, such a drop could have a devastating impact on Amazonia's environment and the 220,000 people representing 180 different indigenous groups who live there,[15] and who have legitimate claim to 20 per cent of Amazonian land.[16]

The 2006 Amazon drought followed on the heels of one the previous year, further encouraged by deforestation, which disrupts the atmospheric water cycle that keeps the trees alive.[17] And were subsequent years to prove as dry, it could tip the entire rainforest into a cycle of destruction and massively accelerate climate change across the world as dying trees release much of the CO_2 stored in their lifetime back into the atmosphere. The rainforest contains 90 billion tonnes of carbon, enough to increase the rate of global warming by 30 per cent.[18] Fires would likely sweep across the dying jungle, and the exposed soil would turn to desert.

The river's annual floods bring vital, enriching nutrients to the land and encourage biodiversity. Water levels of rivers and tributaries rise by as much as 12 m (about 40 ft), which can submerge trees and vegetation for half the year. Through the flooded forest swims the Amazon river dolphin, though it is endangered because of the dangers of hydroelectric dams, deforestation and mining pollution.[19]

Water coursing: the Amazon River surges through the jungle and over giant waterfalls en route to the Atlantic Ocean.

Historically, it is not just a drop in water levels that has threatened Amazonia. The river's very extent, cutting across the continent, has facilitated exploration and the extraction of local resources, which has ultimately contributed to the despoliation of the environment. Europeans first explored and charted the river in the sixteenth and seventeenth centuries, and when a steam-ship service was established in the mid-nineteenth century, the Amazon valley was opened up to colonization. Further sporadic periods of development followed. Today, extensive deforestation and the building of road networks are making a marked impact across Amazonia. In addition, gold mining and agricultural development in the Andean foothills are threatening the spawning grounds of migratory fish. Habitat destruction would have a devastating knock-on effect on fish populations, including those of commercial fisheries thousands of kilometres downstream.

The Amazon Conservation Association (ACA) developed its Amazon Rivers Program to encourage river basin management and conservation biology with a special focus on fish ecology. The Amazon contains the greatest diversity of freshwater fish of any of the world's river basins; up to

Chico Mendes

Francisco (Chico) Alves Mendes Filho was murdered in the Amazon rainforest in December 1988 for campaigning against the wholesale burning of the forest. Where 500 similar murders went unprosecuted, international pressure placed on Brazil brought the gunman to justice.

Mendes, leader of the National Council of Rubber Tappers, had mobilized grassroots, non-violent direct action among rubber tappers in Xapuri, Acre, against cattle ranchers who had stolen land and were burning down trees to make pastures. In 1985, Brazil's government, part prompted by the rubber tappers' campaign, passed the National Plan of Agrarian Reform and seized back land to convert into 'extractive reserves' for the sustainable production of nuts and rubber, among other things, which could be harvested without destroying the trees.

Mendes' activism was inspirational within the global environmental movement and was notable for how it drew the support of a range of interests from local governments to funding agencies and worldwide environmental bodies. In doing so, links were forged between the rainforest environment, the welfare of the people who lived there and the long-term sustainability of trade in forest products.

3,000 species make their home here, many of which rely on submerged fruits and seeds. The fish provide 80 per cent of the protein consumed by local people.[20]

Protecting the Amazon's floodplain rainforests will help to conserve not only the river's freshwater fish but also the other species including monkeys, birds and invertebrates specific to the semi-aquatic habitat. That the local human population is dependent on the fish for survival also emphasizes nature's interconnectedness: concentrating on the protection of one group of animals and their habitat is often beneficial to all.

The intention of the governments of Venezuela, Brazil and Argentina to develop a 9,000 km (5,600 mile) long gas pipeline cutting through the heart of the Amazon has dismayed environmentalists. They claim it would 'ensure [the Amazon's] destruction as a large, operable whole. It would devastate rainforests, water resources, the climate and indigenous populations across a huge swathe of South America.'[21] The conflict between the interests of both the governments and the environmentalists represents the larger battle between the ongoing economic and industrial development of what have been termed 'Third World' countries, and the conservation and environmental protection of previously untapped natural resources and their habitats.

The devastation wrought by the extensive construction work itself, as much as that resulting from the pipeline's actual presence, has motivated campaigners to protest against its building. Inroads must, by definition, be cut into the rainforest, which will draw ranchers and loggers to further exploit the previously pristine woodland. The Amazon's local network of waterways will also likely face pollution from the pipeline's construction and the inevitable leaks that will occur during the pipeline's history.

'It became clear that the murder was a microcosm of the larger crime: the unbridled destruction of the last great reservoir of biological diversity on Earth.'

ANDREW REVKIN, AUTHOR OF
THE BURNING SEASON

The very economic viability of the pipeline has been questioned. Brazil and Argentina both have their own gas fields, which could be exploited to sate domestic need, while Venezuela might not be able to maintain such a steady supply of gas. In addition, gas prices might not be able to be kept low enough to attract consumers while justifying the inevitably huge cost of investment.

Environmentalists point to Peru's Camisea gas pipeline, which similarly cuts through the country's rainforests, as a case in point. It was originally built at the beginning of the twenty-first century with the assurance that it was a model of sustainable development, and that its construction would neither be destructive to the environment nor affect the indigenous people residing in its

Fires were started: clouds of smoke over the rainforest are evidence of deliberate and illegal destruction to make way for soy plantations.

vicinity. In spite of these assurances, the existence of the Camisea pipeline has proved far from beneficial to the land it traverses: 'In three years of operation, it has already experienced five major spills, severely damaging the environment and local communities. Indigenous communities have been devastated by disease, and water resources that they depend upon for drinking and fishing have been fouled.'[22]

Campaigners have appealed to the left-wing credentials of the Venezuelan, Brazilian and Argentinian governments by labelling the pipeline as 'the most antiquated, primitive neo-liberal economic development which the region's governments rally against'.[23] They have called on supporters to write directly to Presidents Hugo Chavez, Luis Inacio Lula da Silva and Nestor Kirchner to cancel the construction programme.

The construction of a road aimed to connect Peru's Amazon region to the Pacific Ocean is further polarizing the country's population as to whether or not its impact will prove beneficial. As award-winning author Ted Conover states:

'Many thoughtful people believe that the fate of the Earth itself depends on keeping nature unpaved. But Peru is mad for new highways. Just as the north–south Pan-American Highway was the infrastructure project of the 20th century for South America, many people see an east–west Carretera Transoceanica – a road joining the Pacific to the Atlantic – as the project of the 21st.'[24]

Without the road, goods from Brazil have to be transported to Atlantic ports and then either shipped or trucked via Argentina to Chile's ports on the Pacific. The 5,600 km (3,500 mile) all-weather highway represents a pact between the governments of Brazil and Peru to link their economies and provide mutual benefits. Of particular importance is the four-lane steel and concrete bridge that crosses the Amazon rainforest's Acre River, replacing a rickety wooden bridge. At its inauguration in January 2006, the bridge was recognized as a key integration project in the region by President Luis Inacio Lula da Silva of Brazil and President Alejandro Toledo of Peru. The paved road already runs from the Atlantic to the Brazilian side of the border river. The planned completion date for paving the next stage from the river's Peru side towards the Pacific is 2010, and it is hoped it will draw trade, people and jobs to the countries' interiors.

Brazil is particularly keen to exploit the already lucrative Asian market; as the key supplier of food to China, 18 per cent of its exports, much of it soybeans, go there. Tropical rainforest is therefore being replaced with soy farms, and also land used for cattle ranching. In the state of Mato Grosso, 62 million hectares (over 150 million acres) of land are already devoted to agriculture, and the Brazilian government is keen for a further 90 million hectares (over 220 million acres) to be planted. The Brazilian government has been developing ties with Chinese investors to develop Brazil's infrastructure;[25] therefore, the expansion of the highway across Peru could bring much-needed revenue into that country too.

However, it is the very economic expansion the highway promises which profoundly concerns environmentalists. The region's already fragile ecosystem would face further threat. Where the highway is built, development and deforestation covering many miles can spread out from it on both sides: this has already occurred on the Brazilian end of the highway, so activists are concerned it will be repeated in Peru, threatening its precious natural habitat. Local indigenous people face having their lives disrupted, and

The Galapagos Islands

The Galapagos Islands have a relatively long history of protection; they were first designated a wildlife sanctuary in 1934 by the government of Ecuador. In 1959, 97 per cent of the islands was declared a national park, and in 1986 the Galapagos Marine Reserve was officially established. However, it effectively took until 1998, when the Special Law for the Galapagos was introduced to protect the islands and their wildlife, for the Marine Reserve, as a part of that law, to gain legal status and protection. At 133,000 sq km (51,300 sq miles), the Galapagos Reserve is the second largest marine reserve in the world.[27]

The Special Law has not been fully implemented, however, and has been consistently threatened by Ecuador's fishing industry, which desires at least the same rights within the Galapagos' protected waters as the islands' local small-scale fishermen. The local fishermen have sought an increase in catch limits, especially on lobster and sea cucumber, as well as the lifting of the ban on shark fishing for export to Asia. Those seeking the protection of these World Heritage Site islands must be on constant alert.

Taking life slowly: the habitat of the Galapagos' giant tortoise is threatened by an increasing human population across the archipelago.

The Galapagos Conservation Trust gives a number of important reasons why the Galapagos Islands are worth preserving in as pristine a state as possible.[28] Both

the Galapagos National Park and Marine Reserve are together recognized as a World Heritage Site, not least because of their iconic place in the history of science as home to Charles Darwin's 1835 visit, and their consequent key influence in his ground-breaking study, *The Origin of the Species*.

While the islands remain the best conserved of the world's tropical archipelagos, their the opening up of access to the rainforest also encourages illegal loggers to move in too.

The construction of Carretera Transoceanica Highway is a microcosm of the conundrum faced by South America and other developing continents over whether or not to improve the lives of its human population while exploiting local natural resources, which ultimately threatens the future of both.

Every minute over the last decade, five football pitches' worth of the Amazon rainforest have been lost, largely for agricultural purposes.[26] The prime causes – illegal logging and cattle ranching – have, in recent years, been overtaken with a vengeance by the cultivation of soy for animal feed,

biodiversity nevertheless remains extremely fragile and at risk from the impact of foreign species, human activity, pollution and climate change; the mangrove finch has already been driven to the brink of extinction by the loss of its habitat.[29] Today, there is a determined effort to remove invasive flora and fauna, and there has been success in getting rid of certain species such as donkeys, pigs and blackberries. After eight years, the Isabela Project, the largest invasive species eradication programme ever undertaken in the world, claimed success in eliminating feral goats from the Galapagos' Isabela and Santiago islands.[30] However, remaining invasive species continue to present a serious threat to the survival and flourishing of native species.

Additionally, pressures from outside threaten to wreak havoc. Ecotourism, as well as a fishing boom, have drawn more and more people to the islands. Between 1990 and 2005 the local population swelled from 10,000 people to over 28,000 residents, and the annual number of visitors grew from 41,000 in 1990 to over 100,000 in 2005.[31] Growing human numbers naturally increases the demand for local resources and threatens to impact the protected areas.

'The Galapagos Islands is a microcosm of the social, political, ecological and economic changes occurring in the world. Throughout the world, human populations are increasing and demands for natural resources are consequently changing. Substantial ecological changes are occurring in the resource base, frequently driven by globalisation and liberalisation of markets. In addition, it has become increasingly recognised that all of these changes are occurring in a complicated socio-political and cultural environment.'

THE GALAPAGOS CONSERVATION TRUST

primarily for Europe's meat industry. In 2003, after an eight-year period of stability and decline in deforestation levels, figures soared by 40 per cent. During the twelve months ending in August 2004, the rate of Amazon rainforest destruction reached the equivalent of over nine football fields every minute – that is, 26,130 sq km (10,089 sq miles) flattened in one year alone.[32] It is not just habitat that is being destroyed. Entire rural communities have been displaced, having sold their land rights and moved to the city.

Ironically, it was Britain's 1995–96 BSE cattle feed crisis that resulted in a switch to the safer soy feed, and European concern to avoid genetically modified produce that directed buyers to Brazil's soybean supplies. The growth in China's meat market to feed the beneficiaries of its economic boom is also fuelling global soy feed demand.

Soy is now Brazil's leading cash crop, its export actively promoted by President Luis Inacio Lula da Silva's government in exchange for debt repayments. But the 2003–04 rate of forest destruction – which resulted in the clearance of an area nearly the size of Belgium – also proved the second highest on record during only the third year of the soy boom. Half of the deforestation occurred in Mato Grosso, a Brazilian state presided over by governor and millionaire Blairo Maggi, who owns Maggi Group, the world's biggest soybean producer.[33] Brazil's top soy exporter is the giant Cargill US grains business.

Pressure has been squarely placed on the soybean industry to quell its expansion, in particular from environmental agency Greenpeace. In 2003, it provided photographic evidence to federal prosecutors showing Cargill's illegal burning of swathes of rainforest to make way for soy plantations in Santarem, Brazil. Legal action was launched.[34]

Significantly, in July 2006 an alliance forged between Greenpeace and leading European food retailers, including Asda, Waitrose, and Marks and Spencer, succeeded in negotiating with Brazil's multinational soy traders an agreement to a two-year moratorium on buying any soy from newly deforested land in the Amazon. This unusual alliance between a conservation body and companies such as fast food chain McDonald's, whose policies it might previously have criticized, followed a three-year Greenpeace investigation into the impact of the soy trade on the rainforest.[35]

Greenpeace proposed that the soy traders work alongside the Brazilian government in halting deforestation, enforcing laws and protecting habitats and the lands of local and indigenous communities. Concerned that the two-year hiatus might prove a mere token gesture, Greenpeace has demanded that laws and governance be established to ensure concrete action. They proposed a working group of traders, producers, NGOs and government representatives be created to carry out an action plan to ensure all commitments are fulfilled.[36]

Slipping away: this tongue of glacial ice is retreating, the water loss threatening millions of people's lives.

The Andes' Disappearing Glaciers

There is rightful concern about the dwindling glaciers of the polar regions and their impact on global sea levels. Yet South America's glaciers also have a crucial function in supplying water to millions of people. It is the glaciers of the Andes Mountains (a range second only to the Himalayas in range and altitude) that provide secure water supplies to communities across the length of the continent, and enable Peru's otherwise rain-starved capital city, Lima, to exist. Without the glacial water source, the city's millions of people would be forced to migrate – or die of thirst.

In the Cordillera Blanca Mountains 400 km (250 miles) north of Lima, the removal of pieces of ice during the annual Qollyur Riti ceremony celebrating Christ's appearance to a shepherd boy in 1870, has had to be restricted as the sacred Qolqepunku glacier has retreated by 183 m (600 ft) in the last twenty years.[37] Local religion blends Catholicism with the worship of Apus, Incan mountain gods that are believed to live in the snow. As the snow disappears so, it is believed, do the Apus – heralding the end of the world.

There is an element of scientific truth in such a myth. Twenty years ago, the lower mountain peaks were *nevados*; that is, snowy mountains. Today, they are reduced to bare rock, which itself acts as an oven, further melting the ice.[38] The loss of snow and ice has a knock-on effect as local mountain flora die without water, and at lower altitudes pastures and crops are also threatened. The Cordillera Blanca Mountains draw climbers from across the world, and a thriving local economy catering to their needs has consequently developed. Without the snowy peaks, the visitors – and their money – will disappear.

Like Lima, La Paz, Bolivia – the world's highest capital city – is also experiencing the decline of neighbouring ice fields of the Cordillera Real Mountains, threatening its water resources. Run-off from the glaciers is accumulated in reservoirs to supply the 1.5 million residents of La Paz and the nearby city El Alto, and also feed the hydroelectric plants that provide the cities' energy.[39]

Rising temperatures and low rainfall are encouraging the rapid melting of local glaciers. The Chacaltaya glacier, renowned as the world's highest ski-field, has lost over 40 per cent of its thickness and surface area.[40] While glaciers across the world are shrinking, those in tropical regions – most of which are found in the Andes – are declining the fastest. While elsewhere, glaciers accumulate snow in the cold winter season, the Andes' low-latitude, high-altitude glaciers accumulate in the summer, when the sun is at its strongest, so have little opportunity to recover the ice that has been lost. They are now melting faster than they are being replenished. Research indicates that those above 5,500 m (18,000 ft) will have disappeared within the next ten years.[41]

Melting glaciers initially produce too much water, overflowing water courses and threatening lives. Flood-bursts – known in Peru as *aluviones* – occur when water stored as a lake inside a glacier shoots out, along with mud

Colombian Harlequin Frogs

lost
and
found

Species of Colombia's harlequin frogs are proving notably hardy against the onslaught of a deadly fungus that is otherwise cutting a swathe through the amphibian population of Central and South America.

In May and June of 2006 three species of rare frog previously believed to be extinct or at least seriously endangered were rediscovered. The Santa Marta harlequin frog and the San Lorenzo harlequin frog had gone unreported for fourteen years before being spotted in Colombia's Eldorado Nature Reserve.[43] What could be the last population of the painted frog was rediscovered in May 2006 in eastern Colombia's Sarna and Toquilla highland deserts by researchers from Boyaca's Pedagogical and Technological University.[44] Last seen in 1995, this discovery gave hope that other species may have survived the killer fungus.

Frogs are important components of ecosystems, namely for consuming insects, and the presence and health of amphibians are good indicators of an ecosystem's viability. But a third of the world's amphibian species are now threatened by a lethal skin fungus exacerbated by deforestation and global warming. As climate temperatures have risen, so has the incidence of the fungus. Conservation International is monitoring the decline of the frogs via its Atelopus Initiative; of the 113 species of Atelopus (or harlequin frogs) found in the Tropical Andes Biodiversity Hotspot, forty-two have seen their populations as much as halved by the disease.[45]

boulders and blocks of ice; they have been known to kill thousands of people.[42] Large ice chunks can split off glaciers into the lakes they feed, triggering devastating floods. But after the deluge comes only drought.

Taking Action

1. Access the global satellite imaging website at http://earth.google.com and observe South America's apparent lack of development, and how the Amazon rainforest appears to cover so much of the continent like a rich green carpet. Home in on any individual region and you can detect the neatly cut edges of often deforested land, as if someone has taken a power mower to the carpet's pile.

2. Eat more Brazil nuts! You'll be supporting an environmentally friendly industry that depends on rainforest preservation rather than its destruction. It reduces poverty in Brazil, Peru and Bolivia. Aim to buy fairly traded brands.

3. Buy fair trade staples such as coffee or chocolate to ensure that the growers are paid a decent wage for their work and their rights are protected. If your local supermarket does not stock fair trade goods, make a point of asking the management to stock them – and get friends to ask too – to indicate that there is local demand for such produce.

4. Help further Greenpeace's success in curtailing soy cultivation in the Amazon rainforest. Greenpeace Brazil's Executive Director, Frank Guggenheim, said:

'We need to keep pushing for an agreement that will really protect the future of the rainforest and the Amazon people. Disputes over land and forest resources have not only destroyed large areas of the Amazon but also claimed thousands of lives. Soya traders must now help bring governance and environmental protection to the entire region.'[46]

Visit www.greenpeace.org to keep abreast of their campaigns and to support their work.

5. Consider becoming a vegetarian, or reduce your weekly consumption of intensively farmed meat. Land devoted to growing feed for animal stocks and ranching – such as that in the Amazon rainforest – could be set aside as natural habitat, and such land elsewhere could be devoted to growing crops to feed the world's hungry people.

6. When buying wood or paper products, choose either those made from recycled fibres, or those with the Forest Stewardship Council logo, which guarantees the source forests are managed in a manner that protects biodiversity and the local indigenous peoples.

7. The unique freshwater fish that take advantage of the Amazon River's flooding are being smuggled illegally out of the continent to supply tropical fish collectors. If you wish to own fish, find out not only how best to keep them but opt for those that are specially bred for sale.

8. 'BirdLife International is a global Partnership of conservation organisations that strives to conserve birds, their habitats and global biodiversity, working with people towards sustainability in the use of natural resources.'[47] Read up on the projects supported around the world at www.birdlife.org/worldwide/index.html .

9. The Amazon Conservation Association's (ACA) Amazon Rivers Program consists of a team of the Amazon Basin's leading aquatic conservation ecologists. The ACA's team advises South American governments, the World Bank, the European Community, NGOs, ecotourism businesses, entrepreneurs and other interests concerned with the conservation and development of Amazonian rivers and floodplains. Encourage your political representatives to support their work.

10. Developing countries such as Bolivia and Peru that are seeing their glaciers disappear require action from the developed world on their behalf to cut carbon emissions. Write to your national political representatives to request that they listen to countries affected by climate change, and promote positive global change.

11. To keep abreast of conservation work and scientific research in the Galapagos Islands, access the webpage www.gct.org/newsreq.html to be put on the monthly emailing list of the Galapagos Conservation Trust. There may also be a member organization of the international Friends of Galapagos network in your own country. Check www.gct.org/fogos.html to find out.

12. If you visit South America, support ecotourism operations that help protect biodiversity by creating incentives to protect it. See http://gosouthamerica.about.com/od/tripplanecotourism/ and http://www.Earthwatch. org .

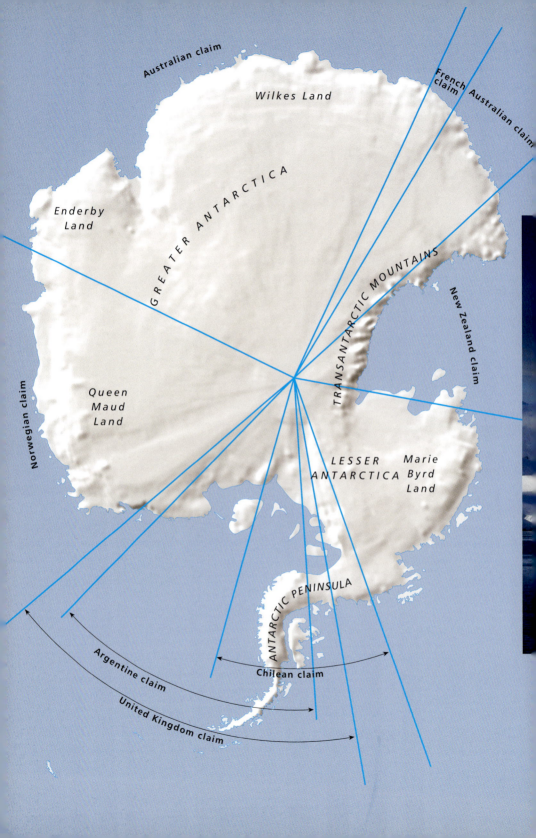

'The international community, not just scientists, need to start thinking of Antarctica not in isolation as something at the bottom of the world but as an integral part of the Earth system.'

Dr John Shears, British Antarctic Survey

Antarctica

CHAPTER 8

Antarctica, the continent that covers the South Pole, is the fifth largest continent. Its land area totals 14 million sq km (5.5 million sq miles), only 280,000 sq km (108,000 sq miles), or 2 per cent, of which is ice-free – and therefore is bigger than Oceania and Europe, and around one and a half times the size of the United States.[1] The Antarctic landmass is completely surrounded by the waters of the Southern Ocean.

To many people, Antarctica, known as the Earth's seventh – or last – continent, situated at the base of the planet, remains an enigmatic ice-bound place. With 30 million cu km (7 million cu miles) of ice containing approximately 87 per cent of the world's ice and 70 per cent of the world's fresh water,[2] even on maps it is not unusual to see the continent represented merely as an outlined white space.

Antarctica wasn't always an icy continent. During the Cambrian Period around 500 million years ago, the continent was in fact located at the equator as part of the Gondwanaland super continent. Over the course of 150 million years this great landmass gradually split apart into the Southern Hemisphere's continental plates. Still attached to Australia, Antarctica drifted southwards during the Mesozoic Era (between 65 and 248 million years ago); at this time its climate was temperate and animals, including dinosaurs, roamed across it. Eventually, Antarctica split away from Australia and alone decamped over the planet's South Pole.[3] Today, 98 per cent of the Antarctic is covered by an ice sheet that averages 2,164 m (1.5 miles) in depth, and is nearly 4,785 m (3 miles) deep in places.[4] The remaining 2 per cent of the continent is bare rock, where fossils have been found recording flora and fauna from the eras when Antarctica was located at warmer latitudes.

There is very little precipitation on the continent. At under 5 cm (2 in) per year it averages less than Africa's Sahara Desert; Antarctica contains the world's largest desert. The South Pole happens to be the coldest, windiest and driest place on Earth – as if each of these properties is magnetically drawn to its most intense level at the planet's southern axis point. The continent's extremes are illustrated by the fact that during summer, more solar radiation reaches the surface at the South Pole than is received at the equator in an equivalent period;[5] however, the lowest temperature ever recorded on Earth – -89.6°C (-128.6°F)[6] – was also at the South Pole.

Previous spread: White-out: coastal mountains edge Antarctica's vast expanse of ice.

Because the vast majority of Antarctica is effectively a frozen desert, it supports very few species of either flora or fauna, though the cold waters that encircle it teem with life forms ranging from the microscopic to the blue whale. Antarctica has never had an indigenous human population, although today there are staffed research stations.

Tourism is a growing industry, and there are stringent regulations as to where visitors are allowed and what interaction they can have with the habitat and actual wildlife of Antarctica. Nevertheless, the explosion in visitor numbers during recent years is raising questions about the potential detrimental impact that tourism might have.

Politically, Antarctica stands as a model of international cooperation to the rest of the world, most notably for the Antarctic Treaty. Emerging out of 1959's International Geophysical Year, the Antarctic Treaty has enabled scientific research to be carried out and national research bases to be established by signatory countries – yet no nation controls any part of the continent.

In recent years, the decline in the ozone layer over the continent and the impact of climate change have received particular attention from research scientists. Global warming has already made an impression on Antarctica. Maps have had to be re-drawn since the Larsen B ice shelf disintegrated in 2002, shattering into tens of thousands of icebergs that drifted into the Weddell Sea.[7] Similarly, penguin and seal colonies have been threatened to the point of starvation as ice has shifted, blocking their routes to the sea and dangerously extending their migration paths.

The loss of Antarctica's vast continental ice sheet as a result of rising atmospheric temperatures would have devastating consequences across the world. That the ice sheet is heavy enough to submerge most of the very land on which it sits to below sea level gives some indication of the sheer amount of run-off water that would pour into the sea. The discovery in early 2007 of vast lakes and river systems beneath the Antarctic ice sheet, which may lubricate the movement of these glaciers towards the sea, has raised new questions about the speed of sea-level rise due to the rate that ice sheets would slide from land into the ocean.[8]

Were the West Antarctic ice sheet to melt, the world's oceans would rise by 4.6–6 m (15–20 ft); though unlikely, were the East Antarctic ice sheet also to melt, the seas would rise by a staggering 61 m (200 ft), swallowing low-lying islands and altering the world's familiar coastlines beyond recognition.[9]

> 'Antarctica represents a more profound manifestation of international peace than any other place in the world – managed in the past half-century through the Antarctic Treaty's unprecedented global cooperation of nearly 50 countries, and formally designated a "natural reserve dedicated to peace and science".'
>
> DENISE LANDAU,
> EXECUTIVE DIRECTOR OF THE
> INTERNATIONAL ASSOCIATION OF
> ANTARCTICA TOUR OPERATORS

James Barnes

The EarthCare Award, the highest international honour of the American environmental group Sierra Club, went to long-time Antarctica activist James Barnes in November 2004.[10] He also received the International Environmentalist of the Year award from the National Wildlife Federation in 1991, and the Order of the Golden Ark from the Dutch Royal Family's foundation in 1998.

Having gained a law degree from the University of Michigan in 1970, Barnes spent the 1970s working as a lawyer and advocate on behalf of a range of human rights and environmental causes at the public interest law firm, the Center for Law and Social Policy. The company specialized in representing 'unrepresented interests', and Barnes was well placed to represent the interests of Antarctica at a time when harvesting krill in the Southern Ocean and drilling for oil were on the international agenda. Barnes recalls, 'There were a lot of closed-door international meetings going on about it – so we at the Center began using legal means to try to open those doors up.'[11]

In 1978, the Antarctic Treaty members began negotiating what would become the Convention on the Conservation of Antarctic Marine Living Resources. Barnes, with other interested parties from across the world, embarked on establishing the Antarctic and Southern Ocean Coalition (ASOC) the same year. Beginning with around twenty-five member organizations, ASOC is now comprised of 240 environmental and conservation groups in over forty countries, including international groups such as Friends of the Earth International, WWF and Greenpeace, and national groups such as the Sierra Club and the Australian Conservation Foundation, with the aim of influencing international politics via lobbying treaty members. Until the emergence of ASOC, the Antarctic Treaty System was a closed political set-up with no organizations permitted to observe their meetings and no reports made public. ASOC also holds the distinction of being the sole environmental NGO at Antarctic Treaty Consultative Meetings, holding official observer status.

Barnes grew aware of the need for an environmental organization devoted exclusively to Antarctica, and in 1982 left the Center for Law and Social Policy to found The Antarctica Project (TAP). Barnes was especially inspired to 'think big about Antarctica' by naturalist Sir Peter Scott, son of Antarctic explorer Robert Falcon Scott. Through TAP, Barnes sought to promote the protection of the continent's unique habitat and better serve ASOC too. Since ASOC is a coalition group, TAP is not only ASOC Secretariat, but remains the only conservation body in the world focused solely on Antarctica and the Southern Ocean.

Barnes went on to become director of international programmes for Friends of the Earth in Washington, DC. He is still on TAP's Board of Directors and is executive director of ASOC, and lives in France.

International Cooperation and Environmental Protection

Antarctica's formal political history emerged out of the success of International Geophysical Year in 1957–58, when scientists from sixty-seven countries cooperated in a unique, full-scale research programme on the continent. Initiated by the United States, the Antarctic Treaty was signed by twelve countries on 1 December 1959 to further this shared work for peaceful purpose only, and entered into force in 1961. The level of cooperation the treaty entails remains unique among international agreements.

Under the treaty's terms, weapons testing, nuclear explosions and radioactive waste disposal are forbidden, and military personnel and equipment are only allowed for logistical support of scientific programmes. Notably, any decisions regarding Antarctica are to be derived by consensus between Consultative Nations, or Treaty Parties – those operating research stations on the continent and islands south of 60° south – at annual Antarctic Treaty Consultative Meetings.[12]

During the 1980s, the international environmental movement sought to have Antarctica designated a World Park to preserve the continent's wilderness status and to prevent exploitation of its fisheries and such mineral resources as platinum and gold, and coal and hydrocarbons. Between 1987 and 1991, Greenpeace established its own small, minimal-impact World Park Antarctic Base to highlight environmental violations on the continent. Greenpeace continued to campaign alongside other environmental groups such as TAP, in particular seeking to overturn the Antarctic Treaty's Convention on Mineral Resources, which sought to regulate mineral exploitation in Antarctica. The convention was eventually dropped when Australia and France declined to ratify it on environmental grounds.[13]

Greenpeace dismantled its base in 1992 after the Antarctic Treaty Parties negotiated what became known as the Madrid Protocol – an environmental protection protocol to the Antarctic Treaty – in October 1991. However, because of the need for each of the twenty-six Treaty Parties to ratify any protocol, it was not until 14 January 1998 that the protocol came into force; Japan had delayed signing until December 1997.

The Madrid Protocol clarified and extended previous environmental policies of the Antarctic Treaty and earlier conventions, formally designating Antarctica and its surrounding marine ecosystems 'a natural reserve, devoted to peace and science'.[14] Notably, a fifty-year ban was placed on any commercial exploitation of Antarctica's mineral resources. It also introduced laws regarding waste disposal, the conservation of flora and fauna, and marine pollution, and demanded that Environmental Impact Assessments be made for all proposed visits to Antarctica regardless of purpose. The Committee on Environmental Protection was established to oversee the protocol's operation.[15]

Particular regions in the Antarctic are under special protection on ecological, historical or scientific grounds, as is Antarctic wildlife, and only permits issued by the appropriate national authority allow access. Protection extends beyond flora and fauna and habitat to designated historic sites and monuments, including remains from celebrated expeditions such as those of Britain's Scott and Shackleton, and of Australia's Mawson's huts. Fishing activities are regulated; any harvesting is based on scientific principles to prevent over-exploitation.

Today, there are forty-six Antarctic Treaty nations, and representatives meet annually to promote scientific cooperation and environmental protection in a continuing climate of peaceful internationalism; no territorial claims are allowed on the continent. The Antarctic Treaty has proved an impressive political model, especially during times of conflict elsewhere between member nations. During the Cuban missile crisis, the Vietnam War and the conflict in the Falkland Islands, scientific communication continued unabated.

The ratification of the Madrid Protocol in the same year as the Kyoto Protocol – which for many environmentalists was a disappointing response to climate change – provided an alternative beacon of hope: 'It shows that countries of the world can, in fact, come together to achieve a meaningful environmental goal,' said Greenpeace's Gerry Leape the day the protocol became law.[16]

Antarctica's Changing Atmosphere

The air above Antarctica is behaving strangely – or at least in a way that has yet to be fully explained by climate models predicting global warming. A 2006 study of archived data collected by weather balloons positioned above the continent over the previous thirty years revealed a heating of Antarctica's atmosphere three times higher than the global average. The greatest temperature rise – of approximately 0.75°C (1.4°F) per decade during winter – was recorded 5 km (3 miles) above the ice sheet in the layer of air known as the middle troposphere.[17]

Baffled climate scientists at the British Antarctic Survey (BAS) concluded that the findings could indicate several things: that there are aspects of climate change still not fully understood; that the modelling was faulty; or that natural climate variability had been recorded.[18] The accrued data was compared with twenty simulations of the climate over the last century, taking account of rising levels of greenhouse gases. These simulations are the same ones used by the Intergovernmental Panel on Climate Change (IPCC) to replicate past climates and make predictions for the future. In all cases, the models failed to simulate the rise in temperatures the BAS research had recorded.[19]

The unexpected warming could have implications for sea levels by affecting levels of snowfall across Antarctica. As the warmed, more moist air blowing across the continent cools to form snow, an extra layer of potential meltwater forms, which would pour into the surrounding ocean once global warming takes effect.

The higher atmospheric temperatures recorded are in themselves unlikely to promote severe melting at the ice sheet's surface, simply because they remain high up in the atmosphere. That the Antarctic atmosphere has warmed up while the continent's surface temperature remains, on the whole, resolutely stable is promoting further scientific research. (An exception is the mountainous Antarctic peninsula, where the temperature has risen 2.5°C [4.5°F] in the last half century, the largest annual warming seen anywhere in the world.[20])

One of the current hypotheses is that Antarctica is especially sensitive to greenhouse gases during its dark winter months. Without sunlight, the surface ice goes unheated, while any heat that is already present at the surface continues to radiate into the atmosphere and is subsequently trapped by the accumulated layer of greenhouse gases. Alternatively, it is possible that air circulation patterns have altered to cause the discrepancy between atmospheric and surface temperatures, though recordings collected at Antarctic weather stations so far dispute this.[21]

While it remains difficult to differentiate between what is occurring naturally and what is due to human activities, the Antarctic research findings nevertheless fit into the jigsaw puzzle that depicts the developing worldwide impact of global warming. They also complement the scientific discoveries made elsewhere about the damage being done to the planet and its atmosphere. For, like its Arctic polar opposite, Antarctica has its own special properties vital to the functioning of all life forms on Earth.

In the middle of nowhere: Antarctica's very isolation makes it a valuable scientific control for calculating the level of pollution from elsewhere.

Drilling ice cores out of Antarctica's continental ice shelf enables scientists to ascertain the climatic history of the shelf and the Earth's natural climate rhythm over hundreds of thousands of years. The layers of ice are as distinct as the annual rings in a tree trunk that are used to measure its age.

In September 2006, data gained from one such 3.2 km (2 mile) long drilling from a thick area of ice known as Dome C revealed rises in carbon dioxide levels that – should the rate of CO_2 rise continue – could see climate change run out of control within ten years, according to BAS scientists. The tiny bubbles of air discovered in an ice core, the oldest part of which was 800,000 years old, showed current levels of CO_2 to be far higher than levels from previous eras held in the same ice core.[22]

Researchers have identified eight cycles of atmospheric change during that 800,000-year period when both carbon dioxide and methane levels soared. These periods of rising gas levels corresponded with the high temperatures of warm, interglacial periods; whenever the levels of carbon dioxide changed, so too did the planet's climate.

> 'The rate of change is probably the most scary thing because it means that the Earth systems can't cope with it. On such a crowded planet, we have little capacity to adapt to changes that are much faster than anything in human experience.'
>
> DR ERIC WOLFF, BRITISH ANTARCTIC SURVEY

During previous cycles, however, CO_2 levels ranged from 180 to 300 parts per million (ppm) of air. Latest levels are 380 ppm, and are largely caused by burning fossil fuels. A 'tipping point' of 440 ppm would send climate change beyond the point of no return.[23] Similarly, whereas methane levels were previously 750 parts per billion (ppb) at their highest, they now stand at 1,780 ppb.

Human activity over the past 200 years has altered the composition of the ice to an unprecedented degree due to the increase in greenhouse gases in the Earth's atmosphere. The level of carbon dioxide has increased by approximately 35 per cent during this period. Before industrialization, CO_2 levels tended towards a steady 5 per cent increase.

Yet it is the sheer rate of change that is most worrying. Whereas increase in CO_2 had never exceeded 30 ppm in 1,000 years, CO_2 in the atmosphere has risen by that amount in merely the last seventeen years.

The Ozone Hole over Antarctica

The ozone hole above Antarctica was first identified by the British Antarctic Survey Expeditions carried out at the Halley Bay research station between 1981 and 1983, and reported in 1985.[24] The international community worked quickly to respond to the findings. A mere two years later, the 1987 Montreal Protocol instigated a global ban on the use of CFCs, the pollutant most damaging to the ozone layer.

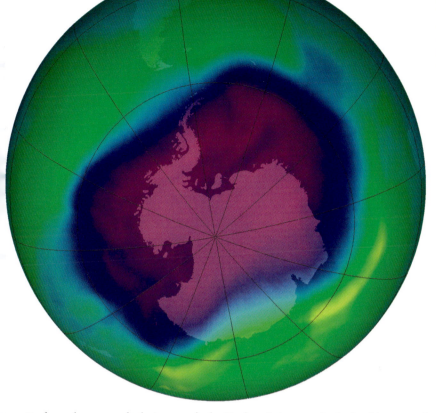

Practically the entire Antarctic landmass is revealed by satellite images of the thinning ozone layer.

In fact, the ozone hole is not a hole. Rather, it is a particularly thin area of the global-wide ozone layer sitting over Antarctica, which tends to occur during the Antarctic spring from September to November. The layer protects the Earth from the sun's UV rays, which would otherwise scorch the planet. Locally, the increased UV light flooding through the so-called hole was found to be adversely affecting the DNA of the icefish, a unique Antarctic fish species. One-celled Antarctic marine plants had also been damaged by ozone depletion. And, in 2002, the Larsen B ice shelf crumbled due to localized atmospheric warming.[25]

On average, the ozone hole is at its largest during October, and its thinning is caused by the impact of atmospheric pollutants. The specific character of the Antarctic weather, however, makes the ozone layer above it susceptible to damage at a level nowhere else experienced; seasonally, the layer can be reduced by as much as 70 per cent.[26]

During Antarctica's dark winter months, strong winds blowing over the continent combine to form the polar vortex that separates the Antarctic's air from that of the rest of the world. Within this isolated weather system polar stratospheric clouds form at an altitude of about 24,000 m (80,000 ft), where the atmospheric temperature drops below -73°C (-99°F).

The only clouds in the entire stratosphere, they are also known as 'nacreous clouds' owing to their mother-of-pearl sheen; unfortunately, the ice crystals they attract react with pollutants, such as bromine, and chlorine atoms from CFCs, and so damage the ozone layer. By the following spring, the thinning of the ozone layer is re-established – and further damaged by the return of extreme sunlight to the pole.

In 2006, the ozone hole measured 28m sq km (10.6m sq miles) – rivalling 2000's record ozone hole extension and 1998's record shallow levels[27] – and there was a loss of 40 million tonnes of ozone over the southern continent, beating 2000's 39 million tonne decline. Extremely low temperatures in the stratosphere over Antarctica, the lowest recorded since 1979, combined with sunlight to eat away at the layer.[28] While the ozone hole is an especially Antarctic phenomenon, the ozone layer is thinning worldwide, and a lesser ozone hole, its rate of damage limited by warmer stratospheric temperatures than in the South, occurs over the Arctic from March to May during the Northern Hemisphere's spring months.

Collapse of the Larsen B Ice Shelf

The March 2002 disintegration of the Larsen B ice shelf was directly linked to global warming and the ozone hole over Antarctica.[29] In the space of a month, the entire 3,250 sq km (1,254 sq mile) ice shelf – a physical feature larger than Luxembourg, up to 200 m (650 ft) thick and weighing 500 billion tonnes – which had been stable for thousands of years, splintered into tens of thousands of icebergs and collapsed into the Weddell Sea. More ice was dumped into the Southern Ocean that month than the icebergs of the past fifty years combined.[30]

Polar scientists concluded that stronger westerly winds in the northern Antarctic peninsula, largely the result of human-induced climate change, were responsible for marked regional summer warming that led to the retreat and collapse of the northern Larsen ice shelf.[31] This monumental event proved that a major disaster was caused by global warming.

On days when the strengthened westerly winds forced warm air eastward over the natural barrier of the Antarctic peninsula's 2 km (1.2 mile) high mountain chain, summer temperatures in the north-east peninsula warmed by about 5°C. This heating led to meltwater draining into the Larsen B ice shelf's crevasses: the key to its collapse.[32] Over the past half-century, the western Antarctic peninsula has shown the greatest increase in temperatures (primarily in winter) observed anywhere on Earth.

Owing to the slow decline of pollutants in the atmosphere, it is not expected that the ozone hole over Antarctica will have fully recovered before 2050. CFC emissions must continue to be held at bay by appropriate and enforced regulations; however, this alone will not solve the problem. Greenhouse gases raise surface temperatures, but conversely result in the long-term cooling of the stratosphere, increasing the amount of polar stratospheric cloud, the creation of which would turn back any healing of the ozone layer that otherwise might have occurred.

Wildlife Under Threat

Antarctica is often regarded as a particularly pristine part of the world, a perception emphasized by the blown white appearance of the region. Because of its extreme climate, flora and fauna can only survive on the edges of the continent.

Flora are notably vulnerable and low-lying; a footprint on a mossbed may remain unchanged for a decade.[33] The Antarctic hair grass and a pearlwort found on the west coast of the Antarctic peninsula, south of 56°S, are the only vascular plants able to grow under such severe conditions. Additionally, approximately 150 lichens, thirty mosses, fungi and one liverwort have also been identified, as well as over 300 species of non-marine algae.[34]

Despite its remote location, the continent is subject to the impact of more developed and industrialized parts of the globe. Indeed, its very lack of a human population allows scientists to monitor environmental impact that has clearly come from elsewhere. Yet, increasingly this once-pure outdoor laboratory is being threatened by the impact of people, whether scientist or tourist.

Depending on the time of year, the total population of Antarctica's research stations varies between approximately 1,000 and 4,000 personnel, with over a quarter of those at the US base during the peak December to February summer season, plus a further thousand or so working onboard ships.[35] These scientists cannot help but contribute to local pollution of the environment in the course of their work; human habitation accumulates its own waste such as litter and vehicle fuel emissions, which is not always easily removed. Additionally, what has become known as the 'cold rush' is placing further pressure on the continent. India plans to build a year-round scientific base – the sixtieth on the ice cap – on the Larsemann Hills, a region already suffering human-induced contamination and degradation. America has constructed a 1,600 km (1,000 mile) motorway between its McMurdo base and the South Pole, while Australia is planning to operate flights to the ice.[36]

Perhaps the most notorious example of pollution introduced from elsewhere was in the case of the chemical DDT[37] being detected in penguin eggs in 1966. More recently, the impact of global warming on ice floes created havoc among penguin colonies. Abnormally extensive sea ice floes and the movement of massive icebergs are threatening entire populations with starvation. If coastal areas become choked with ice, the route to the sea and its fish is extended, such as occurred at Cape Crozier in November 2002.

Cape Crozier's emperor penguin colony is Antarctica's most renowned colony of birds. First recorded in 1902 by the British National Antarctic Expedition (1901–04) led by Captain Robert Falcon Scott, it came to fame as the subject of *The Worst Journey in the World*,[38] an account of the 193 km (120 mile) round-trip journey from Cape Evans to Cape Crozier, a spin-off from Captain Scott's Terra Nova expedition (1910–13). In June 1911, three men – Edward Wilson, Henry Bowers and Apsley Cherry-Garrard (who was to author the book) – braved ferocious winds and bitter cold to visit the emperor penguins' breeding colony and return with a number of eggs, which they then believed provided the missing link between birds and dinosaurs, for embryological studies.[39]

Today part of the New Zealand Ross Sea Dependency, both the adelie penguins based on Cape Crozier's ice-free land and the metre-high emperor penguins that crowd at the foot of the Ross ice shelf to breed (the southernmost bird colony on Earth) have been heavily scrutinized by scientists. Long-term studies of population dynamics and social behaviour, however, took second place to climate change studies in December 2001, when ice blockaded the coastline, lengthening the migratory journey to the sea and threatening to starve the adelie penguins in particular.

Two massive icebergs, known as B-15 and C-19, first broke away from the Ross ice shelf in March 2000 and floated east to create a barrier that altered wind and current patterns. These grounded icebergs and extensive amounts of sea ice in Antarctica's Ross Sea cut off the adelies feeding in the open sea from their breeding grounds.[40] Whereas normally at that time of year the sea ice extends from 24 to 32 km (15 to 20 miles) north of the United States' McMurdo Station on Ross Island, in 2000 the sea ice stretched 128 km (80 miles) beyond the station.[41]

Rather than swim home to their colonies, the birds had to walk. Trekking an average 1–2 km/h (0.6–1.2 mph) compared to their average swimming speed of 7–8 km/h (4.3–4.9 mph),[42] they struggled to survive the journey; the mates and chicks waiting for their return to the colony also faced death. Numbers of breeding pairs of adelie at Cape Crozier declined to the low end of the normal range of approximately 130,000 pairs most years; the small colony of adelies at Cape Royd, a colony monitored annually since 1959 and the southernmost group of adelies, failed.

Additionally, between August and October 2002, a colony of around 2,400 adult emperor penguins and 1,200 chicks also at Cape Crozier scattered into five sub-groups due to the grounding of the icebergs and subsequent disturbance of their habitats. Numbers of chicks and breeding pairs were greatly reduced.[43] Of the chicks that did survive, their development wa

The Decline of the Albatross

Memorably depicted as a mythic herald of doom for seamen in Coleridge's *The Rime of the Ancient Mariner*, the albatross, as the largest of the world's seabirds, is also a magnificent sight for seafarers in Antarctica as it makes its journey across thousands of miles to feed.

Along with the snow petrel, the albatross belongs to the most prominent bird order in Antarctica. In addition to the albatross, approximately thirty-five bird species live or migrate among the sub-Antarctic islands of Kerguelen and South Georgia, including cormorants, gulls and terns.

Within the last twenty years, however, the number of albatrosses has declined so dramatically that the species is now facing extinction. The main cause of the loss of these impressive birds is the introduction by fishing fleets of 'long-lining', a method involving a line of squid-baited hooks being trailed behind a fishing boat for up to 130 km (80 miles). As many as 100,000 albatrosses are killed from long-lining every year; the seabirds become caught on the line and are then drowned. Because albatross pairs mate for life and raise only one chick at a time, the remainder parent and offspring are invariably doomed too.

The Amsterdam species of albatross – named after the French southern territory of Amsterdam Island, the only place in the world it exists – is most threatened with disappearance. Of the eighty or fewer remaining birds, only twenty pairs are breeding each year.[44] Conservation bodies are seeking to save the species. Tying blue threads to the lines has been promoted as a low-cost means of making the lines visible to the birds.[45]

In 2004, WWF-Australia joined forces with Peregrine Shipping, an Antarctic expedition cruise operator, in a direct bid to protect albatrosses. Their joint project, International Cooperation for the Conservation of Albatrosses and Petrels, was established under the umbrella of the global WWF Endangered Seas programme. Combining WWF's sound conservation strengths and Peregrine's financial and physical backing, the partnership's particular focus was on illegal – that is, unregulated and unreported (IUU) – fishing in the region, the greatest threat to the albatross's future. WWF sees the teamwork as a new model for corporate partnerships, while Peregrine plans to inspire other tourism operators to be committed to responsible tourism.[46]

slowed because of a reduction in food sources. It was feared that a missing group of emperors was crushed by locking ice plates.[47]

Research backed by the National Science Foundation, which manages the US Antarctic Program, aims to re-establish the strength and resilience of both species in the light of such ice conditions.[48]

Tourism in Antarctica

Besides climate change, a more prosaic threat to Antarctica's environment is mass tourism. The Antarctic Treaty grants freedom of access to any individual, organization or government, but has no legally binding regulations on commercial tourism. In the ten years between 1994–95 and 2005–06, numbers of tourists visiting Antarctica soared by 350 per cent, from 8,000 to 28,000 people. Around 80 per cent of the visitors in 2005–06 set foot on the Antarctic Peninsula as part of a cruise trip.[49] Congestion from too many cruise ships at sea, and crowds of people on land are the inevitable consequences; some of the ships can carry as many as 1,000 passengers as well as transport helicopters. While a high percentage of tourists are there because they value the wildlife, its habitat and the sheer beauty of the continent itself, ironically their very presence places great pressure on the highly vulnerable natural landscape and its waters.

Black and white issue: ice floes blocking or extending the seasonal migratory route of emperor penguins between their feeding and breeding grounds threaten the survival of whole colonies.

To counter any potential damage such as sea and coastal pollution, littering and disruption of breeding patterns and sensitive research activities, site-specific ecological studies have been carried out to ascertain how human proximity affects local flora and fauna. Recommendations to lessen the damage have included introducing paths that direct tourists and limit where they can go, allocating guidelines for distances allowed between visitors and wildlife, and establishing refuge sites where tourists are not allowed at all.[50]

The first incidence of commercial tourism occurred in 1957, although it was not until 1969, with Lars-Eric Lindblad's purpose-built Antarctic tour-ship, *Lindblad Explorer*, that trips to the continent became regular.[51] Today, visitors are increasingly attracted to Antarctica for the opportunity to climb, ski, snowboard, hike and go snow-mobiling.

This troubles environmentalists, who, through the Antarctic and Southern Oceans Coalition (ASOC), are calling for tourism to be covered by the Antarctic Treaty's environmental protocol. ASOC director James Barnes commented:

'Land-based tourism could have severe repercussions because nowhere is out of bounds. If tourists start treating Antarctica as an activity theme park, instead of respecting its status in international law as a natural reserve dedicated to peace and science, we've got a serious problem.'[52]

Policies are in place to regulate such activities. The Antarctic Treaty's 1991 Madrid Protocol on Environmental Protection[53] places responsibilities on tour companies and private expeditions. They are legally obliged to undertake an environmental impact assessment, and guidelines are provided for waste management, prevention of marine pollution, avoiding disturbance to wildlife and plants, and avoiding damage to historic buildings, including Mawson's, Shackleton's and Scott's huts.

Additionally, in 1994, the Antarctic Treaty Consultative Meeting (ATCM) recommended a policy of 'Guidance for Visitors to the Antarctic'.[54] Areas designated as 'Antarctic Specially Protected and Managed Areas' have further strictures, and some are only accessible for scientific and management purposes.

In 1991, the self-regulating International Association of Antarctica Tour Operators (IAATO) was established by seven private tour companies to encourage environmentally responsible and safe practices among members. Today, members number eighty companies – more than 95 per cent of operators – and IAATO is an official observer to the ATCM. Their guidelines and bye-laws include limiting the size of ships cruising Antarctic waters and the number of people disembarking at particular coastal sites.[55]

However, there is nothing to prevent non-member tour operators that do not adhere to such regulations from taking tourists to Antarctica. Additionally, smaller private expeditions are growing in popularity; however,

lost and found

Antarctica's Undersea World

The collapse of the Larsen A and Larsen B ice shelves in 1995 and 2002, respectively, exposed 6,476 sq km (3,900 sq miles) of the Weddell Sea's floor – and a wealth of new species, including '15 shrimp-like amphiphods, four possible new species of cnidarians (organisms related to coral), jellyfish and sea anemones'.[56] Striking undersea images beamed round the world featured ghostly blue icefish, bright orange twelve-limbed starfish and herds of slothful sea cucumbers, their individual members all heading in the same direction across the floor as if they were going to war.[57]

Global warming is believed to be responsible for the destruction of the 5,000-year-old ice shelves within a decade of each other. Ironically, it is global warming that has made such biodiversity accessible to scientific research for the first time. The findings proved a valuable contribution to the Census of Antarctic Marine Life, an International Polar Year project involving forty-seven scientists from twelve countries.[58]

As a result of the ten-week voyage of discovery around the Antarctic peninsula by the research icebreaker, *Polarstern*, scientists were able to observe wildlife that previously was only visible via holes drilled in the ice. Creatures were recorded at a depth of 853 m (2,800 ft) that are usually associated with seabeds three times that deep.[59] Fast-growing sea squirts, which look like gelatinous bags, appeared to have colonized the area only after the ice shelves collapsed. However, other recorded fauna, such as large, slow-growing glass sponges found at Larsen A, indicate that they were present before the ice shelf collapsed.[60]

some practitioners underestimate the continent's sheer wilderness qualities and, unprepared when disaster strikes, are entirely dependent on costly rescue services provided by research bases or passing shipping. They have also been known to leave broken-down vehicles, including crashed planes, and abandoned equipment in their wake. Yet a well-organized and responsible small-scale expedition can have minimal impact, and there is concern that in a bid to regulate independent travel on the continent, something of what has characterized human endeavour on this vast ice-bound space might be lost.[61]

Taking Action

1. To gain a clear perception of the Antarctic continent, look up Antarctica in a quality atlas such as *The Times Atlas of the World* (Collins Bartholomew) at your local library.

2. Learn more about the Antarctic Treaty at www.antarctica.ac.uk/About_Antarctica/index.html .

3. Contact the Antarctic Treaty Secretariat at secret@ats.aq to find out whether your own nation is a member of the Antarctic Treaty system – and the level of its involvement.

4. Access the website of the Antarctic and Southern Ocean Coalition to keep abreast of the environmental status of the continent and to support ASOC's work. Go to www.asoc.org .

5. Find out about Antarctic environmental campaigning with Greenpeace at www.greenpeace.org/international and Friends of the Earth International at www.foe.org .

6. Contact www.onceextinct.com to add your name to the campaign to save the albatross.

7. Antarctica's adelie penguins have been contaminated with chemicals used in paints and preservatives. To learn more about how to reduce contaminants in your own life which threaten humans and wildlife, log on to http://detox.panda.org/reduce-your-risks/index.cfm for a helpful list of suggestions.

8. Visit NASA's interactive Learning Technologies Project, 'Live from Antarctica 2' at http://quest.nasa.gov/Antarctica .

9. Take the Ozone Hole tour, a virtual trip around the topic developed by members of the Centre for Atmospheric Science at the University of Cambridge: www.atm.ch.cam.ac.uk/tour .

10. For a basic scientific explanation of the creation of the Antarctic ozone hole, visit Washington University's Science Outreach pages about 'The Ozone Hole over Antarctica' at www.so.wustl.edu .

11. Keep abreast of the Antarctic weather and climate by visiting the website of the Antarctic Automatic Weather Station Project, and the Antarctic Meteorological Research Center at http://uwamrc.ssec.wisc.edu .

12. If you choose to visit Antarctica, ensure your tour operator is affiliated with IAATO.

Europe

ICELAND

NORWAY

SWEDEN

FINLAND

Stockholm

ESTONIA

DENMARK

LITHUANIA

IRELAND

UNITED
KINGDOM

BELARUS

Amsterdam

Berlin

Warsaw

London

GERMANY

POLAND

BELGIUM

Rhine

CZECH
REPUBLIC

UKR

Paris

SLOVAKIA

FRANCE

Bern

AUSTRIA

HUNGARY

A L P S

CROATIA

ROMANIA

Danube

Bucharest

SERBIA

PORTUGAL

SPAIN

ITALY

BULGARIA

Madrid

Rome

GREECE

Athens

'Ecology isn't something we
can only leave to politicians.'

MIKHAIL GORBACHEV

Europe is a continent consisting of forty-one different countries, and contains both the world's largest country, Russia, in the east, and the smallest country, the tiny Vatican City, surrounded by Rome in the south-west. The continent stretches to Iceland in the north-west and extends north beyond the Arctic Circle. It is bordered by the Arctic Ocean to the north and the Atlantic Ocean to the west. A chain of seas, including the Mediterranean, Aegean, Black and Caspian, separate it from the continents of Africa and Asia to the south. On land, Europe meets Asia at the Ural and Caucasus mountain ranges.

Europe has a politically shifting sense of itself. Split apart by two World Wars in the first half of the twentieth century, as recently as 1989 it was divided by the 'Iron Curtain' to its east; on the one side was Western democracy and on the other, Soviet Communism. The opening of the Berlin Wall in November of that year did not simply establish the beginning of the end of an old world order. The once heavily patrolled border region has been transformed into a so-called 'Green Curtain' – a haven for local wildlife – the remaining physical evidence of the east–west divide creating a veritable chain of nature reserves.

In 1949, the Council of Europe was founded to unite disparate nations. While it remains distinct from the European Union (EU), formed in 1957, no country has ever joined the EU that was not first a member of the Council. Today, countries are gradually being admitted into the European Union. All will be influenced by – and will be able to contribute to – the EU's environmental policy:

'Protecting the environment is essential for the quality of life of current and future generations. The challenge is to combine this with continuing economic growth in a way which is sustainable over the long term. European Union environment policy is based on the belief that high environmental standards stimulate innovation and business opportunities. Economic, social and environment policies are closely integrated.'[1]

Previous spread: Traditional methods: small-scale farmers grow their crops against the backdrop of Europe's foothills.

Climate change is already having a dramatic impact on the continent. Spain and Portugal experienced prolonged drought in 2005, which expanded into central and southern Europe the following summer.[2] The traditional English country garden is being ravaged by heat, and Britain's National Trust Heritage Gardens will in turn be threatened as temperatures rise.[3] Yet the hotter weather looks set to be a temporary blip; a possible shift in the Atlantic Ocean's warming Gulf Stream away from the European landmass would see a notable drop in temperature, as the water keeps Europe warm.

Elsewhere across Europe it will be a surplus of water that will cause havoc. Waters are already rising in Venice, and it has been proposed that the lagoon within which the city sits be sealed off from the sea before floodwaters threaten to bury the city in all its architectural glory.

London's Thames Barrier is already being raised far more often than originally planned,[4] and flood risk management must be vigilantly maintained to prevent full-scale flooding of the capital city. Along England's south-east coast, seawalls built to keep out the North Sea are being ripped down to allow sea water to reclaim marshes, which act as natural flood barriers by absorbing excess waters, and attract wetland birds.[5]

Similarly, in Holland, 500,000 hectares (1.2 million acres) of land – 'an area more than twice the size of Greater London'[6] – is to be strategically flooded, and people are to move from permanent to floating homes in a considered response to the crisis. Yet, in contrast, the British government has given the go-ahead for developers to build 200,000 homes across what has been named the Thames Gateway region. Concerned environmentalists point out that it also happens to be the Thames floodplain, and that there are good reasons why it has not previously been developed.[7]

The roof of Europe is also at risk from the impact of climate change as the snow-capped Alps gradually lose their cover, threatening the skiing industry and therefore the local economies that rely on it. Alpine flora and fauna are also endangered as pressure is placed on remaining habitats, which are increasingly being squeezed between a rising treeline and the bare rock above.

A Green Curtain Across the Continent

The 'Iron Curtain' of the c. 1946–89 Cold War years was not simply a metaphor made famous by Winston Churchill to describe the military, political and ideological division at the heart of Europe between the Soviet Bloc countries in the East and the Western nations.[8] It was the name given to the very real and solid 6,400 km (4,000 mile) trail of heavily patrolled barbed-wire fencing, minefields and walls that split the continent in half.

This barren 'no man's land' with its high-level security allowed nature to retain a toe-hold, and laid the groundwork for peacetime nature reserves to be established and planned along the longest continuous stretch of undeveloped land in central Europe.[9]

Since the Berlin Wall fell in 1989, the curtain has progressively become park. Germany spearheaded the movement by protecting over half of the 1,400 km (870 mile) one-time border between East and West Germany.

Finland and Russia protect the largest stretch of the curtain by joining two national parks at their shared Arctic border.[10]

In 2003, the IUCN drew environmental and community development groups from all the border countries, including Green Cross International president, Mikhail Gorbachev (ex-president of the USSR), to meet in Bonn, Germany. They discussed the feasibility of replacing the one-time Iron Curtain with a chain of parks, nature reserves and organic farms stretching from the Arctic coastline south to the shared Bulgaria and Greece border, and fully encircling Albania.[11]

Under Soviet-era collectivism, many wetlands were drained and grasslands were ploughed up to make way for intensive farming. In Hungary, thousands of such acres are now restored, drawing birdlife and allowing for cattle grazing too. Officials at both Hungary's Ferto-Hansag National Park and Austria's adjoining Neusiedler See National Park coordinate wildlife and habitat management including Lake Ferto and farms within the parks. It is hoped this well-negotiated balance established between local human needs and the environment can be replicated along the curtain. Encouraging local farmers and landowners to develop environmentally friendly practices is regarded as

Sir Peter Scott, Conservation Pioneer

In 1912, trapped in his tent by an Antarctic blizzard and knowing he would not see his loved ones again, Captain Robert Falcon Scott ('Scott of the Antarctic') wrote this in his diary, offering advice to his wife Kathleen on how to bring up their infant son, Peter: '… make the boy interested in natural history if you can. It is better than games…'

Peter Markham Scott was to become one of the twentieth century's foremost conservationists, and, in 1973, the first person to be knighted for services to conservation and the environment. He was also an author, working on many books with his wife Philippa, as well as a renowned artist; he illustrated Paul Gallico's *The Snow Goose* (1946) and designed the World Wildlife Fund's original panda logo. And, as it happened, he proved to be good at games too. In 1936 alone, he won a bronze medal at the Olympics for single-handed sailing; the Prince of Wales' Cup for dinghy racing; and he made his first BBC broadcast about that sport. He was also a championship-level skater and glider.

In 1940, he joined the British Royal Navy as sub-lieutenant on HMS *Brooke*, and was mentioned in dispatches for his role in rescuing the crew of the burning HMS *Comorin* in 1941. In 1942, he was awarded the MBE (Member of the Order of the British Empire) and was appointed lieutenant commander. In 1945, he left the navy for an intended career in politics but was an unsuccessful candidate in that year's General Election.

the most promising 'bottom-up' method of protecting the envisioned green belt. However, not all local farmers are enamoured by the restrictions newly imposed upon them such as not using chemical pesticides.

Myriad political differences among the eighteen European countries that the curtain crosses reflect the continent's chequered past – differences that must be overcome to complete the Green Curtain project. Greece, Macedonia and Albania together require careful diplomacy, and Croatia and Serbia are still nursing wounds from the 1991–95 Yugoslav civil war which saw them on opposing sides. Remaining divides such as the fence along the Poland-Belarus border are creating environmental problems elsewhere in Europe.

Today, the Green Curtain is a very physical symbol of cross-country environmental connectiveness, yet past legislation also took steps to limit the countries' negative impact on the environment. As early as 1967, the European Council introduced legislation on the industrial risks of dangerous substances and technologies including asbestos, and pentachlorophenol (PCP), polychlorinated biphenyls (PCBs) and terphenyls (PCTs), which are converted to the poisonous chemical compound dioxin by fire – such as occurred at Seveso, Italy, in 1976.[12]

In 1946, he founded the Severn Wildfowl Trust at Slimbridge, Gloucestershire, which was to become the Wildfowl (latterly 'and Wetlands') Trust (WWT). In 1961, he established the World Wildlife Fund (WWF) and his autobiography, *Eye of the Wind*, was published. Also in that year, he set up the Loch Ness Investigation Bureau to study reports of monster sightings. In 1962, he originated the World Conservation Union's (IUCN) 'Red Data' books identifying endangered species, and was also to found many local and regional environmental bodies, including the Gloucestershire Trust for Nature Conservation and the Falkland Islands Foundation (later Falklands Conservation).

In 1966, he first visited Antarctica, his father's last resting place, to make a film for the BBC, and two years later was guest lecturer on Eric Lindblad's pioneer cruises to the continent. His environmental expertise proved instrumental in the establishment of the 1971 Ramsar Convention, the world's first intergovernmental treaty on the conservation and wise use of wetlands, especially as waterfowl habitat.

In 1977, Scott, along with Jacques Cousteau, was awarded the UN's International Pahlavi Environment Prize, and he also received the IUCN John Phillips Medal and the WWF Twentieth Anniversary Special Award in 1981. In 1986, the year of WWT's fortieth anniversary, Scott was awarded the JP Getty Prize and the WWF Gold Medal. In 1988, a coral fish – *Cirrilabrus scottorum* – was named after Sir Peter and Lady Scott. He died in 1989, shortly before his eightieth birthday.[13]

On 10 July 1976, a chemical reactor at a pesticide and herbicide manufacturing plant in the town released a toxic cloud of dioxin, contaminating an area of over 16 sq km (10 sq miles). Approximately 2,000 people were treated for dioxin contamination. In the wake of this incident, legislation was drawn up to prevent and control similar chemical accidents: the Seveso Directive regarding 'major-accident hazards of certain industrial activities' was adopted in 1982. But further major chemical accidents followed, including 1984's Union Carbide factory leak at Bhopal in India, and 1986's fire

The EU Greenhouse Gas Emission Trading Scheme (EU ETS)

The world's largest multi-country, multi-sector greenhouse gas emission trading scheme began operating in January 2005, the culmination of an EC directive that entered into force on 25 October 2003.[14] The scheme targets large emitters of CO_2, responsible together for around half of the EU's total CO_2 emissions.

Under approval and guidance from the European Commission, each member state must implement a national allocation plan (NAP), which establishes a system of carbon dioxide emission allowances and determines how they will be distributed among an initial 12,000 industrial plants. These allowances can be traded between plants; the first trading period lasted from 2005 to 2007, but subsequent ones will be five years long.[15] When a plant emits more CO_2 than it has allowances for, it must buy further allowances – from any installation that has produced less CO_2 than its allocation so has surplus to sell. Member states can also purchase internationally traded carbon allowances created through emission reduction projects under the Kyoto Protocol's Clean Development Mechanism or Joint Implementation arrangements.[16]

The second trading period, 2008–12, notably coincides with the deadline for the EU and its member states to meet Kyoto Protocol targets for reducing greenhouse gas emissions, so ETS NAPs will come under especial scrutiny from the European Commission.[17] Projected emissions and fuel prices, and the reductions in emissions from outlined policies and measures must all be presented. In turn, the EC reports on the progress of the ETS to the Council of Europe and the European Parliament.

A well-established, successful emissions trading scheme across Europe could lead to an international carbon market. However, over-allocation of allowances by some countries during the first trading period brought carbon prices crashing and threatened the viability of the scheme. In 2005, Germany – a heavy polluter – was left with 44.1 million tonnes of CO_2 allowances, while the UK – the only country to emit more than its quota that year – had to buy over 30 million tonnes of extra allowance. The future allocation of allowances at a European-wide level could prove more effective.[18]

at the Sandoz warehouse in Basel, Switzerland, which led to the Rhine's severe pollution and the death of half a million fish.

The Seveso Directive was amended in 1987 and 1988 to take account of storage of materials, and eventually replaced in December 1996 by the Seveso II Directive. In 2003, it was further applied to thousands of industrial organizations where dangerous substances exceeded directive thresholds.[19]

Acid rain pollution is another environmental issue requiring transnational cooperation. The EU's action to limit acid rain was one of the first examples of successful cooperation regarding trans-boundary pollution. In 1985, under the Convention on Long Range Transboundary Air Pollution, the First Sulphur Protocol was signed by twenty-one countries. In 1988, the EU's Large Combustion Plant Directive required that sulphur dioxide emissions from existing large power stations be reduced overall by 58 per cent from a 1980 baseline by 2003. New plants were to be faced with a ceiling on their allowed SO_2 and NO emissions.[20]

The Warming of Europe

The European Alps appear an iconically fresh and pristine mountain range. Yet 14 million people are packed into this seemingly empty 190,000 sq km (74,000 sq miles), two-thirds of them living in urban areas. Only 17 per cent of the Alps and its valleys is protected.[21]

The skiing industry has its own environmental impact and is also being affected by climate change. Tourists put huge pressure on mountain

The hills are alive: a picturesque Alpine village nestled in the lee of one of its mountains.

communities by demanding an infrastructure of roads, hotels and chalets, and ski-lifts and ski-runs to support their sport. However, climate change is taking its toll on the mountain snows that are so vital to attracting visitors and their money. Resorts at lower altitudes face eventual closure as the snows melt away. Already snowfall in such regions has declined by an average of 40 per cent. The snow line is predicted to rise 200–300 m (650–980 ft) in the next 30–50 years, and soon only ski stations higher than 1,500 m (4,900 ft) will be able to host winter sports.[22] To stave off the accelerating melting of ice sheets, a number of Swiss resorts such as Verbier and Andermatt have taken to covering sections of local glaciers through the summer – with successful results.[23]

In late 2006, the World Meteorological Organisation recorded alpine winter snowfalls at a third of their usual level and temperatures up to 3°C higher than normal. In some resorts, it was too warm for even artificial snow-making machines to work.[24] The Organisation for Economic Co-operation and Development revealed Europe's highest mountain chain was heating up three times as fast as the world as a whole.[25]

Developers moving facilities further up the Alps to protect the ski industry impinge on previously untouched wildlife habitats. The edelweiss nestling among high rocks and meadows are probably the most well-known alpine flora. Like other mountain plants, edelweiss is extremely vulnerable to climate change because the habitat in which it thrives is hemmed in between the woodland below and the bare mountain rock above. A modest 2°C rise in average temperature would lead to a 300–400 m (980–1,300 ft) raising of the treeline[26] and reduce the land area where it can flourish, thus increasing the species' fragility.

Even the bare rock beneath the alpine snow is not safe from climate change. In July 2006, a 400,000 cu m (14.1 million cu ft) limestone slab broke away from the Eiger mountain.[27] It had been loosened by the retreat of the Grindelwald glacier over the previous twenty-five years; the revealed limestone was prey to water erosion, and fissures widened until the rock split away. Melting permafrost also destabilizes the Alps and promotes rockfalls.

Increasing temperatures have also had negative repercussions elsewhere on the continent. In August 2003, 15,000 people died in Paris due to an unprecedented two-week-long heatwave. Daytime temperatures soared to 40°C (104°F) for nine consecutive days[28] while night-time temperatures remained as high as 25.5°C (78°F) for several nights running.[29]

The death rate, double that of August 2002, caused political conflict. The government was criticized for its delayed response and for past cuts in funding to medical services that now proved unable to cope. Dr Lucien Abenhaim Director General for Health, resigned. Parisians, many of whom leave the city in August, were slammed for neglecting elderly relatives; older people with existing medical conditions living alone were notably at risk, although 19 per cent of fatalities lived in care homes lacking air-conditioning.[30]

The Paris heatwave took place during a period of exceptionally high temperatures across Europe that led to a total 35,000 deaths. Wildfires raged across regions of Portugal, Croatia, Greece, Italy, the Netherlands and France.[31]

There is no universal definition of a heatwave; it is inevitably categorized as a period of particularly high, sustained temperatures impacting human mortality figures, ecosystems and regional economies. Projected future heatwaves will be more intense, frequent and longer lasting beyond 2050 as greenhouse gases exacerbate the atmospheric circulation patterns causing even higher temperatures than presently recorded.[32] In Europe, heatwaves currently tend to occur more readily in the Mediterranean region. Climate change will increase their severity in the south, but areas currently not as susceptible such as France, Germany and the Balkans will also face periods of high temperatures.[33]

Cooling off: Paris residents take advantage of ornamental fountains to fend off the impact of increasingly hot weather.

Thawing Arctic Wastes

The Arctic tundra – Finnish for 'open plain' – lies north of the boreal woodland, the conifers of which link Canada, Russia, Siberia and the taiga of Scandinavian birch forests like a planetary green necklace. The tundra sits like a waterlogged carpet of vegetation atop the permafrost soil. In the winter it is covered in snow, and in summer the plant life thrives. An estimated 250 species of moss, lichens, grasses, shrubs, herbs and sedges re-sprout; migratory birds and herbivores such as caribou and reindeer take advantage of these nutrients.[34]

Tundra flora and fauna have adapted to the north's extreme climate but are prey to global warming. Beyond local environmental concern, the world's largest frozen peat bog, covering the entire sub-arctic region of western Siberia, is thawing, threatening to release billions of tonnes of methane (CH_4), a gas twenty-three times more potent than CO_2, into the atmosphere. In western Siberia, temperatures have risen 3°C in forty years, a rate faster than that of anywhere else on Earth. The once-frozen landscape is riddled with mud and lakes. In eastern Siberia, methane hotspots were discovered where methane was bubbling up to the surface of the permafrost so quickly that the soil could no longer freeze over.[35]

> '*The higher the temperature gets, the more permafrost we melt, the more tendency it has to become a more vicious cycle. That's the thing that is scary about this whole thing. There are lots of mechanisms that tend to be self-perpetuating and relatively few that tend to shut it off.*'
>
> CHRIS FIELD, DIRECTOR OF GLOBAL ECOLOGY AT THE CARNEGIE INSTITUTION OF WASHINGTON

Since forming at the end of the last ice age, Siberia's peat bogs have produced CH_4, the by-product of bacterial decomposition in the soil. Rather than be released into the air, the gas became locked in the permafrost; 70 billion tonnes of methane – a quarter of that stored in the ground across the Earth – is estimated to be held there.[36] Siberia's permafrost, known as *yedoma*, has also trapped CO_2, and it is calculated to contain 100 times the amount released each year by the burning of fossil fuels.[37]

The thaw, which apparently began in the twenty-first century's opening years, has forced an upwards revision of global temperature predictions. In 2006, the Arctic permafrost was found to be releasing five times more CH_4 into the atmosphere than was previously calculated.[38] The resulting accelerated warming was itself promoting the melting of the peat bogs, releasing even more methane.[39]

The fragile biodiversity within an apparently barren landscape is recognized by initiatives like the Arctic Council's Program for the Conservation of Arctic Flora and Fauna[40] and Norway's protection of the Svalbard Archipelago wilderness.[41]

The Flooding of the Continent

Sea-level rise and an increase in storm intensity and associated surges around Europe's coasts will drastically impact local human populations and threaten the continent's biodiversity. The Mediterranean wetlands and Baltic coasts will be particularly vulnerable to flooding, their loss affecting wintering shorebirds and marine fish numbers.[42]

Already, 150 million Europeans live within 20 km (12.4 miles) of the Mediterranean Sea. By 2020, 350 million people – the approximate population of North America – are expected to live there.[43] Half the coast will be built on, including most of the region's shores, while scarce water resources will be diverted to hotels and golf courses, promoting drought inland. Further pollution and the loss of sensitive species such as turtles and cetaceans (whales, dolphins and porpoises) is likely.

The Threat of POPs

The Arctic's colder temperatures make local ecosystems susceptible to deposits of industrial chemicals, by-products of industrial processes and pesticides, or Persistent Organic Pollutants (POPs). POPs pose a global threat. Transported in the atmosphere across international boundaries from industrialized southern temperate regions, they stay in the environment for a long time and accumulate via the food web to toxic levels in humans and animals, and are suspected to cause cancer and limit fertility.

The protocol to the regional United Nations Economic Commission for Europe (UNECE) Convention on Long-Range Transboundary Air Pollution (CLRTAP) on POPs[44] opened for signatures in June 1998 and eventually entered into force on 23 October 2003. It was shadowed by the Stockholm Convention on Persistent Organic Pollutants, a global treaty that entered into force on 17 May 2004 that was intended to protect human health and the environment from POPs.[45] Governments implementing the treaty aim to eliminate or reduce the release of such pollutants into the environment. The European Community signed both agreements, ratifying the protocol on 30 April 2004, and the Stockholm Convention on 16 November of the same year.[46]

Sea-level rise will exacerbate the problem. Already significant inhabited coastal areas in countries such as the Netherlands, England, Denmark, Germany, Italy and Poland are below normal high-tide levels. Many of Europe's largest cities, including London, Hamburg, St Petersburg and Thessaloniki, are built on estuaries and lagoons.[47]

The Netherlands' waterlogged history – a quarter of the country is below sea level and it sinks a little lower each year – has led to creative responses to climate change that draw engineers and architects from the world's low-lying regions. Houses along the Maas dyke were built to float as water level rises, and sink down again as the level falls. The houses are attached to poles sunk into solid ground so that they do not float away. Land adjacent to Dutch rivers designated as a flood zone can now be built on, but the buildings must be amphibious. Rising water *and* human habitation can therefore co-exist.[48]

London's Thames Barrier opened in 1983 namely to protect the city from a risky combination of tidal surges and high spring tides. Its development accompanied a 200 km (124 mile) network of dikes in the Thames estuary, the UK's most complex and costly flood defence system.[49] In January 2007, the barrier was closed three times in four days to block the highest tidal surge since it was built. London's clay foundations, along with the gradual tipping of south-east England into the sea and rising sea levels, increase the flood risk

Against the tide: without further development, London's Thames Barrier, for all its engineering majesty, will prove a poor future match for tidal surges and encroaching sea-level rise.

facing over a million residents and workers, 500,000 properties, thirty-eight Underground and light railway stations, and City Airport.[50] Designed for use until 2030, the barrier's defence abilities will decline as waters rise. In 2008, the UK Environment Agency will publish 'Thames Estuary 2100' (TE100), a study of projected necessary flood defence, including a proposed 16 km (10 mile) barrier with gates.[51]

Floodgates are also being planned to protect the historic Italian city of Venice which, located among islands in a lagoon fed by the Adriatic Sea, is notably at risk from sea-level rise. Flooding in Venice has long been a problem, whether due to a build-up of silt from local rivers during the fifteenth century, or to the subsidence of the very land on which the city stands. High water, or *acqua alta*, occurs when storm winds from the south force sea water into the lagoon; St Mark's Square succumbs for about a third of every year.[52] The proposed 'MOSE' (Modulo Sperimentale Elettromeccanico, or Experimental Electromechanical Module) will involve seventy-nine underwater, mobile gates that shut to block the three lagoon inlets in the event of a 0.3–0.5 m (12–20 in) rise in sea level. Should water levels rise further, the gates would remain closed more often, effectively serving as permanent barriers.[53] However, environmentalists fear that MOSE will quickly become obsolete and the increasing need to close the floodgates – thus restricting the flow of water between the lagoon and the sea – will threaten the lagoon's ecosystem. Pollutants will accumulate in the lagoon waters and poison wildlife.[54]

Fuelling Europe's Energy Needs

It is imperative that individual European countries develop their own energy sources. The continent is fearfully dependent on Russian gas and oil supplies, making it vulnerable to the former Soviet Union's wranglings with the neighbouring countries through which the pipelines run. In January 2007, a dispute between Russia and Belarus saw the latter state closing the Druzhba pipeline, thus preventing Russian oil from reaching Germany, Poland or the Ukraine.[55] Prior to that, in January 2006, Russia cut natural gas supplies to the Ukraine, threatening supplies in Germany and Hungary.[56]

A growing consensus among European politicians sees developing nuclear power as a viable means of both tackling climate change and securing energy. The European Union's Euratom Treaty calls for all member states to fund nuclear research.[57] However, in 2006 a coalition of European NGOs led by groups from Austria, France, Holland and Finland pointed out the dangers, costs and unsustainability of the nuclear industry, and drew up an anti-nuclear petition for which they wished to attract a million signatures.[58] The processes of nuclear fuel sourcing, construction and waste management are all extremely carbon-intensive, and the uranium vital to nuclear energy production is a finite resource that must be mined.

The petition was launched on the twentieth anniversary of the world's worst nuclear accident on 26 April 1986, when a reactor exploded following a

The Common Agricultural Policy

The European Community (EC) established its Common Agricultural Policy (CAP), in operation since 1962, to protect member countries' farmers from foreign imports and to ensure the availability of food locally. Yet the EC ensured future problems by buying up farm produce whenever market prices dipped. CAP encouraged overproduction – notably leading to surplus wine 'lakes' and butter 'mountains'. The use of fertilizers and pesticides also helped to fuel overproduction. When the EU dumped surpluses on the world market, however, this caused produce prices to drop, undermining farmers in the developing world already penalized by Europe's taxes on agricultural imports. Since the 1990s, there have been moves to reduce overproduction and subsidies, and also to encourage rural economic diversity. Yet it is huge agribusinesses, such as sugar company Tate and Lyle, and hereditary landowners that most benefit from CAP funds.[59]

On 26 June 2003, EU farm ministers formally adopted a fundamental reform of CAP. The link between subsidies and levels of food production was severed and replaced with 'Single Farm Payments' dependent on meeting high standards of food safety, animal welfare and environmental protection. To receive funding, European farmers must respond to market needs and consumer demands, while keeping farmland in good agricultural and environmental condition – a condition known as 'cross-compliance'.[60] Farmers are also paid to leave land fallow, or 'set aside', though again it must be ensured that the land is 'in good agricultural and environmental condition and that the environment is protected'.[61]

routine safety check at the Chernobyl power plant in the Ukraine, part of the then Soviet Union. Hundreds of thousands of people within a 32 km (20 mile) contaminated area were evacuated from their homes, to which they were never able to return. In the next ten days, around 40 per cent of Europe experienced radioactive fall-out, although the Ukraine, Russia and Belarus were especially affected.

Rates of leukaemia, cancers – especially thyroid – and iodine deficiency increased among local children; tens of thousands designated as 'Chernobyl affected children' received financial assistance from the government.[62] Twenty years later, three million people continued to suffer the consequences.[63] As far west as the UK, the movement and sale of sheep remain restricted on 359 Welsh farms, fourteen Scottish farms and nine farms in England.[64] The estimated eventual death toll is contested; the World Health Organisation suggests a figure of 9,000,[65] while Greenpeace claim as many as 93,000 people[66] will have fallen victim to the nuclear accident.

Those environmentalists against nuclear power want energy needs met by energy efficiency and renewable energy. Their hopes were raised by a groundbreaking EU summit in March 2007 which agreed that by 2020, 20 per cent of Europe's energy would be produced from renewable sources. The EU governments also aimed to cut greenhouse gases by 20 per cent below 1990 levels by 2020, and by a 30 per cent reduction if countries such as Russia, the USA and China followed suit at the G8 summit in June 2007.[67]

In 2005, renewables accounted for less than 7 per cent of European energy, so the EU summit decision was a call to industry to invest in renewable energy options. It also positioned Europe as a global leader in the fight against climate change. German Chancellor Angela Merkel, who led the summit, wielded particular influence in 2007 as the chair of the EU presidency and the internationally powerful G8 group. Warning against the imminent threat of global warming, she said, 'It's not five minutes to midnight, it's five minutes after midnight.'[68] She went on to stress that urgent measures had to be taken, and a commitment to use more renewable energy sources was needed.

Within weeks, the EU's strident environmental commitment was undermined by its own transport ministers' 'open skies' agreement allowing any European airline to fly to the USA from any part of Europe. In five years, an estimated extra twenty-six million passengers would fly across the Atlantic,[69] adding to an extra yearly 3.5 million tonnes of CO_2 emissions.[70]

The British government's radical draft Climate Change Bill of March 2007 set up Britain to be the first country in the world to establish legally binding targets to cut CO_2 emissions. Under the bill, a system of five-year 'carbon budgets' would be introduced to cap total emissions by between 26 and 32 per cent by 2020, and 60 per cent by 2050.[71] While campaigners welcomed the initiative, the challenge will be to ensure that the bill is not watered down as it progresses through Parliament before becoming law in 2008. Opposition parties are seeking to commit the government to an 80 per cent cut in CO_2 emissions by 2050.[72]

Europe's Wildlife

When a two-year-old brown bear named Bruno was shot dead in the Bavarian Alps in June 2006, it made the news across Europe. As the first bear sighted in Germany for 170 years, its killing was considered a deeply inappropriate act by many.

    The bear was part of an Italian programme to reintroduce bears into the wild; it had crossed into Germany via the Austrian Alps. Its presence was initially hailed as representing a landmark achievement of endangered species protection,[73] but the German authorities changed their tune when the bear killed dozens of sheep. Fearing the bear's threat to humans, they planned to capture 'rampant brown bear JJI' alive. Although bears are legally protected under the 1979 Bern Convention on the Conservation of European Wildlife and Natural Habitats, only hours after a ban on shooting the bear with live ammunition had been lifted, it was killed. Bruno, stuffed, would be displayed at Bavaria's Museum for Man and Nature in Munich.[74]

Bear necessity: the Bern Convention on the Conservation of European Wildlife and Natural Habitats legally protects bears – but must be tightly enforced if the dwindling species is to survive.

A bear believed to be from the same Italian region of Trentino was sighted in the Swiss Alps the previous summer. Between 1999 and 2002, Trentino's diminishing local bear population was boosted by the import of brown bears from Slovenia. That they travel along green corridors into neighbouring countries indicates the programme's success and the relative health of the alpine environment, since it can accommodate such large mammals. In the Austrian Alps, wild brown bears roam freely, far from humans.

Rare sightings of bears attract tourists, but livestock is being lost. Farmers must relearn how to protect animals after decades of not needing to while bears were regionally extinct. By simply fencing in farm animals and using guard dogs to frighten away bears, and instructing tourists to take care and leave no food waste, Europe's largest mammals can co-exist alongside alpine human communities.[75]

> *'The Bavarian government's decision was wrong, because it was based only on the fact that the bear was getting close to human habitation. If this is to be the yardstick for the right to life of brown bears then the outlook is bleak for European bears.'*
>
> GABRIEL SCHWADERER, DIRECTOR OF THE EUROPEAN NATURE HERITAGE FUND

Slovenia has been instrumental in helping European countries revitalize their bear numbers, but an increase in hunting quotas on its own soil could decimate its brown bear population. In 2007, the government announced that that year's quota would be 106 bears, out of a total population of between 500 and 700. Taking account of road mortalities could push the death rate up to a third of Slovenia's bears in one year. In response, WWF declared the hunting quota alone of 20 per cent of the population to be unsustainable and unscientific. As Slovenia is taking over the EU presidency in early 2008, WWF suggested it instead follow EU guidelines on managing large carnivores, thus promoting the new EU member (it joined in 2004) as a leader in conservation.[76]

While Russia is home to most of the world's brown bears – it is, in fact, the national symbol – it was those in Moscow Zoo that garnered attention during the winter of 2006. For the first time, they did not hibernate until late in December with a tiny fall of snow; normally they are asleep in their dens in November with that month's usual continuous snow cover. However, in December 2006, Moscow's temperature was 5°C (41°F) – the warmest in the city since records began in 1879 – when ordinarily it would be *minus* 5°C (23°F). In December 2005, temperatures dropped as low as -29°C (-20°F).[77] In light of the late hibernation of the brown bear, Russia's emergency minister warned that their waking up early due to further mild weather could make them aggressive.[78]

While in Scandinavia's woods, bears were still awake in January 2007, it is their very biological make-up that enables them to cope and adapt accordingly. As long as food remains plentiful, hibernation can be postponed. Similarly bird migration occurs whenever winter falls, sending flocks in search of food. In fact, it is human input such as street lighting that has a more pervasive impact on wildlife by disorientating mammals and disrupting birds' sleeping patterns.[79]

In addition to the brown bear, the Iberian lynx is also at risk. An infectious disease in rabbits, viral haemorrhagic pneumonia, has decimated the Iberian lynx population. But *human* modification of the cat's habitat for game reserves and the building of transport infrastructures, irrigation schemes and dams has proved negative too. Indeed, a WWF report published in early 2006[80] highlighted the inherent conflict between the European Union's respected advanced level of support for conservation and biodiversity via such legal frameworks as the Birds, and Habitat Directives,[81] and EU-funded construction work threatening vulnerable species across the continent.

No future? The Iberian lynx is the world's most endangered cat.

The replacement by southern Europe's wine growers of traditional cork stoppers with plastic screwtops has forced a slump in the cork industry, which maintains the local forests. Without this work, the 80,000 employees are likely to cut down trees to plant more profitable crops – and therefore wipe out the world's most endangered cat.[82]

Fear of the Iberian lynx's consequent extinction led the Standing Committee of the Convention on the Conservation of European Wildlife and Natural Habitats to recommend that Spain and Portugal urgently implement measures to conserve the species, and that the EU protect the Mediterranean forests, or *dehesa*, one of the richest wildlife habitats in Europe, where the beast makes its home.[83] In 2003, the Standing Committee also recommended the implementation of a pan-alpine conservation strategy for the Eurasian lynx.[84] Once nearly extinct in Scandinavia, protection policies have revived numbers to around 2,500 across Norway, Sweden and Finland.[85]

While the wolf is technically fully protected across Europe by such legislation as Appendix II (strictly protected species) of the 1979 Bern Convention – the Convention on the Conservation of European Wildlife and Natural Habitats[86] – individual countries can reserve the right not to apply the provisions of the species' listing in Appendix II. Switzerland proposed that the Eurasian wolf's status be reduced to Appendix III, giving it less protection, even though the country has one of the most vulnerable wolf populations in Europe, with only three to four individuals as of 2005.[87] Norway's controversial licensed culling of five of its national population of roughly twenty wolves in Hedmark County in early 2005 was heavily criticized for its lack of scientific insight, notably by wolf experts in neighbouring Sweden, who have recorded a debilitating lack of genetic diversity in the countries' shared wolf population of over 100 beasts.[88]

Yet there are several hundred of the mammals in both Poland and Latvia, and around 3,000 across Spain and Italy. Instead of a uniform Europe-wide protection status, WWF proposed a differential listing related to population levels in any given country and a regular assessment of wolf numbers to promote their return to all suitable habitats.[89]

The creatures that edge the continent and live in its waters are also hugely vulnerable to human pressures. Numbers of the Mediterranean monk seal, for example, have declined sharply. It is now classed as critically endangered; only 400–500 individuals remain, existing in small and vulnerable cave-based colonies.[90]

Europe's seas have experienced long-term over-fishing and consequent dwindling stocks. Atlantic cod catches have dropped by 70 per cent in the last thirty years. Illegal catches, wasteful methods and destructive industrialized fishing techniques are decimating fish populations in European waters. WWF's European fisheries campaign reported that as much as 80 per cent of some catches, notably plaice and sole, were thrown overboard because the fish were either too small or not valuable enough. This results in an annual cull of millions of fish for no reason whatsoever.[91]

European fisheries represent approximately 16 per cent of world catches, and thousands of jobs depend on it. Such is the level of depletion, that fish stocks spanning the North Sea, the north-east Atlantic Ocean and the Mediterranean have dwindled to 10 per cent of 1970s levels. Fleets of European boats have begun fishing for shrimp and squid in West African waters where there are as yet no maximum quotas or supervision.[92]

Tuna were once exported to feed Japan, but growing European demand for sushi so threatens stocks that fishing grounds would require seasonal closure to replenish tuna numbers. The British alone eat 600 tonnes a year. In September 2006, the European Parliament's fishing committee warned that eastern Atlantic and Mediterranean stocks of bluefin tuna were on the verge of commercial collapse unless urgent act was taken. Spanish tuna fishermen reported that their local stocks had declined by 80 per cent.[93] The price of tuna has soared and individual fish can sell for thousands of pounds, putting further pressure on stocks and encouraging illegal netting above quotas. Imposing regulations and monitoring the industry will not completely stamp out such theft, but to ensure that stocks are maintained sustainably, WWF's European fisheries campaign called on European governments to urgently tighten their fisheries management.[94]

Sea Eagles

The world's fourth largest eagle, and northern Europe's biggest bird of prey, the white-tailed sea eagle is a startling success story. In the space of six years up to 2006, the bird has gone from being IUCN-designated 'Near Threatened' to 'Least Concern',[95] though work on protecting the species goes back over twenty-five years.

In Britain, white-tailed sea eagle numbers had been decimated to the point of extinction by sheep farming and sporting interests in the early twentieth century. In a spirit of pan-European cooperation, young birds were taken from their nests in Norway, reared, and released on Scotland's island of Rum in 1975.[96] They soon settled on the neighbouring islands of Mull and Skye, though it was not until 1987 that a pair of the sea eagles on Skye attempted to breed. In 2006, the 200th wild-bred white-tailed sea eagle chick – one of the first-ever record of triplets on Skye – fledged. While it had taken twenty-five years from the 1975 reintroduction to record 100 wild-bred birds, it only took a further six years for that figure to double.[97] Such has been the success of the Scottish programme that, in December 2005, English Nature approved a scheme to release white-tailed sea eagles in East Anglia and on the Suffolk coast.[98]

The sea eagle population has similarly prospered throughout Europe. Numbers have quadrupled in Sweden; the birds have recolonized Denmark; and they can be seen in Poland and Finland. After DDT was banned in Europe in 1976, Germany recorded a major increase in the species' population where previously offspring rarely survived.[99]

In full flight: the sea eagle has seen a drastic turnaround in fortune due to cross-continent conservation cooperation.

Taking Action

1. To keep abreast of reports on Europe's climate and weather, access the European Organisation for the Exploitation of Meteorological Satellites (EUMETSAT) at www.eumetsat.int/Home/Main/Media/News .

2. For the European Union's list of environmental policies and their related themes, access http://ec.europa.eu/environment/policy_en.htm and http://climatechange.eu.com .

3. The Eco-Schools programme is a predominantly Europe-wide initiative aimed at promoting environmental awareness via action and education in schools. Is your local school part of this valuable network? Encourage your local authority to link with www.eco-schools.org so that your education is Green-tinged.

4. Encourage any children you know to delight in the world's flora and fauna.

5. Europe's once-widespread wolf population historically gained a bad reputation for taking livestock. Today's conservation challenge is for peaceful coexistence between humans and threatened wild animals. Be mindful of the intrinsic worth of the world's less popular creatures, and campaign for their survival.

6. Help to look after sea eagles in the Baltic Sea on a conservation holiday in Germany. Access the website http://work4travel.co.uk/Conservation%20and %20Environmental%20Work.htm for details of travel opportunities that will promote sustainable conservation of the planet's wildlife.

7. Drink more wine with natural corks! Help support the Spanish cork industry and by doing so help maintain the habitat of 'Europe's tiger', the endangered Iberian lynx.

8. For information on the impact of the Chernobyl disaster and present conditions in the affected areas, access www.chernobyl.info and http://chernobyl.undp.org, and for details about the Chernobyl Forum initiative, go to www-ns.iaea.org/meetings/ rw-summaries/chernobyl_forum.htm .

9. France's Camargue region, designated a 'wetland of international importance' under the 1971 Ramsar Convention on Wetlands, is famed for its distinct white horses. Believed to be descended from prehistoric horses that lived during the Paleolithic era over 17,000 years ago, they are one of Europe's few remaining original horse breeds and are strictly protected. For a list of six groups responsible for the protection and conservation of the Camargue horse, access www.logassist.com/english/regions/camargue_decouv.asp .

10. Where does your salary go? Spend a month itemizing what you spend your money on, and adapt your purchasing habits to reduce your impact on the environment.

11. Live within your means. The problem with carbon trading is that wealthy countries and individuals can buy themselves out of having to alter their lifestyles, thus fuelling their wasteful lives on the poor's lack of economic power. If carbon trading is to work, then allocations must be reduced periodically so that *everyone* has to reconsider their lifestyle's impact on the planet. Start at home, but also keep tabs on your political representatives to ensure caps are imposed.

12. Do not encourage your garden to grow at the expense of the wider environment. Buy only composts labelled as peat-free, or make your own from household food waste.

Oceania

PAPUA NEW GUINEA

Port Moresby

Darwin

AUSTRALIA

GREAT VICTORIA DESERT

Brisbane

Darling

Perth

Sydney

Canberra

Melbourne

Tasman

Australasia

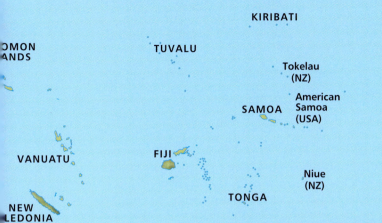

KIRIBATI

OMON
ANDS

TUVALU

Tokelau
(NZ)

American
Samoa
(USA)

SAMOA

FIJI

VANUATU

Niue
(NZ)

NEW
LEDONIA
(France)

TONGA

'*I wake up in the morning thinking there are lots of times when people have woken up feeling like this, like the Old Testament prophets. I try to find a way out of it, but I can't. It's life-changing to realise what is going on.*'

PROFESSOR TIM FLANNERY

Auckland

NEW ZEALAND

Wellington

The continent of Oceania consists of the states of Australia, Fiji, French Polynesia, Kiribati, New Caledonia (French), New Zealand, Papua New Guinea, the Solomon Islands, Tonga, Tasmania, Tuvalu and Vanuatu.

A continent is technically a large continuous area of land. But Australasia – or Oceania, as it is often now known – notably incorporates the islands and atolls of the Pacific Ocean that neighbour the larger and therefore seemingly more prominent states of Australia and New Zealand.

Besides the United States and its neighbour, Mexico, Australia and New Zealand are unusual among the majority of the world's developed nations for bordering member states of the developing world. Oceania's environmental status reflects that contrast. Its industrialized, resource-rich south has the wealth to implement positive measures if the political will is there, while elsewhere in the region there is little capacity to deal with very real threats such as deforestation and sea-level rise.

However, the common ecological traits particular to Oceania represent its value and strength. Its sheer diversity and strikingly high level of endemism are balanced by the local human population's high level of economic and cultural dependence on the natural environment, whether that be based on tribal lifestyles that have existed for thousands of years or on modern concepts of tourism, in which people travel to view the beauty of a landscape and its wildlife. The loss of any of this richness – be it a particular plant or animal species or a washed-away atoll – is a unique loss to the whole world.

Australia, for example, is as likely to experience such losses (though on a different scale) as the tiny Pacific Ocean atolls, which points to the need for a combined effort of action and skills-sharing to support individual states' management of their natural resources. Independent conservation body WWF-Australia, for example, works to complement local knowledge with expert advice on conservation management and planning that is backed by scientific research.

Pacific states such as Papua New Guinea, the Solomon Islands, French Polynesia, Fiji and Tonga were until recently symbols of exotic, faraway Eden-like destinations, their names perhaps most familiar to many through the pages of old stamp albums. International air travel has made them seem closer

Previous spread: Fire island: Uluru, also known as Ayers Rock across the world, glows like a hot coal beneath Australia's sky.

(Tuvalu's Funafuti International Airport charmingly has the destination code FUN), and the internet has further shortened the distance between the islands and the wider world.

Indeed, in 2000 Tuvalu chose to lease its internet domain name '.tv' for $50m in royalties over the next twelve years to bring some much-needed income to the state. Ironically, just as it has been able to afford to upgrade its population's standard of living, the nine-island state is struggling to survive against a rising ocean tide. If water level trends continue, by 2050 Tuvalu could well be depopulated by the sea.

It is relatively tiny countries such as Tuvalu and the Solomon Islands whose destiny could have a major impact on global environmental policy, or at least prove a barometer of how successful (or not) it has been. Appearing like pinheads on the face of the globe when compared with most other landmasses, their size belies their environmental importance. As the Pacific Ocean increasingly batters and swamps their lands, it is as though the impact of global warming and climate change across the world is highlighted here. Vanuatu's island of Tegua will be the first community in the world to be forced out by rising sea levels.[1] As the islands are gradually washed away by the sea, their fate tolls out a clear warning to the rest of the world to change our ways.

The Tuvaluan government's appeal to the wider world through its representation at Kyoto Protocol discussions marks the latest of the region's political activism. In 1971, on the initiative of the island of Fiji, the South Pacific Forum was established as a focus for debate on common interests among local governments. The forum focused particularly on nuclear testing in the region, and paved the way for the 1985 Treaty of Rarotonga, which established the Pacific Nuclear Free Zone, of which Australia and New Zealand are the most high-profile Oceania signatories. Australia also leads the world in cetacean – and particularly whale – conservation policy.

Rising Temperatures on Land

A cycle of bush fires and drought is inevitable amidst a harsh, dry land such as Australia. However, the summer of 2002–03, which saw Canberra's environs set ablaze, was the hottest on record for over a century. It was directly attributed to climate change caused by the burning of fossil fuels.[2]

The state's already extreme climate makes it particularly susceptible to climate change. Higher maximum temperatures and drier conditions plus strong winds fuelled the treacherous fires that devastated the region. Over $200m worth of property suffered damage, and the local timber industry faced losses of around $65m. Such destruction indicated the cost to communities, agriculture and ecosystems that could be wrought across the world by a widespread rise in temperatures.

'This is the first Australian drought where the impact of human-induced global warming can be clearly observed.'

Conclusion of a study by representatives of the IPCC, Monash University and WWF

Opposite: Burning bushes: Canberra's firefighters battle a tinder dry landscape set ablaze by 2002/03's hottest summer on record.

New South Wales farmers have particularly suffered from a five-year-long drought – its worst for a century – in which fires raged, riverbeds dried up, including sections of the Darling, Australia's longest river, and land was left parched. In October 2006, farmers were reported to be committing suicide at a rate of one every four days as crops failed, paddocks were reduced to dustbowls, and stock was being sold in record numbers in an attempt to relieve debt. Almost the entire south-western state – 92 per cent of it – was in a drought that gave little indication of ending. The Australian government promised $350m (£141m) in aid to the stricken region.[3]

Australia's Commonwealth Scientific and Industrial Research Organisation (CSIRO) predicts that the country's average temperature will have risen by between 0.4° and 2°C by 2030, and between 1° and 6°C higher by 2070.[4] This will put intense pressure on agriculture, fisheries, forest and water resources and their further ability to withstand increased heat levels. Bush fire rates will also intensify.

Whereas the planting of trees has often been cited as a means of both replenishing resources and offsetting carbon pollution, a fire-prone country such as Australia is unsuitable for such a policy. Burning trees instead *release*

Tim Flannery

Born in 1956, Professor Tim Flannery is a world-renowned mammalogist and palaeontologist, and is currently based at Macquarie University's Department of Environmental and Life Sciences. He is also climate change adviser to Premier Mike Rann of South Australia.

His doctoral research focused on the evolution of Australian mammals, and he identified twenty-nine new kangaroo species, including eleven new genera and three new sub-families. He also discovered and described the world's oldest kangaroo fossils, and went on to classify the entire fossil record of phalangerids, Oceania's dominant possum family.[5]

In the 1980s, he was involved in a number of dinosaur site discoveries on Victoria's south coast, including being a member of the 1985 group that discovered Australia's first cretaceous mammal fossils, taking the country's mammal fossil record back a further 80 million years.[6] Further studies in New Guinea drew him to consider long-term human impact on rainforests, and was to inspire his future environmental writings.

During the 1990s, Flannery led a research programme surveying Melanesia's mammals; sixteen new species and many sub-species were discovered in the course of the study, including two new tree kangaroos. As a result conservation programmes for the most endangered creatures were initiated. In 1995, the Australian Federal

Parliament sought Flannery's advice on conservation and population issues, and in 1999 he spent a year as Visiting Chair of Australian Studies at Harvard University. He has also been a one-time Principal Research Scientist at the Australian Museum, and Director of Adelaide's South Australian Museum.

Flannery is author of a number of influential books on conservation and the environment. In the best-selling *The Future Eaters* (1994), he suggested the replacement of Australia's European-style farming with a return to farming native species such as emu, kangaroo and crocodile; drew attention to Aboriginal fire control practices in preventing widespread bushfires; and proposed a population control policy for Australia based on environmental sustainability.[7]

In 2005 he published *The Weather Makers*, a book about the impact of climate change, in which he warns that Australia's dry climate makes it especially susceptible. He predicts that by 2050 Sydney will have 60 per cent less water, and Perth will become a 'ghost metropolis'. The contribution to be made by Australia and other industrialized nations to combat the impending disaster, he suggests, is to develop environmentally responsible technology to be transferred to emerging Asian manufacturing nations, while abandoning previous investment in coal power stations and dams. 'They are developing nations. They will be buying technology options off the shelf. If they buy what we are using now, we will be well and truly in the deep end, without a way out.'[8]

He was the Council of Australian Humanist Societies' Humanist of the Year in 2005, and was also nominated for the 2007 Australian of the Year Award.

the principal greenhouse gas, CO_2, into the atmosphere, thus exacerbating the problem.

Entering the new millennium, Australia had the highest level of greenhouse gas emissions per person of any industrialized country, second only to the United Arab Emirates, owing to its dependency on coal-fired energy, a rate 30 per cent higher than that of the USA;[9] the Australian government's continued refusal to ratify the Kyoto Protocol suggests that, like the US, it does not want to place perceived control on economic development. The Australian government is, however, committed to limiting emissions to 108 per cent of 1990 levels between 2008 and 2012.[10]

Inland Water Resources

Australia's rivers, as well as its groundwater systems and wetlands, are under threat from over-development and degradation in a severe climate. To remain ecologically healthy, some of these freshwater resources need extra water. If the inland water sources are to survive, it is important too that people recognize their value in terms of the wealth of wildlife they encourage as well as their importance to local communities.

'Human behaviour, much more than ozone depletion, determines the overall effect of UV on people in Australia.'

2001 AUSTRALIA STATE OF THE ENVIRONMENT REPORT

WWF-Australia, for example, has concentrated its Wetland Watch conservation project on the Swan Coastal Plain in Western Australia since April 2004.[11] The south-west district of Western Australia is one of the twenty-five most biodiverse regions in the world, due largely to its wetland systems. They contain many rare plant and animal species plus an estimated 80 per cent of the region's threatened ecological communities. Such wetlands filter out pollutants from the catchment water; can be appreciated for their beauty and the birdwatching and bushwalking opportunities they provide; and are often of cultural value to local indigenous communities.

However, it is estimated that since European settlement from the late 1700s, 70–80 per cent of the wetlands of the Swan Coastal Plain have been lost. Of the remainder, only 15 per cent retain high conservation value to this day – and these lands could also face destruction within the next ten to twenty years if urban and rural development continues unabated.[12] Often, local communities are simply unaware of the value of the environment on their doorstep.

As a result, WWF representatives operate on the principle of a 'bottom up' approach by involving landowners and community groups in their conservation projects, developing incentives for promoting and protecting wetland biodiversity and therefore establishing a long-term policy of conservation and management among local residents. Residents 'own' the project, and consequently care deeply about its outcome.

Too Much Sunlight?

Australians have the highest rate of skin cancer in the world: for every three people who live to the age of seventy-five, two of them are likely to develop some form of the disease.[13] Over-exposure to UV radiation is the prime factor in the increase in skin cancer, and there are a range of reasons why Australians may be particularly susceptible in comparison to people living in other parts of the world.

The depletion of the ozone layer – especially the seasonal enlargement of the ozone hole recorded in the atmosphere above Antarctica which, at its largest, stretches over the southern edges of Australasia too – has in recent years been blamed for the high incidence of skin cancer across Australia. With only 0.3 per cent of the world's population, the country's population accounts for 6 per cent of all the lethal forms of skin cancer diagnosed globally; approximately 1,200 people die annually from skin cancer in Australia.[14]

Yet Australians are, on the whole, a fair-skinned race. The Aboriginal peoples who originally inhabited the land today make up only 2 per cent of Australia's 18 million people.[15] The protection their dark skin provides them from the sun's rays is not available to most of the country's people.

Australians are traditionally an outdoors society, enjoying the warmth and sunshine of the local climate, even before the ozone layer became damaged in any way. For those who emigrated from one-time 'mother country', the often grey and wet Britain, Australia's long hours of tropical sunlight are a particular contrast – and it is tempting to indulge. Plus, the country's numerous Baby Boomers have increased the rates of cancer among the population, especially as they enter their fifties.

The 2001 Australia State of the Environment Report stated:

'Because of the very long lead time between exposure to UV radiation and the related occurrence of skin cancer, the increasing incidences of skin cancers in Australia from 1980 to 1996 are thought to be associated primarily with behaviour in relation to exposure to UV radiation that presumably took effect before there was any significant depletion of the ozone layer… The Australian climate, with high levels of UV radiation, is conducive to elevated incidences of sunburn and other UV-related medical problems, such as melanoma. Human behaviour, much more than ozone depletion, determines the overall effect of UV on people in Australia.'[16]

While ozone depletion in the stratosphere allows UV radiation to penetrate and reach Australia, therefore increasing the risk of skin cancer, Australians have had to accept that a tanned skin, once believed to be a sign of health, is now an invitation to severe sun-damage. Current government policy is encouraging the population to protect itself, and is providing medical care for those affected. Australia's skin cancer rate may well fall in the future as people become increasingly aware of the risks and protect themselves more.

The future of the Northern Territory's Daly River is of national consequence as, ironically, it remains in relatively good health. With year-round flow and good water quality, it is home to forty-eight species of freshwater fish, including the threatened sawfish and whipray, as well as the largest number of freshwater turtles in any Australian river. Its estuary and lower floodplains are internationally important wetlands.

If development and land and water management are not carefully monitored, however, land clearing and over-extraction of water for irrigation could be the death of the Daly. Its long-term health is particularly important for the Aborigines, who own half the river's catchment area, and who are also fishermen and landowners. The Northern Territory government made an election pledge to provide legal protection for the Daly River through its Living Rivers Strategy, and the electorate need to ensure that it carries out its commitments.[17]

Within Oceania, as far as is possible, the smaller – and invariably poorer – Pacific states must develop strategies to respond to the seemingly inevitable heightened environmental impact that development, and eventually climate change, will have on their communities. Such planning is already underway. In October 2005, for example, after consultation with local communities, Papua New Guinea's government announced it would nearly double the country's protected areas. As a result, some of the Earth's most biologically diverse environments – incorporating forests, wetlands and some of the world's richest coral reefs – would be made more secure against large-scale logging operations, mining and over-fishing.

The proposed protected areas – or Wildlife Management Areas (WMAs) – with rules developed by the local villages that own the land, are designed to ensure the sustainable use of wildlife and its habitats for subsistence and cash income including tourism, as well as strengthen land rights and cultural sites including protecting sacred areas. By 2010, Papua New Guinea's government is committed to including 10 per cent of the state's land in protected area zones.[18]

Additionally, local representation at international conventions – such as Papua New Guinea's at the Convention on Biological Diversity in March 2006 in Brazil[19] – puts pressure on the world's industrialized nations to fulfil their global responsibilities of curbing pollution. However, the states themselves also need to work together, particularly in sharing information on how to diversify their economic base so that they are less dependent on their reefs and, where they are able, to shift away from coastal residency. As sea levels rise, ultimately entire populations will need assistance in rehabilitation and repatriation elsewhere.

The Protection of Local Flora and Fauna

The Australian government, often lambasted by environmentalists worldwide for its refusal to ratify the Kyoto Protocol, nevertheless has a far-sighted approach that establishes it as one of the world leaders in the conservation and management of its native species of plants and animals.

Of the world's eighty species of cetaceans, at least forty-three occur in Australian waters. Australia's policy towards these migratory mammals therefore has a major impact on how they are regarded elsewhere. Today, Australia is a world leader in the protection of its species, at domestic, regional and international levels. Under the 1999 Environment Protection and Biodiversity Conservation (EPBC) Act all cetaceans are protected throughout Australian waters to the 320 km (200 mile) limit of the Exclusive Economic Zone, establishing this area as essentially a sanctuary.[20]

Before 1978, Australia had a commercial whaling industry; however, the vulnerability of the whale population to large-scale hunting led to a turnaround commitment to whale conservation. It has since established a national framework – in force until 2010 – to protect cetaceans while ensuring people are able to enjoy and learn about them on their journey through Australian waters.

Freestyle swimming: cetaceans migrating through Australian waters benefit from full legal protection.

Protecting the Great Barrier Reef

The world's most famous reef, Australia's Great Barrier Reef is home to as many as 2,000 different species of fish; every year a new one is discovered. An estimated 4,000 different types of mollusc are found there, amidst 350 varieties of hard or reef-building coral.[21]

In October 2005, the Australian government received WWF's 'Gift to the Earth' award, its highest accolade, for the establishment of the Great Barrier Reef Marine Park zoning plan as a benchmark for developing marine protection areas across the world. A third (11 million hectares or 27 million acres) of the Marine Park and World Heritage Area is now under strict protection. Commercial and recreational fishing are banned, and tourism and non-extractive activities are allowed only within a network of protected areas.[22]

It remains to be seen, however, whether this valuable commitment to a recognized natural 'wonder of the world' off the coast of Queensland is enough to protect the Great Barrier Reef from a similar fate from global pollution being faced by coral reefs elsewhere.

Rainbow nation: the vibrant colours of the Great Barrier Reef are as rich as the wealth of marine-dwelling species that make their home there.

Tourism and fishing are the bedrock of most Pacific island states' economies; both 'feed' on local coral reefs so will be directly affected by the reefs' gradual death. The small states have little scope to adapt to the forthcoming decline in income and employment from tourism that will emerge as seawaters increase in temperature and the reefs disappear; coral bleaching will decimate entire coral ecosystems.

Local fisheries will also become depleted as the marine food chain breaks, potentially posing a health risk to subsistence communities, and perhaps even leading to starvation among remote tribespeople. Industrial reef fisheries and pelagic (that is, ocean travelling) fisheries, including those containing tuna, will also experience the knock-on effect of reef damage as fish stocks decline.

Beyond the Great Barrier Reef, Oceania's coral reefs provide a protective barrier, especially around the low-lying atolls such as Tuvalu and Kiribati, and prevent coastal erosion. Any break in the defences of the reef threatens these islands' future.

Permits are issued by the Ministry of Environment and Heritage for activities within the sanctuary that might affect cetaceans. Beyond these waters, the EPBC Act provides further protection over approval of actions that might have significant impact only after a rigorous assessment process. Actions requiring careful consideration include seismic operations, which involve the surveying for and extraction of oil and natural gas beneath the seafloor.

Since 2000, the whale watching industry has grown by 15 per cent per year, and in 2003 was worth an estimated annual $29m. Because it is land-based, it poses no threat to the whales' natural behaviour; the public are able to observe baleen whales on their round trip from their Antarctic feeding grounds to warmer, tropical breeding grounds, and humpback and southern whales pass closely along the coastline. Whereas previously their numbers were decimated through hunting, whale populations, especially of endangered species such as the blue whale and southern right, are able to re-establish themselves.[23]

Although they have legal protection, whales are still prey to human activities within Australian waters. Strandings and entanglements in marine debris are hazards; a Sightings and Strandings Database has been established to collect information about such phenomena. There also remains a lack of knowledge about population levels, migratory patterns, habitat degradation and the effects of climate change. Satellite monitoring is key.

Australia continues to work with other nations in the International Whaling Commission towards a permanent global ban on commercial whaling and 'whaling' under the guise of science. There are now viable alternatives for all whale products, and Australian scientists have developed a range of non-lethal research techniques to be used in all circumstances.[24]

Kangaroos are also protected under the same act by legislation in all the country's states and territories. Four of the approximate sixty species can be commercially harvested in the wild, primarily for the export of skins and fur but only by licensed hunters under a National Code of Practice. Kangaroos remain an essential part of the Australian ecosystem, and their conservation remains a priority. Their numbers have increased dramatically due to European farming methods and the extra water available to them.

The numbers harvested are based on annually reviewed quotas determined by the population size and trends of long-term climate predictions. Depending on seasonal conditions, the population size within the harvested areas has fluctuated between 15 and 50 million over the last twenty years.[25]

Perhaps because of Australia's island nature, there seems to be particular concern about the damage caused by non-native species, whether flora or fauna, and an especial value given to those species that are unique to its shores. For example, invasive garden plants 'escape' and taint bushlands and agricultural land, making up to 70 per cent of weeds there. The country spends approximately $4 billion annually on its weed problem in an attempt to prevent alien disease and pollution.[26]

In March 2007, the Northern Territory Parks and Wildlife Service called for a drastic cull of wild camels after they rampaged through remote communities in a desperate search for water. Thousands had already died of thirst. Severe drought had exacerbated the already detrimental impact made across the desert by around a million of the beasts – the world's largest feral camel population. Imported in their thousands into Australia from the 1840s onwards, they helped build the nation. Eventually released into the wild, numbers have since soared; their population is expected to double by 2015.

While live camels are exported to South-East Asia, where they are slaughtered for their meat, there is no licensed camel abattoir in Australia. Such is the size and damage wrought by the species, especially in Western Australia, that a national management plan will consider using them for pet food, and further exporting the camels. A level of culling would be unavoidable.[27]

It is in its clear recognition of the conflict between non-native and local species that Australia has a range of positive and negative experience to offer to the rest of the world. The Tasmanian devil's history is of being hunted almost to extinction across Australia because it was regarded as a pest for attacking poultry and other small farmstock; a protected species, it is now limited to south-western Tasmania. In recent years, population numbers have been decimated by devil facial tumour disease, and the species is now listed as vulnerable.[28] First noticed in north-eastern Tasmania in the mid-1990s, the disease has since spread across the state. It appears to kill most devils once they reach adulthood; in high-density populations there has been 100 per cent mortality within twelve to eighteen months of the disease's onset.[29]

However, government animal welfare policy is not always welcomed. The United States Fish and Wildlife Service declared koalas an endangered species in 2000.[30] The Australian government, however, saw no threat to them, although it does ban their hunting and commercial use.

Yet when the creatures' over-enthusiasm for eucalyptus was seen to be killing trees on Kangaroo Island, an ecotourism haven south-west of Adelaide, they were sterilized and shipped back to the mainland from whence they had come in the 1920s, to much outcry.[31] Koala numbers have fallen due to wood chip production, dogs, foxes, cars and urbanization, but shifting them around the country to encourage breeding is no answer since there are several sub-species that interact differently. Many too have succumbed to disease and infertility via the voracious spread of chlamydia.[32]

New Zealand is designated a biodiversity hotspot; from its national bird – the kiwi – down, the country has a rich variety of endemic species. None of its mammals, amphibians or reptiles, as well as two species of bats, can be found anywhere else in the world.[33]

Though humans have only lived on the islands for 700 years, they all but immediately began to make a detrimental impact on the local birdlife in particular. Notably, the world's largest bird, the flightless moa, was hunted to extinction by the Maori; none are believed to have remained by the time Captain Cook landed in 1769.[34]

Invasive species remain a major threat to New Zealand's state's flora and fauna today, and deforestation and wetland drainage are also destroying habitats. Once all but covered by rainforest, today only approximately a quarter of the forest remains; the New Zealand government's Department of Conservation has designated a third of the nation either national or forest parkland.

The Impact of Sea-level Rise on Low-lying States

Oceania's low-lying atolls are at the forefront of a wave of disaster. High tides are normal and to be expected at the full moon and new moon of each month, but rising sea levels and strong winds mean that the flooding they cause has grown more severe in recent years. It undercuts buildings and foundations, and washes away the coastline, emphasizing the sheer vulnerability of the inhabitants of these tiny islands in the midst of the vast Pacific Ocean.

Tuvalu is a tiny island group of nine coral atolls, which is home to almost 11,700 people, and is one of the most vulnerable nations in the world to sea-level rise and coastal erosion. Its total area is 26 sq km (10 sq miles), its highest point a mere 5 m (16 ft) above sea level.[35] Its high tide currently peaks at 2.5 m (8 ft), but there has been a steady rise in sea level of just over 6 mm (0.2 in) per year since 1993.[36] Temperatures too are rising, bringing severe storms, cyclones and winds and ocean currents out of season.

At such times, the country becomes saturated. Rainstorms overflow its fresh water tanks, and the water table beneath the atolls becomes contaminated by the seeping sea water. Sewage from septic tanks washes into Funafuti's (the capital city's) lagoon, and pollutes the water and surrounding

Knee-deep: homes on the Pacific Ocean's low-lying atolls such as Tuvalu must be built on stilts to avoid regular flooding.

The Wollemi Pine

lost
and
found

When, in September 1994, David Noble – an officer with the New South Wales National Parks and Wildlife Service – chanced upon some trees he did not recognize in a canyon of Australia's Greater Blue Mountains, Wollemi National Park, he made a discovery of international significance. The sighting was later compared to finding a dinosaur alive. The species, a member of the *Araucariaceae* family and a relative of the monkey puzzle tree, since named *Wollemia nobilis* or the Wollemi pine, was thought to have died out between 90 and 200 million years ago during the Jurassic period. Fossil remains have been discovered in Australia, New Zealand and Antarctica.[37]

Fewer than 100 trees are now known to remain in the wild, their location a closely guarded secret. The tree is close to extinction and human beings pose its biggest threat. A management strategy, the Wollemi Pine Recovery Plan, has been developed to protect the species by methods including minimizing the threat of introducing pathogens such as a root fungus to any site.[38]

Plantings have been made in botanical gardens across Australia and Tasmania, including the first in the Rare and Threatened Plant Garden at Sydney's Royal Botanic Gardens in 1988, and internationally at London's Kew Gardens, Vienna University's Botanical Garden, and the United States Botanic Garden in Washington.[39]

beaches. Root crops such as pulaka, once a staple in the Tuvaluan diet, are poisoned from beneath.

The increasing incidence of flooding, notably into the Funafuti atoll, occurs when high tides and winds correspond. Tuvalu's only airstrip has to be closed at such times, and its foundations require regular repairs due to erosion. Interlocked concrete blocks placed at the edge of the atoll's lagoon are aimed to prevent erosion and stem the force of the water. However, in August 2002, a storm surge from the unprotected Pacific Ocean side of the atoll ate away and measuring 500 m (1,640 ft) wide and 300 m (984 ft) deep just beyond the end of the runway.[40]

A number of islets that lie on the outer edge of Te Namo lagoon have already been severely damaged by the Pacific Ocean's encroachment, although they are within Tuvalu's conservation zone. Tepuka Islet's coral sand beaches have suffered recent erosion, and coconut and pandanus palms have been brought down – the first stage in destroying the islet's protective barrier against the waves. Its fate is likely to reflect that of neighbouring islet Tepuka Vili Vili which, as a result of 1997's Cyclone Meli, has been reduced to a small, bare rock where once it was the image of a palm-topped paradise.

It is feared that Tuvalu could be 'the first sovereign state since Atlantis to vanish beneath the waves'.[41] Severe flooding across the state is predicted within the next twenty years, followed by the island's complete submersion by the end of the century. In 2001, an appeal from the Tuvalu government for a new home for its people met with an agreement from neighbour New Zealand to accept refugees from 2002 over the forthcoming decades.[42]

The Tuvaluans are a devoutly Christian people, many of whom believe that when God displayed a rainbow in the sky as a sign to Noah that He would never flood the Earth again, this remains true for them today too. The plight of the Tuvaluan people – their island at risk of disappearing in part due to the effects of global warming – points further to the need for industrialized nations to minimize their global emissions.

New Zealand's willingness to take the Tuvaluan people presents a model of response to environmental migration, an issue proving to be of growing international concern as climate change takes hold across the planet. This is not the first time New Zealand has made a notable stand regarding an issue of environmental concern. In 1987, the Labour government passed the New Zealand Nuclear Free Zone, Disarmament and Arms Control Act to establish the nation as an entirely nuclear-free state.[43]

Taking Action

1. On a map or globe of the world, identify Oceania's tiny atolls and islands that dot the Pacific Ocean.

2. Directly support WWF's work in the region by donating money specifically to WWF-Australia at www.org.au or WWF-South Pacific Programme at www.wwfpacific.og.fj .

3. View the full New Zealand Nuclear Free Zone, Disarmament and Arms Control Act 1987 at www.middlepowers.org/pnnd/docs/nukefree.html . For its place in the context of New Zealand's history, visit NZ History.net at www.nzhistory.net.nz/politics/nuclear-free-nz .

4. Keep abreast of Tuvalu's news at www.tuvaluislands.com .

5. Contact your local politicians and let them know you will support a campaign to reduce carbon emissions in your country for the sake of people like the Tuvaluans who are dependent on the actions of the rest of the world.

6. Grow your own Jurassic Park! Contact www.wollemipine.com for further details. You can also sign up for the Wollemi pine newsletter and join the Wollemi Pine Conservation Club.

7. To financially support research into Tasmanian devil facial tumour disease, email the Devil Facial Tumour Disease Project for further information: DevilDisease.Enquiries@dpiw.tas.gov.au .

8. Get to grips with your own local wetlands, streams or rivers. Contact your local volunteer conservation group for work projects.

9. Enjoy the sunshine but cover up and use suncream. Try to find natural ways of keeping cool rather than resorting to energy-hungry air-conditioning, which only makes the climate hotter.

10. Make cutting back on fossil fuels fun! Have a 'power cut evening', in which you make your own entertainment by candlelight. If it's too dark, use mirrors to spread light around the room. Children will love it. And if ever there's a *real* power cut, you'll be prepared...

11. In February 2007, the Australian government declared that incandescent lightbulbs would be phased out within three years[44] to cut greenhouse gas emissions. If you can afford them, by all means switch – but low energy lightbulbs are a false economy if you are more wasteful with them than ordinary lightbulbs. They are not as easy to manufacture or recycle, either. Does every room need to be lit? Does every member of the family need to be in a separate room using separate gadgets? If your workplace leaves its lights on during the night when no one is there, get a staff campaign going to request that the company 'Switch Off'.

12. Join a conservation project in Oceania. Check out www.worktravelcompany.co.uk in the UK or www.responsibletravel.com for New Zealand conservation project holidays, or visit www.environaki.co.nz/nz-conservation-corps.html for details of the New Zealand Conservation Corps.

Organizations

Note: all polar organizations are listed under 'Chapter 8: Antarctica'

Chapter 1: The Earth's Atmosphere

American Geophysical Union
www.agu.org

American Meteorological Society
www.ametsoc.org

Carbon Dioxide Information Analysis Center (CDIAC)
cdiac.esd.ornl.gov

Centre for Atmospheric Science, Cambridge University
www.atm.ch.cam.ac.uk/cas

European Organisation for the Exploitation of Meteorological Satellites (EUMETSAT)
www.eumetsat.int

European Space Agency
www.esa.int

Hadley Centre for Climate Prediction and Research, Met Office, UK
www.metoffice.com/research/hadleycentre

NASA Goddard Institute for Space Studies
www.giss.nasa.gov

National Aeronautics and Space Administration (NASA)
www.nasa.gov

National Center for Atmospheric Research (NCAR)
www.ncar.ucar.edu

National Oceanic and Atmospheric Administration (NOAA)
www.noaa.gov

Royal Meteorological Society
www.royal-met-soc.org.uk

Tyndall Centre for Climate Change Research, UK
www.tyndall.ac.uk

UN Intergovernmental Panel on Climate Change (IPCC)
www.ipcc.ch

UN World Meteorological Organization (WMO)
www.wmo.ch

Chapter 2: The Earth

BirdLife International
www.birdlife.org

Conservation International
www.conservation.org
*For CI's material on Biodiversity Hotspots go to
www.biodiversityhotspots.org*

Earth Policy Institute
www.Earth-policy.org

Earthwatch Institute
www.Earthwatch.org

Environmental Defense Fund
www.environmentaldefense.org

Environmental Literacy Council
www.enviroliteracy.org

Forest Stewardship Council (FSC)
www.fsc.org

Foundation for Environmental Education (FEE)
www.fee-international.org

Friends of the Earth International
www.foei.org
*For national groups, check
www.foei.org/groups/members*

Green Cross International
www.greencrossinternational.net

Greenpeace International
www.greenpeace.org/international/
For national groups, access your country's group via the above web address.

International Permafrost Association (IPA)
www.geo.uio.no/IPA

Leonardo DiCaprio Foundation
www.leonardodicaprio.org

United Nations www.un.org

United Nations Environment Programme (UNEP)
www.unep.org

World Conservation Union (IUCN) www.iucn.org

World Resources Institute
www.Earthtrends.wri.org

World Wildlife Fund
www.wwf.org
Also www.panda.org

Worldwatch Institute
www.worldwatch.org

Chapter 3: The Oceans

Atlantic Salmon Federation
www.asf.ca

Commission for the Convention of Antarctic Marine Living Resources
www.ccamlr.org

The Cousteau Society
www.cousteau.org

Deep Sea Conservation Coalition (DSCC) www.savethehighseas.org

European Cetacean Bycatch Campaign (ECBC)
www.eurocbc.org

Global Whale Alliance
www.global-whale-alliance.org

International Council for the Exploration of the Sea (ICES)
www.ices.dk

International Hydrographic Organisation
www.iho.shom.fr

International Whaling Commission (IWC) www.iwcoffice.org

Marine Conservation Society, UK (MCS) www.mcsuk.org

Marine Stewardship Council (MSC) www.msc.org

NASA Physical Oceanography DAAC
http://podaac-www.jpl.nasa.gov

National Hurricane Center, USA
www.nhc.noaa.gov

National Oceanic and Atmospheric Administration (NOAA)
www.noaa.gov

National Oceanographic Data Center www.nodc.noaa.gov

North Atlantic Salmon Conservation Organization (NASCO) www.nasco.int

Oceans Alive
www.oceansalive.org

Pacific Tsunami Warning Center, Hawaii (PTWC)
www.prh.noaa.gov/ptwc

Scripps Institution of Oceanography, California
www.sio.ucsd.edu

Chapter 4: Asia

Asia-Pacific Center for
Environmental Law
law.nus.edu.sg/apcel

Bangladesh Meteorological
Department (BMD)
www.bangladeshonline.com/bmd

Centre for Science and
Environment, New Delhi (CSE)
www.cseindia.org

China's State Environmental
Protection Agency (SEPA)
www.sepa.gov.cn

Friends of River Narmada
www.narmada.org

IRC International Water and
Sanitation Centre   www.irc.nl

Chapter 5: Africa

African Conservation Foundation
(ACF)
www.africanconservation.org

African Wildlife Foundation
(AWF)   www.awf.org

Bushmeat Crisis Task Force
www.bushmeat.org

Ethiopian Wolf Conservation
Programme, Oxford University
www.ethiopianwolf.org

Green Belt Movement
www.greenbeltmovement.org

Mo Ibrahim Foundation
www.moibrahimfoundation.org

Mountain Gorilla Veterinary
Project (MGVP)   www.mgvp.org

Movement for the Survival of the
Ogoni People (MOSOP)
www.dawodu.net/mosop.htm

Chapter 6: North America

Arctic National Wildlife Refuge
arctic.fws.gov and
www.anwr.org and
www.savearcticrefuge.org

Canadian Wildlife Service
www.cws-scf.ec.gc.ca

Caribbean Conservation
Association   www.ccanet.net

End Mountaintop Removal Action
and Resource Center
www.ilovemountains.org

Forest Stewardship Council, USA
(FSC)   www.fscus.org
FSC Canada   www.fsccanada.org

National Audubon Society
www.audubon.org

National Religious Partnership for
the Environment   www.nrpe.org

National Resources Defense
Council (NRDC)   www.nrdc.org

National Wildlife Federation
(NWF)   www.nwf.org

Nature Conservancy
www.nature.org

NOAA National Marine Fisheries
Service (NOAA Fisheries Service)
www.nmfs.noaa.gov

Parks Canada   www.pc.gc.ca/agen

Sierra Club   www.sierraclub.org

Sierra Club Canada
www.sierraclub.ca

Society for the Conservation and
Study of Caribbean Birds
(SCSCB)   www.scscb.org

Union of Concerned Scientists
(UCS)   www.ucsusa.org

United States Permafrost
Association
www.uspermafrost.org

US Department of Energy
www.energy.gov

US Environmental Protection
Agency   www.epa.gov

US Fish and Wildlife Service
www.fws.gov

Wilderness Society
www.wilderness.org

Wildlife Watch, Inc.
www.wildwatch.org

WWF Canada   www.wwf.ca

WWF US   www.worldwildlife.org

Chapter 7: South America

Amazon Conservation Association
www.amazonconservation.org

Chico Mendes Committee
www.chicomendes.org

Galapagos Conservation Trust
www.gct.org

Naturereserve   www.natureserve.org

Organization for the Conservation
of Penguins   www.seabirds.org

Chapter 8: Antarctica

Alfred Wegener Institute for Polar
and Marine Research   www.awi.de

Antarctic and Southern Ocean
Coalition (ASOC) and The
Antarctica Project (TAP)
www.asoc.org

Antarctic Automatic Weather
Station Project and Antarctic
Meteorological Research Center
www.amrc.ssec.wisc.edu

Antarctic Treaty Secretariat
www.ats.org.ar

Arctic Climate Impact Assessment
www.acia.uaf.edu

Arctic Council   www.arctic-
council.org

Australian Antarctic Division
www.aad.gov.au

British Antarctic Survey (BAS)
www.antarctica.ac.uk

Centre for Polar Observation and
Modelling, University College
London   www.cpom.org

International Arctic Research
Center, University of Alaska
Fairbanks   www.iarc.uaf.edu

International Arctic Science
Committee (IASC)   www.iasc.se

International Association of
Antarctic Tour Operators
(IAATO)   www.iaato.org

International Polar Foundation
(IPF)   www.polarfoundation.org

International Polar Year
(IPY: 2007–08)   www.ipy.org

National Snow and Ice Data
Center (NSIDC) nsidc.org

Polar Bears International
www.polarbearsinternational.org

Scientific Committee on Antarctic
Research (SCAR)   www.scar.org

Scott Polar Research Institute,
Cambridge, UK (SPRI)
www.spri.cam.ac.uk

World Data Centre for Glaciology
wdcgc.spri.cam.ac.uk

Chapter 9: Europe

Alpine Network of Protected Areas (ALPARC) www.alparc.org

Arctic Council www.arctic-council.org

Central and Eastern European Working Group for the Enhancement of Biodiversity (CEEWEB) www.ceeweb.org

Centre for European Protected Area Research www.bbk.ac.uk/ce/research/cepar

Chernobyl Children's Project International www.chernobyl-international.org

Chernobyl Forum www-ns.iaea.org/meetings/rw-summaries/chernobyl_forum.htm

Council of Europe www.coe.int

Eco-Schools www.eco-schools.org

European Environment Agency www.eea.europa.eu

European Federation for Transport and the Environment www.transportenvironment.org

European Spatial Planning: Adapting to Climate Events (ESPACE) www.espace-project.org

European Union europa.eu

Eurosite www.eurosite-nature.org

Green Balkans www.greenbalkans.org

The Greens/European Free Alliance in the European Union www.greens-efa.org

International Commission for the Protection of the Alps (CIPRA) www.cipra.org

International Scientific Committee for Alpine Research (ISCAR) www.alpinestudies.ch/iscar

Large Carnivore Initiative for Europe (LCIE) www.lcie.org

Mediterranean Information Office for Environment, Culture and Sustainable Development (MIO-ECSDE) www.mio-ecsde.org

Chapter 10: Oceania/Australasia

Australian Conservation Foundation (ACF) www.acfonline.org.au

Boomerang Alliance www.boomerangalliance.org

Commonwealth Scientific and Industrial Research Organisation (CSIRO) www.csiro.au

Cooperative Research Centre for Australian Weed Management (CRC Weed Management) www.weeds.crc.org.au

Earthwatch Australia www.Earthwatch.org/australia

Greenpeace Australia Pacific www.greenpeace.org/australia

National Centre for Aquatic Biodiversity and Biosecurity, NZ www.niwascience.co.nz/ncabb

New Zealand Government Department of Conservation www.doc.govt.nz

Royal Forest and Bird Protection Society of New Zealand www.forestandbird.org.nz

SaveTheKangaroo.com www.savethekangaroo.com

South Pacific Forum www.forumsec.org.fj

Wildlife Protection Association of Australia www.wildlifeprotectaust.org.au

Wollemi Pine Conservation Club www.wollemipine.com

WWF-Australia www.wwf.org.au

WWF-South Pacific Programme www.wwfpacific.org.fj

Glossary

agribusiness   A large-scale factory farming business, as opposed to traditional agriculture.

agro-forestry   A system of land use in which harvestable trees or shrubs are grown among crops or on pastureland.

Antarctic Treaty   A 1959 agreement signed by twelve countries which prohibited military actions on the continent and provided for the exchange of scientific data. Member countries now number forty-six.

anthropogenic climate change That which occurs as a result of human activities.

aquaculture   The controlled cultivation and harvest of aquatic plants or animals, whether marine or fresh water.

archipelago   A group of many islands in a large body of water.

biodiversity   The variety of life on Earth at all its levels, or within a given area.

biomes   Distinct ecological communities of plants and animals, such as deserts, forests, grasslands and tundra.

boreal   Relating to the north; such as the north wind or forest areas of the north.

bush meat   Wild animals killed for food, often illegally.

carbon footprint   The sum of all greenhouse gas emissions induced by human activities and measured in units of CO_2.

cetaceans   Marine animals with teeth, including whales, porpoises and dolphins.

Coriolis effect   The deflective effect of the Earth's rotation – to the right in the Northern Hemisphere, to the left in the Southern Hemisphere – on all free-moving objects, including the atmosphere and oceans.

counter-clockwise gyre   A broad, circular system of currents.

diffuse pollution   The result of the accumulation of polluting materials from a range of sources, including acid rain, pesticides, run-off and others.

ecotourism   Travel undertaken to witness sites or regions of unique natural or ecological quality.

endemic   Flora and fauna found nowhere else on earth.

feedbacks   Mechanisms that act to intensify or reduce the effects of a change in a climate system (such as solar radiation); can be positive or negative.

Gaia Theory   Theory proposed by James Lovelock that the Earth is a self-regulating organism. All life and inorganic material of the planet are part of a dynamic system that regulates conditions to support life.

geosphere   The soils, sediments and rock layers of the Earth's crust, both continental and beneath the ocean floor.

Gondwanaland super-continent A giant landmass existing 500–550 million years ago made up mostly of the continents in today's Southern Hemisphere.

Greenhouse Effect   The warming of the atmosphere by the trapping of long-wave radiation being radiated to space. The gases most responsible for this effect are water vapour and carbon dioxide.

hypoxia   A deficiency of oxygen in the tissues.

ion   An atom or group of atoms that has gained or lost one or more electrons and thus acquired a net negative or positive charge.

Larsen B ice shelf   A 10,000-year-old mass of mostly solid ice inhabited only by Weddell seals.

micro-habitat   A very small, specialized habitat, such as a clump of grass or a space between rocks.

monoculture   The cultivation of a single crop on a farm, region or country without diversity.

organochlorines   A range of synthetic and natural chemicals that contain carbon, chlorine and sometimes other elements. They pose many human health risks, and most were banned in the 1980s.

permafrost   Permanently frozen subsoil.

phytoplankton   Microscopic, free-floating plants such as algae.

POPs   According to the UNEP, 'chemical substances that persist in the environment but accumulate through the food web, and pose a risk of causing adverse effects to human health and the environment'.

renewables   Energy resources that are replaced rapidly by natural processes such as sunlight, wind and wave.

subduction zones   Geographical features beneath the Earth's crust where the tectonic plates are diving beneath each other into the Earth's interior.

taiga   A moist sub-arctic coniferous forest dominated by spruces and firs located south of the tundra.

tectonic plates   Segments of the lithosphere that comprise the surface of the Earth.

thermohaline circulation   Large-scale density-driven circulation in the ocean, caused by differences in temperature and salinity.

tundra   A treeless permafrost plain between the icecap and the treeline of Arctic regions.

ungulates   Hoofed mammals, which are mainly grazing herbivores, many of which have horns and double stomachs.

zooplankton   Microscopic animals that float or drift in great numbers in fresh or salt water.

List of Acronyms

ACA Amazon Conservation Association

ACF African Conservation Foundation

ASOC Antarctic and Southern Ocean Coalition

ATCM Antarctic Treaty Consultative Meeting

BAS British Antarctic Survey

CAP Common Agricultural Policy

CCA Caribbean Conservation Association

CCAMR Convention on the Conservation of Antarctic Marine Living Resources

CI Conservation International

CPRA Coastal Protection and Restoration Authority

CSE (New Delhi's) Centre for Science and Environment

EC European Community

EEZ Exclusive Economic Zone

ENSO El Niño Southern Oscillation

EPA Environmental Protection Agency

EPBC Environment Protection and Biodiversity Conservation (Act)

ETS Emissions Trading Scheme

EU ETS EU Gas Emission Trading Scheme

FAO United Nations' Food and Agriculture Organisation

GPS Global Positioning System

IAATO International Association of Antarctica Tour Operators

IBA Important Bird Area Program (of the Nature Conservancy, BirdLife International)

IPCC Intergovernmental Panel on Climate Change

IPY International Polar Year

IUCN International Union for the Conservation of Nature

IWC International Whaling Commission

IWMI International Water Management Institute

MOSOP Movement for the Survival of the Ogoni People

MSC Marine Stewardship Council

NAP National Allocation Plan

NOAA National Oceanic and Atmospheric Administration

NRDC National Resource Defense Council

NWF National Wildlife Federation

POP Persistent Organic Pollutant

SCSCB The Society for the Conservation and Study of Caribbean Birds

SPAW (Protocol for) Specially Protected Areas and Wildlife

TAP The Antarctica Project

TAR IPCC's Third Assessment Report

UNEP United Nations Environment Programme

UNFCCC UN Framework Convention on Climate Change

USGS US Geological Survey

WCD World Commission on Dams

WMO World Meteorological Organization

WWF World Wildlife Fund

WWT Wildfowl and Wetlands Trust

YOTO Year of the Ocean

References

Please note that due to the nature of web-based information, some information in internet-based references below is subject to change.

Introduction

1. von Ruhland, Catherine, *Going Green: A Christian Guide*, Marshall Pickering, 1991.

Chapter 1: The Earth's Atmosphere

1. Connor, Steve, '*The Independent* Guide to the Weather' [wallchart], *The Independent*/Met Office, 2006.

2. 'The Atmosphere', www.littleexplorers.com/subjects/astronomy/planets/Earth/Atmosphere.shtml

3. IPCC, 'About IPCC: Mandate and Membership of the IPCC' www.ipcc.ch/about/about.htm

4. Alley, Richard; Berntsen, Terje; Bindoff, Nathaniel L. et al., *Climate Change 2007: The Physical Science Basis. Summary for Policymakers*, Contribution of Working Group 1 to the Fourth Assessment Report of the Intergovernmental Panel on Climate Change, Intergovernmental Panel on Climate Change, February 2007, p. 5, www.ipcc.ch/SPM2feb07.pdf

5. Ibid., p. 10.

6. IPCC, *Technical Summary of the Working Group 1 Report*, www.ipcc.ch/pub/wg1TARtechsum.pdf

7. 'Solar Variation Theory', http://solar-center.stanford.edu/images/solactivity.jpg

8. archive.newscientist.com/secure/article/article.jsp?rp=1&id=mg16622370.800

9. 'Global Warming', http://dictionary.laborlawtalk.com/Global_warming

10. The text of the Protocol is available at www.unfccc.int

11. Hare, B., 'Assessment of Knowledge on Impacts of Climate Change – Contribution to the Specification of Art. 2 of the UNFCCC: Impacts on Ecosystems, Food Production, Water and Socioeconomic System', UNFCCC, 2003, www.wbgu.de/wbgu_sn2003_ex01.pdf

12. Stern, Sir Nicholas, 'Stern Review on the Economics of Climate Change', HM Treasury, 30 October 2006, www.hm-treasury.gov.uk/Independent_Reviews/stern_review_economics_cliimate_change/sternreview_index.cfm

13. Ibid.

14. Meinshausen, Malte, 'On the Risk of Overshooting 2°C', Swiss Federal Institute of Technology, Zurich, 2005, http://regserver.unfcc.int/seors/file_storage/FS_871540246

15. Friends of the Earth International, 'Climate Change Treaty One Year Old, but Emissions Still on the Rise', 15 February 2006, www.foei.org/media/2006/0215.html

16. UNFCCC, United Nations Climate Change Conference, 6–17 November 2006, http://unfccc.int/2860.php

17. Tearfund, 'Climate Change Proposals Display "Staggering Complacency"', 17 November 2006, www.tearfund.org/News/Latest+news/Climate+change+proposals+display+staggering+complacency.htm

18. NCDC/NOAA, 'A Paleo Perspective… on Global Warming', www.ncdc.noaa.gov/paleo/globalwarming/what.html

19. 'GeoTopics: Environmental Problems/Global Warming', www.geography.learnontheinternet.co.uk/topics/globalwarming.html

20. 'The Nobel Prize in Chemistry, 1903', Nobel Web AB, 2006, nobelprize.org/nobel_prizes/chemistry/laureates/1903

21. Highwood, Dr Eleanor, 'Climate Change – How Do We Know It's Happening?' [Event review of The Cafe Scientique], Reading Lifelong Learning Partnership, 23 May 2005, www.readingllp.co.uk/cafesci/climate_review.htm

22. Connor, Steve, 'Methane Emissions Soar as China Booms', *The Independent*, 28 September 2006, p. 26.

23. Highwood, Dr Eleanor (above, n. 21)

24. Steinfield, Henning; Gerber, Pierre; Wassenaar, Tom et al., *Livestock's Long Shadow: Environmental Issues and Options*, Food and Agriculture Organization of the United Nations, 2006.

25. Steele, Paul et al., 'Contribution of Anthropogenic and Natural Sources to Atmospheric Methane Variability', *Nature*, 28 September 2006, p. 439, www.nature.com/nature/journal/v443/n7110/index.html

26. Hoffman, Ian, 'Global Warming Could Trigger Methane Release', ANG Newspapers, 2006, www.geo.oreganstate.edu/events/Press_2006/20060905_global_warming.pdf

27. Connor, Steve, 'Global Warming: Our Worst Fears are Exceeded by Reality', from 'The Year in Review 2006' [supplement], *The Independent*, 29 December 2006, p. 4.

28. UNFCCC Secretariat, 'Greenhouse Gas Data, 2006', United Nations Framework Convention on Climate Change, Bonn, 30 October 2006.

29. UNFCCC Secretariat, '2006 UNFCCC Greenhouse Gas Data Report Points to Rising Emission Trends' [press release], United Nations Framework Convention on Climate Change, Bonn, 30 October 2006.

30. Romanowicz, Goska, '"First World" Emissions on the Rise', Faversham House Group, 1 November 2006,

www.edie.net/news/news_story.asp?id=12202

31. UNFCCC Secretariat (above, n. 28)

32. Bows, A.; Anderson, K.; and Upham, P., 'Contraction and Convergence: UK Carbon Emissions and the Implications for UK Air Traffic', Tyndall Centre Technical Report 40, Tyndall Centre, UK, 2006.

33. Lucas, Caroline, 'MEP and EU Rappoteur on Aviation and Climate Change. Airlines Must Lose Their Right to Pollute the Skies', *The Independent*, 22 June 2006.

34. Harrison, Michael, 'Branson Pledges 43bn to Combat Global Warming', *The Independent*, 22 September 2006, p. 6.

35. US Department of Energy, 'Breaking the Biological Barriers to Cellulosc Ethanol: A Joint Research Agenda', A Research Roadmap Resulting from the Biomass to Biofuels Workshop Held by the Office of Science and Office of Energy Efficiency and Renewable Energy in December 2005, Rockville, Maryland, DOE, 2006.

36. US Environmental Protection Agency, 'Why is the Ozone Hole over Antarctica?', www.epa.gov/ozone/science/hole/whyant.html

37. Ibid.

38. Environment News Service, 'Ozone Loss Reaches New Record', www.ens-newswire.com/ens/oct2006/2006-10-02-01.asp

39. Ozone Secretariat, 'Montreal Protocol', http://ozone.unep.org/Treaties_and_Ratification/2B_montreal_protocol.asp

40. 'A Hole Lot Bigger', *New Scientist*, 16 September 2006, www.newscientist.com/article/mg16722561.100-a-hole-lot-bigger.html

41. UNEP, 'New Report Projects Later Recovery of Ozone Layer' [press release], 18 August 2006,

www.unep.org/Documents.Multilingual/Default.asp?DocumentID=484&ArticleID=5335&I=en

42. Gleason, Karin L., 'Science: The Antarctic Ozone Hole', NOAA, updated 3 March 2006, www.ozonelayer.noaa.gov/science/ozhole.htm

43. US Environmental Protection Agency, 'Substitutes for ODS in Aerosol Solvents and Propellants', www.epa.gov/ozone/snap/aerosol/list.html

44. US Environmental Protection Agency, 'Effects of Acid Rain – Human Health', www.epa.gov/airmarkt/acidrain/effects/health.html

45. Hames, Ralph S.; Rosenberg, Kenneth V.; Lowe, James D. et al., 'Adverse Effects of Acid Rain on the Distribution of the Wood Thrush *Hylocichla mustelina* in North America', *Proceedings of the National Academy of Sciences of the United States of America* (PNAS), Vol 99, No 16, 12 August 2002.

46. US Fish and Wildlife Service, 'Amphibian Declines and Deformities', Division of Environmental Quality, 2006, www.fws.gov/contaminants/issues/Amphibians.cfm

47. Sacquet, Anne, 'Emissions of Sulphur Compounds', *World Atlas of Sustainable Development: Economic, Social and Environmental Data*, Editions Autrement, 2002, pp. 34–35.

Chapter 2: The Earth

1. Hamilton, Calvin J., 'Earth Introduction', www.solarviews.com/eng/Earth.htm

2. Coble, Charles R.; Murray, Elaine G.; and Rice, Dole R., *Earth Science*, Prentice-Hall, 1987, p. 102.

3. Christian Aid, 'The Climate of Poverty: Facts, Fears and Hope', May 2006, www.christian-aid.org.uk/indepth/605caweek/index.htm

4. Thomas, Chris D.; Cameron, Alison; Green, Rhys E. et al., 'Extinction Risk from Climate Change', *Nature*, Vol 427, No 6992, 8 January 2004, pp. 145–148.

5. Bryant, Dirk; Nielsen, Daniel; and Tangley, Laura, *Last Frontier Forests: Ecosystems and Economies on the Edge*, World Resources Institute, 1997. Can be downloaded from, www.wri.org/biodiv/pubs_description.cfm?pid=2619

6. 'Hawaii's Ecosystems', HawaiiNatureGuides.net, 13 January 2006, www.hawaiinatureguides.net/ecosystems01.htm

7. Hawaii Forestry Extension, 'Native Plants in Public Places: Hawaii's Unique Biological Heritage', College of Tropical Agriculture and Human Resources, University of Hawaii at Manoa, 2002, www.ctahr.hawaii.edu/forestry/Past/Workshops/NativePlants/index.asp

8. Trigger, Robert, 'When a World Loses its Wonder', *The Disappearing World: 100 Things Your Grandchildren May Never See*, Part 2: Planet in Peril, *The Independent*, 18 October 2005, p. 5.

9. Ibid.

10. Lovelock, J.E. and Margulis, L., 'Atmospheric Homeostasis by and for the Biosphere: The Gaia Hypothesis', *Tellus*, Vol 26, No 1, 1974, pp. 2–10.

11. Lovelock, J.E. and Epton, S.R., 'The Quest for Gaia', *New Scientist*, 6 February 1975.

12. Lovelock, James, *Gaia – A New Look at Life on Earth*, Oxford University Press, 1979.

13. Ibid.

14. American Geophysical Union, First Chapman Conference on the Gaia Hypothesis, San Diego, 1988.

15. Watson, A.J. and Lovelock, J.E., 'Biological Homeostasis of the Global Environment: The Parable of Daisyworld', *Tellus* 35B, 1983, pp. 284–289.

16. Lovelock, James, *The Revenge of Gaia: Why the Earth is Fighting Back – and How We Can Still Save Humanity*, Basic/Allen Lane, 2006.

17. Lovelock, James, 'The Earth is About to Catch a Morbid Fever That May Last as Long as 100,000 Years', *The Independent*, 16 January 2006, p. 31.

18. Annan, Kofi, 'Climate Change is Not Just an Environmental Issue', *The Independent*, 9 November 2006, p. 39.

19. Lambert, Jean (Green MEP for London), 'Refugees and the Environment', Speech to the World University Service, 26 October 2001, www.jeanlambermep.org.uk/downloads/speeches/0110Environrefwus.doc

20. Tearfund, 'Climate Change will Create Millions More Refugees', 20 October 2006, www.tearfund.org/News/World+news/Climate+change+will+create+millions+more+refugees.htm

21. Tearfund, 'Feeling the Heat', Tearfund, 20 October 2006, www.tearfund.org

22. Burke, Eleanor J.; Brown, Simon J.; and Christidis, 'Modeling the Recent Evolution of Global Drought and Projections for the Twenty-First Century with the Hadley Centre Climate Model', *Journal of Hydrometeorology*, Vol 7, Issue 5, October 2006.

23. McCarthy, Michael, 'The Century of Drought: Hunger. Thirst. War. Migration. Death. How Climate Change Will Affect the World', *The Independent*, 4 October 2006, p. 2.

24. Thornton, Philip, 'Wheat Prices Soar on Drought Fear', *The Independent*, 11 October 2006, p. 44.

25. FAO, '40 Countries Face Food Shortages Worldwide' [press release], 9 October 2006, www.fao.org/newsroom/en/news/2006/1000416/index.html

26. Barlow, Maude, 'Introduction', *Blue Gold: The Global Water Crisis and the Commodification of the World's Water Supply*, A Special Report Issued by the International Forum on Globalization, Spring 2001, www.thirdworldtraveler.com/Water/Blue_Gold.html

27. Ekklesia, 'Time to Get Tough with World Bank and IMF, Says Christian Aid', 7 July 2006, www.ekklesia.co.uk/content/news_syndication/article_06077imfwb.shtml

28. Barlow, Maude, 'Conclusion', *Blue Gold: The Global Water Crisis and the Commodification of the World's Water Supply*, A Special Report Issued by the International Forum on Globalization, Spring 2001, www.thirdworldtraveler.com/Water/Conclusion_BG.html

29. DEFRA, E-digest Statistics about: Global Atmosphere, 'Agreements to Limit Greenhouse Gas Emissions', Department for Environment, Food and Rural Affairs, 2005, www.defra.gov.uk/environment/statistics/globatmos/gaemlimit.htm

30. Lynas, Mark, *High Tide: How Climate Crisis is Engulfing our Planet*, HarperPerennial, 2005.

31. Lovelock, James (above, n. 16)

32. Monbiot, George, *Heat: How to Stop the Planet Burning*, Allen Lane, 2006.

33. Christian Aid, Statement on the Close of the Nairobi Climate Change Conference, 20 November 2006, www.christian-aid.org/news/stories/061120s.htm

34. Division of Environmental Conventions, United Nations Environment Programme, 2004, www.unep.org/dec/about_dec.html

35. 'Millennium Ecosystem Assessment', World Health Organisation, 2001, www.maweb.org

36. 'International Polar Year 2007–2008', International Council for Science/WMO, 2006, www.ipy.org

Chapter 3: The Oceans

1. Raloff, Janet, 'Venting Concerns: Exploring and Protecting Deep-Sea Communities', *Science News*, Vol 170, No 15, 7 October 2006, p. 232.

2. MBL, 'MBL Scientists Embark on International Effort to Uncover Microbial Diversity in World's Oceans: First Global Effort to Acquire Information about Diversity and Distribution of Single-Celled Organisms and Associated Viruses' [press release], Marine Biological Laboratory, Woods Hole, Massachusetts, 29 November 2004, www.mbl.edu/inside/what/news/press_releases/2004/2004_pr_11_29.html

3. Welch, Charles, 'Oceans', www.solcomhouse.com/oceans.htm

4. Matthews, Professor Jack (former director of the Scottish Association for Marine Science), 'Climate Crisis Could Devastate Oceans', *The Independent*, Letters to the Editor, 20 September 2006, p. 32.

5. UNEP, 'Further Rise in Number of Marine "Dead Zones" [press release], 19 October 2006, www.unep.org/Documents.Multilingual/Default.asp?DocumentID=486&ArticleID=5393&i=en

6. National Environment Research Council, 'What are "Acid Oceans" and Why is Acidification Important?', 2006, www.nerc.ac.uk/research/issues/climatechange/acidification.asp

7. Fry, Carolyn, 'Acid Oceans Spell Doom for Coral', BBC News, 29 August 2004, http://news.bbc.co.uk/1/hi/sci/tech/3605908.stm>

8. IPCC, *IPCC Third Assessment Report – Climate Change 2001*, www.grida.no/climate/ipcc_tar

9. Friends of the Earth, 'Potential Sea Level Rise Worse Than Previously Expected' [Climate Clinic press release], 19 September 2006,

www.foe.co.uk/resource/press_rele ases/potential_sea_level_rise_w_ 19092006.html

10. 'EarthPulse: If You Feel Like Your Favorite Beach Keeps Getting Skimpier Each Time You Visit, It's Not Your Imagination', National Geographic Society, 2001, www.nationalgeographiv.com/ngm/ 0102/Earthpulse

11. Gribbin, John, 'Ocean Forces Threaten Our Climate', FirstScience.com, 2005, www.firstscience.com/ site/articles/gribbin.asp

12. Ibid.

13. Ibid.

14. Sample, Ian, 'Alarm Over Dramatic Weakening of Gulf Stream', *Guardian Unlimited*, 1 December 2005, www.guardian.co.uk/science.story/ 0,3605,1654803,00.html

15. Leake, Jonathan, 'Britain Faces Big Chill as Ocean Current Slows', *The Sunday Times*, 8 May 2005.

16. Bryden et al., 'Slowing of the Atlantic Meridional Overturning Circulation at 25°N', *Nature*, Vol 438, 1 December 2005, pp. 655–657.

17. CIA, 'Pacific Ocean', *The World Factbook* [online edition], last updated 19 December 2006, www.cia.gov/cia/publications/ factbook/geos/zn.html

18. Sample, Ian (above, n. 14)

19. WHO Media Centre, 'El Niño and its Health Impact', Fact sheet No 192, revised March 2000, www.who.int/mediacentre. factsheets/fs192/en

20. 'Environmental Issues of the Galapagos', www.galapagosislands.com/html/ environment.html

21. Oshima, Kenzo, 'Statements to the Economic and Social Council on the Implementation of the International Strategy for Disaster Reduction (ISDR) and International Cooperation to Reduce the Impact of the El Niño Phenomenon', UNISR,

25 July 2001, www.unisdr.org/eng/media-room/statements/stmts-2001-25-july-USG.doc

22. 'Atlantic Ocean' [encyclopedia entry], *The Columbia Electronic Encyclopedia*, 6th ed., Columbia University Press, 2006, www.infoplease.com/ce6/world/ AO856755.html

23. Ibid.

24. Ibid.

25. Sacquet, Anne, 'Emissions of Sulphur Compounds', *World Atlas of Sustainable Development: Economic, Social and Environmental Data*, Editions Autrement, 2002, pp. 34–35.

26. 'Hurricane Nursery', *New Scientist*, 5 August 2008, p. 4.

27. Grammatico, Michael, 'Major Hurricanes (Category 3 or Higher) to Enter the Gulf Coast (1900–2005)', www.geocities.com/hurricaneme/ gulfcoast.htm

28. CIA, 'Indian Ocean Geography', *The World Factbook* [online edition], www.cia.gov/cia/publications/ factbook/geos/xo.html

29. Union of Concerned Scientists, 'Global Warming 101: Hurricanes and Climate Change', 17 November 2005, www.ucsusa.org/global_warming/ science/hurricanes-and-climate-change.html

30. Lovgren, Stefan, 'Tsunamis More likely to Hit US Than Asia', National Geographic News, 3 January 2005, http://news.nationalgeographic. com/news/2005/01/0103_050103_ US_tsunami.html

31. Ibid.

32. CIA, 'Geography and Map of Southern Ocean', *The World Factbook* [online edition], www.cia.gov/cia/publications/ factbook/geos/xo.html

33. Young, Emma, 'Ozone Hole Alters Antarctic Sea Life', *New Scientist*, 22 July 2006, p. 18.

34. Maw, Marianne, 'Sierra Club Honours Antarctica Activist' [press release], 15 November 2004, http//www.asoc.org/Documents/E arth%care%20Release111504.pdf

35. '"Last Chance" for Southern Ocean', BBC News, 23 January 2004, http://news.bbc.co.uk/ 1/hi/sci/tech/3421313.stm

36. CIA (above, n. 32)

37. Roach, John, 'Can Satellites Aid Earthquake Predictions?' National Geographic News, 20 July 2004, http://news.nationalgeographic. com/news/2004/07/0720_040720_ earthquake.html

38. Hedley, Chris, 'Compendium of Legal Texts', *Internet Guide to International Fisheries Law*, IGIFL and Chris Hedley, 2000–2001, www.oceanlaw.net/texts

39. Castle, Stephen, 'EU Trawlers Buy Fishing Rights off Africa for £350m', *The Independent*, 24 July 2006, p. 17.

40. Browne, Anthony, 'Melting Ice Starts Rush for Arctic Resources', *The Times*, 28 January 2006.

41. Worm, Boris et al., 'Impacts of Biodiversity Loss on Ocean Ecosystem Services', *Science*, Vol 314, No 5800, 3 November 2006, pp. 787–790.

42. Marine Stewardship Council, 'Fisheries', http://eng.msc.org/ html/content_530.htm

43. 'Marine Stewardship Council – Not Dolphin Safe', European Cetacean Bycatch Campaign, updated February 2006, www.eurocbc.org/ecbc_ci_marine_ stewardship_council_page1255.html

44. 'Ocean Data Confirms Fishing Puts Targeted Species in Double Jeopardy', Scripps Institution of Oceanography, University of California San Diego, 18 October 2006, http://scrippsnews.ucsd.edu/ article_detail.cfm?article_num=752

45. Connor, Steve, 'Revealed: How Conservation Efforts May Be Exacerbating the Crisis in the Seas', *The Independent*, 19 October 2006, p. 6.

46. WWF, 'Fish Dish: Exposing the Unacceptable Face of Seafood', WWF European Fisheries Campaign Report, September 2006.

47. WWF, 'Atlantic Salmon – Ecology', www.worldwildlife.org/salmon/ecology.cfm

48. Rigor, I.; Shiklomanov, A.; Stroeve, J. et al., State of the Arctic Report, NOAA OAR Special Report, NOAA/OAR/PMEL, Seattle, WA, 2006.

49. Buis, Alan, 'NASA Sees Rapid Changes in Arctic Sea Ice' [press release], NASA Jet Propulsion Laboratory, Pasadena, CA, 13 September 2006, www.nasa.gov/home/hqnews/2006/sep/HQ_06315_sea_ice.html

50. 'Arctic Sea Ice Shrinks as Temperatures Rise', NSIDC News, The National Snow and Ice Data Center, University of Colorado Boulder, 3 October 2006, http://nsidc.org/news/press/2006_seaiceminimum/20061003_press releases.html

51. 'International Polar Year 2007–2008', International Council for Science/WMO, 2006, www.ipy.org

52. Adam, David, 'UK Scientists Attack Oil Firms' Role in Huge Arctic Project', The Guardian, 18 April 2006, pp. 1–20.

53. USGS, 'World Energy Project – World and Region Assessment Summaries', US Geological Survey, 24 March 2000, http://energy.cr.usgs.gov/energy/worldEnergy/weptotal.htm

54. Piskur, Michael, 'Energy Spotlight Falls on the Arctic', Asia Times Online, 22 August 2006, www.atimes.com/atimes/Global_Economy/HH22Dj01.html

55. Granier, Claire; Niemeier, Ulrike; Jungclaus, Johann H. et al., 'Ozone Pollution from Future Ship Traffic in the Arctic Northern Passages', Geophysical Research Letters, Vol 33, No 13, 8 July 2006.

56. 'Earth's Most Diverse Marine Life Found off Indonesia's Papua Province' [press release], Conservation International, 17 September 2006, www.conservation.org/xp/news/press_releases/2006/091706.xml

57. Kirby, Terry, 'Dozens of New Species Found in Underwater Wonderland', The Independent, 18 September 2006, p. 1.

58. 'Scientists Discover Dozens of New Species in "Lost World" of Western New Guinea' [press release], Conservation International, 7 February 2006, www.conservation.org/xp/news/press_releases/2006/020706.xml

Chapter 4: Asia

1. Zhonghua, Yan, 'World's Largest Dam Completed on China's Yangtze River', China View, 20 May 2006, http://news.xinhuanet.com/english/2006-05/20/content_4575432.htm

2. Gurulev, S.A., 'The Face of Baikal – Water', Baikal World, 2006, www.bww.irk.ru/baikalwater/pollution.html

3. 'India: Environmental Issues', US Government Energy Information Administration, February 2004, www.eia.doe.gov/emeu/cabs/indiaenv.html

4. Ibid.

5. Centre for Science and Environment, 'Sunita Narain: Professional Experience', www.cseindia.org/html/au/au12_sunitabio.htm

6. IRC International Water and Sanitation Centre, 'Sunita Narain Awarded Padma Shri', 11 February 2005, www.irc.nl/page/16325

7. Pearce, Fred, 'The Parched Planet', New Scientist, 25 February 2006, pp. 32–36.

8. Ibid.

9. Europa, 'European Commission and China Step up Co-operation on Clean Coal Technologies and Other Energy Issues'

[press release], European Commission, 20 February 2006, Reference IP/06/190, http://europa.eu/rapid/pressReleasesAction.do?reference=IP/06/190

10. Sacquet, Anne, 'Natural Disasters', World Atlas of Sustainable Development: Economic, Social and Environmental Data, Editions Autrement, 2002, pp. 32–33.

11. Revkin, Andrew C., 'Gauging Disaster: How Scientists and Victims Watched Helplessly', New York Times, 31 December 2004, http://poseidon.uprm.edu/NYTimes.pdf

12. Roach, John, 'Pulse of the Planet: Earthquake Prediction Remains a Moving Target', National Geographic News, National Geographic Society, 14 July 2004, http://news.nationalgeographic.com/news/2004/07/0714_040714_earthquakeprediction.html

13. Tearfund, 'A Year on from Kashmir Quake – Tearfund is Reducing the Risk of Disasters in Vulnerable Communities' [press release], 2 October 2006, www.tearfund.org/News/Latest+news/

14. Owen, James, 'Science and Space: Satellite Global Disaster Alert System Planned', National Geographic News, National Geographic Society, 24 January 2005, http://news.nationalgeographic.com/news/2005/01/0107_050107_tsunami_index.html

15. Ahmed, Sabihuddin, 'For My People, Climate Change is a Matter of Life and Death', The Independent, 15 September 2006, p. 4.

16. ESCAP, 'Integrating Environmental Considerations into the Economic Decision-Making Process: II – Flood Loss Reduction and Review of Past Experiences', United Nations Economic and Social Commission for Asia and the Pacific,

www.unescap.org/drpad/publicatio
n/integra/modalities/bangladesh/
4b102a02.htm

17. Ahmed, Sabihuddin (above,
n. 15)

18. United Nations Development
Programme, *Human Development
Report 2006: Beyond Scarcity –
Power, Poverty and the Global
Water Crisis*, November 2006,
hdr.undp.org/hdr2006

19. Coonan, Clifford, 'Tibet's
Lofty Glaciers Melt Away', *The
Independent*, 17 November 2006,
pp. 32–33.

20. WWF Nepal Program, *An
Overview of Glaciers, Glacier
Retreat, and Subsequent Impacts in
Nepal, India and China*, An
overview report of a regional-level
project initiated by WWF Nepal
Program, WWF India and WWF
China Program, and compiled by
Joe Thomas K. and Sandeep
Chamling Rai, March 2005,
http://assets.panda.org/downloads
/himalayaglaciersreport2005.pdf

21. Coonan, Clifford (above,
n. 19)

22. United Nations Development
Programme (above, n. 18)

23. Helmholtz Beijing Office,
'Rising Temperature Exacerbates
Shrinkage of Glaciers in Western
China', *Science News from Chinese
Media in November 2006*, Xunhua
Net, China Highlights, November
2006, www.intec-online.net/
uploads/media/China_Highlights-
2006_November.pdf

24. Brown, Lester R., 'China
Losing War with Advancing
Deserts', Earth Policy Institute, 5
August 2003, www.earth-
policy.org/Updates/Update26.htm

25. French, Howard W., 'China's
Growing Deserts are Suffocating
Korea', *New York Times*, 14 April
2002.

26. Yang, G.; Xiao, H.; and Tuo,
W., 'Black Windstorm in
Northwest China: A Case Study of
the Strong Sand-Dust Storm on
May 5 1993' in Yang, Y.; Squires, V.;
and Lu, Q. (eds), *Global Alarm:

Dust and Sandstorms from the
World's Drylands*, Asia Regional
Coordinating Unit, Secretariat of
the United Nations Convention to
Combat Desertification, Bangkok,
Thailand, 2001, chapter 3.

27. Lynas, Mark, *High Tide: How
Climate Crisis is Engulfing Our
Planet*, Harper Perennial, 2005,
p. 138.

28. United Nations Development
Programme (above, n. 18)

29. Pearce, Fred (above, n. 7)

30. Ibid.

31. International Water
Management Institute, 'The Socio-
Ecology of Groundwater in India',
2004, www.iwmi.cgiar.org/
waterpolicybriefing.files/
wpb04.doc

32. Brown, Lester, 'World Creating
Food Bubble Economy Based on
Unsustainable Use of Water', Earth
Policy Institute, 13 March 2003,
www.Earth-policy.org/Updates/
Update22.htm

33. Xinhua News Agency, 'Political
Advisors Call for Efforts to Save
"Dying" Sea', China View, 9 March
2006, http://news.xinhuanet.com/
english/2006-03/09/
content_4280616.htm

34. Gangulyiagra, Meenakshi, 'At
the Taj Mahal, Grime and
Grandeur', *Time* Magazine, Time
Inc, 10 September 2001,
www.time.com/time/magazine/
article/0,9171.1000714,00.html

35. Bashkin, Vladimir and
Radojevic, Miroslav, 'A Rain Check
on Asia', Royal Society of
Chemistry, 2001,
www.chemsoc.org/chembytes/
ezine/2001/bashkin_jun01.htm

36. Connor, Steve, 'Methane
Emissions Soar as China Booms',
The Independent, 28 September
2006, p. 26.

37. US Environmental Protection
Agency, 'International
Agreements: Stockholm
Convention on Persistent Organic
Pollutants (POPs)',
www.epa/gov/oppfead1/
international/agreements.htm

38. Watts, Jonathan, 'Rapid City
Growth Means China Faces
Rubbish Crisis by 2020', *The
Guardian Unlimited*, 10 January
2007,
http://environment.guardian.co.uk/
waste/story/0,,1986582,00.html

39. Zhao, Michael, 'Pollution Costs
Equal 10 Per Cent of China's
GDP', *Shanghai Daily*, 5 June
2006, http://chinadigitaltimes.net/
2006/06/pollution_costs_equal_
10_of_China's_gdp_shanghai_
daily.php

40. The Bhopal Medical Appeal
and Sambhavna Trust, 'What
Happened in Bhopal?' (summary),
www.bhopal.org/
whathappened.html

41. Coonan, Clifford, 'China's
Green Revolution', *The
Independent*, 23 November 2006,
pp. 36–37.

42. BOCOG, 'Green Olympics in
Beijing: BOCOG's Environmental
Efforts', Beijing Organizing
Committee for the Games of the
XXIX Olympiad, 3 July 2006,
http://en.beijing2008.cn/68/80/
article212028068.shtml

43. Coonan, Clifford (above,
n. 41)

44. Marven, Peter. 'Three Gorges
River Valley, China', *The
Disappearing World: 100 Things
Your Grandchildren May Never See*,
Part 2: Planet in Peril, *The
Independent*, 18 October 2005,
p. 14.

45. The South Asian, 'Repression
in Tipaimukh Project in Manipur',
17 December 2006,
www.thesouthasian.org/archives/
2006/repression_in_tipaimukh_
projec_1.html

46. Coles, Peter and Bavadam,
Lyla, 'A Barrage of Protest', *The
UNESCO Courier*, April 2000,
www.unesco.org/courier/
2000_04/uk

47. Karko, Kate, 'The Nomads of
Tibet', *The Disappearing World:
100 Things Your Grandchildren
May Never See*, Part 2: Planet in
Peril, *The Independent*, 18 October
2005, p. 37.

48. Organization of the Petroleum Exporting Countries, 'OPEC Share of World Crude Oil Reserves', 2004, www.opec.org/home/PowerPoint/Reserves/OPEC%20share.htm

49. World Resources Institute, 'Population, Health and Human Well-Being Data Tables: Trends in Mortality and Life Expectancy', EarthTrends: The Environmental Information Portal, 2003, http://Earthtrends.wri.org/text/population-health/datatable-68.html

50. United Nations Development Programme, '21: Energy and the Environment: Carbon Dioxide Emissions – Per Capita (metric tonnes)', *Human Development Report 2006: Beyond Scarcity: Power, Poverty and the Global Water Crisis*, http://hdr.undp.org/hdr2006/statisics/indicators/202.html

51. Sacquet, Anne, 'Industrial Pollution and Disasters', *World Atlas of Sustainable Development: Economic, Social and Environmental Data*, Editions Autrement, 2002, pp. 34–35.

52. 'Lebanese Oil Slick', *New Scientist*, 5 August 2006, p. 5.

53. Sacquet, Anne, 'Conflict', *World Atlas of Sustainable Development: Economic, Social and Environmental Data*, Editions Autrement, 2002, p. 28.

54. Marven, Peter, 'Wild Cedar Groves of Lebanon', *The Disappearing World: 100 Things Your Grandchildren May Never See*, Part 2: Planet in Peril, *The Independent*, 18 October 2005, p. 11.

55. McGrath, Kimberley A. and Travers, Bridget E. (eds), 'Agent Orange', *World of Invention* (2nd ed.), Thomson Gale, 1998.

56. Sacquet, Anne (above, n. 53)

57. World Wildlife Fund, 'WWF: 3 Really Scary Truths this Halloween', 27 October 2006, y125fd.bay125.hotmail.msn.com/gi-bin>

58. Huggler, Justin, '"Kick-boxing" Orang-utans are Flown Home to Borneo', *The Independent*, 23 November 2006, p. 38.

59. Morpurgo, Michael, 'Orang-utans', *The Disappearing World: 100 Things Your Grandchildren May Never See*, Part 2: Planet in Peril, *The Independent*, 18 October 2005, p. 10.

60. Wildlife Conservation Society, 'Orangutan Numbers Plummeting Worldwide: Species May Vanish from the Wild in Ten Years', 27 February 2001, www.wcs.org/353624/194744

61. Morpurgo, Michael, *Kensuke's Kingdom* (new ed.), Egmont, 2003.

62. Morpurgo, Michael (above, n. 59)

63. 'China Reports Panda Breeding Boom', BBC News, 17 November 2005, http://news.bbc.co.uk/2/hi/asia-pacific/4445318.stm

64. World Wildlife Fund, 'New Survey Reveals Nearly 1,600 Giant Pandas in the Wild' [press release], 10 June 2004, www.wwfchina.org/english/panda central/htm/wwf_at_work/panda_survey/press_release.htm

65. Liou, Caroline, 'China's Third National Panda Survey Helps Create a New Generation of Conservationists', WWF, 2004, www.wwfchina.org/english/pandacentral.htm/wwf_at_work/panda_survey/feature.htm

66. Ibid.

67. House of Commons, *International Whaling Commission*, House of Commons Hansard, United Kingdom Parliament, Column 499W-500W, 28 June 2000, www.publications.parliament,uk/pa/cm199900/cmhansard/vo000628/text/00628w02.htm

68. The Humane Society of the United States, 'Fisheries Factsheet', 2007, www.hsus.org/marine_mammals/what_are_the_issues/commerical_fisheries_and_marine_mammals/fisheries_factsheet.html

69. 'Japan Gains Key Whaling Victory', BBC News, 19 June 2006, http://news.bbc.co.uk/2/hi/science/nature/5093350.stm

70. Roach, John, 'Majority Votes to Legalize Whaling', National Geographic News, 19 June 2006, http://news.nationalgeographic.com/news/2006/06/060619-whaling-ban.html

71. Environmental Literacy Council, 'Indo-Burma', 2002, www.enviroliteracy.org/article.php/498.html

72. Environmental Literacy Council, 'Indonesia', 2002, www.enviroliteracy.org/article.php/493.html

73. Jones, Geraint, 'Parsi Funerals', *The Disappearing World: 100 Things Your Grandchildren May Never See*, Part 2: Planet in Peril, *The Independent*, 18 October 2005, p. 43.

74. IUCN, 'Asian Vultures – A Glimmer of Hope', *2006 IUCN Red List of Endangered Species*, International Union for Conservation of Nature and Natural Resources, 2006, www.iucn.org/themes/ssc/redlist2006/fighting_extinctioncrisis.htm

75. Langley, Nick, 'Vultures in India Continue to Decline – Though There are Encouraging Signs', BirdLife International, 2005, www.birdlife.org/news/news/2005/12/2005_review.html

76. Pearce, Fred (above, n. 7)

77. www.mahatmagandhi.org.in/quotes/quotes.jsp?link=qt

78. Friends of the Earth, 'FAQs: "I've heard that products containing palm oil are seriously damaging rainforests. How can I avoid such products?"', April 2005, www.foe.co.uk/resource/faqs/questions/palm_oil.html

Chapter 5: Africa

1. Quammen, David, 'The Human Footprint', *National Geographic* Special Issue: *Africa – Whatever You Thought, Think Again*, Vol 208, No 3, September 2005, p. 21.

2. Diamond, Jared, 'The Shape of Africa', *National Geographic*

Special Issue: *Africa – Whatever You Thought, Think Again*, Vol 208, No 3, September 2005, p. 29.

3. Ibid.

4. United Nations Environment Programme, 'New Report Underlines Africa's Vulnerability to Climate Change' [press release], 5 November 2006, www.unep.org/Documents.Multilingual/Default.asp?DocumentID=485&ArticleID=5409&l=en

5. Dowden, Richard, 'On Offer: A Huge Prize in a Land of Poverty', *The Independent*, 26 October 2006, p. 31.

6. Gwin, Peter, 'Making the Connection', *National Geographic* Special Issue: *Africa – Whatever You Thought, Think Again*, Vol 208, No 3, September 2005, p. 37.

7. www.moibrahimfoundation.org/mif_prize.html

8. Thornton, Philip, 'India Put on Hold as Africa Challenges to be the Latest Outsourcing Hotspot', *The Independent*, 6 June 2006, p. 36.

9. 'Africa: The Benefits and Dangers of These Gifts from the East' (Editorial), *The Independent*, 7 September 2006, p. 34.

10. Counsell, Simon, 'Africa's Rainforests for the Chop in World's Biggest Illegal Giveaway' [press release], Rainforest Foundation, 9 November 2005.

11. World Development Movement, 'Date with Climate Disaster – 8 January 2007' [press release], 8 January 2007, www.wdm.org.uk/news/climatecalendar08012007.htm

12. Bloomfield, Steve, 'Nomads with No Future: The Crisis in the Horn of Africa', *The Independent*, 8 September 2006, pp. 38–39.

13. Hollow, Mike (ed.), 'Climate Change: Voices', *Global Action*, Tearfund, Autumn 2006, pp. 6–7.

14. Selva, Meera, 'Drought Threatens the People and Wildlife of East Africa: On the Brink of Starvation', *The Independent*, 21 February 2006, p. 2.

15. Milmo, Cahal, 'Drought in Africa: Ethiopia's Bitter Harvest', *The Independent*, 24 October 2006, pp. 22–23.

16. Selva, Meera (above, n. 14)

17. Ekklesia, 'Churches Respond to Kenya Flood-Drought Dilemma', 7 November 2006, www.ekklesia.co.uk/content/news_syndication/article_06117kenya.shtml

18. Oxfam, 'The Sahara', www.oxfam.org.uk/coolplanet/ontheline/explore/nature/deserts/prtgeograph.htm

19. Arthur, Charles, 'Snows of Kilimanjaro Immortalised by Hemingway "Will Have Melted by 2020"', *The Independent*, 18 October 2002.

20. Ohio State University, 'Snows of Kilimanjaro Disappearing, Glacial Ice Loss Increasing', 13 February 2006, www.newswise.com/articles/view/518036

21. Oxfam, 'Desertification', www.oxfam.org.uk/coolplanet/ontheline/explore/nature/deserts/prtconserve_desertifcation.htm

22. Quaschning, Volker and Blanco Muriel, Manuel, 'Solar Power – Photovoltaics or Solar Thermal Power Plants?' VGB Congress Power Plants 2001, Brussels, 10–12 October 2001, www.volker-quaschning.de/downloads/VGB2001.pdf

23. Okafor, Ugo, 'African Deserts a Potential Clean Energy Goldmine?', www.africanarchitecture.blogspot.com/2006/04/african-deserts-potential-clean-energy.html

24. Lean, Geoffrey, 'Our Rivers are Drying to Death', *The Independent on Sunday*, 12 March 2006, p. 16.

25. Selva, Meera (above, n. 14)

26. Masibo, Joseph, 'Masai Mara (Kichwa Tembo) 9/22/2005', Migration Update, www.wildwatch.com/sightings/migration.asp

27. Masibo, Joseph, Masai Mara (Kichwa Tembo) 8/23/2005', Migration Update,

www.wildwatch.com/sightings/migration.asp

28. Colours of the Nile, 'Why the Colours of the Nile Expedition is Happening', www.niletrip.com/purpose.html

29. Selva, Meera (above, n. 14)

30. African Wildlife Foundation, 'Anthrax Cause of Death of Grevy's Zebra of Samburu Heartland', 28 December 2005, www.awf.org/news/66476

31. Taylor, Jerome, 'Climate Change May Drive Lemurs to Extinction', *The Independent*, 30 September 2006, p. 36.

32. Stony Brook University, NY, 'Rain Key to Survival of Baby Lemurs' [press release], 14 November 2005, http://news.mongabay.com/2005/1114-wildmadagasgar.html

33. Shea, Neil, 'Bush Meat', *National Geographic* Special Issue: *Africa – Whatever You Thought, Think Again*, Vol 208, No 3, September 2005, p. 41.

34. FAO Regional Office for Africa, 'Promoting the Business of Grasscutter Production in West-Africa', 12 December 2005, www.fao.org/world/regional/raf/news/events_detail_en.asp?event_id=32757&year=2005

35. African Conservation Foundation, 'Overview', www.africanconservation.org/aboutacf.html

36. WWF, 'Africa: Wildlife, Habitats and Threats', www.wwf.org.uk/core/wildlife/fs_0000000037.asp

37. 'Gold Mining "Hits" Poor Countries', BBC News, 11 May 2006, www.news.bbc.co.uk/2/hi/in_depth/4760707.stm

38. 'Gold Mining Threatens Environment and Communities in East Africa', *Drillbits and Tailings*, Vol 5, No 15, 19 September 2000, www.moles.org/ProjectUnderground/drillbits/5_15/2.html

39. Garbutt, Nick, 'A Golden Curse', *BBC Wildlife*, July 2002.

40. Connor, Steve, 'Rabies Vaccine May Save Rarest Wolf from Extinction', *The Independent*, 12 October 2006, p. 9.

41. Oxford University, 'Targeted Vaccine Programme Cuts Rabies in Endangered Ethiopian Wolves' [press release], 12 October 2006, www.admin.ox.ac.uk/po/061012.shtml

42. Schaller, George, 'Buying a Mobile? First Read This…', *BBC Wildlife*, May 2001.

Chapter 6: North America

1. 'Asia-Pacific Countries Join US, Australia to Control Climate', Environment News Service, 7 February 2006, www.ens-newswire.com/index.asp

2. Matthiessen, Peter, '*Time* 100: Rachel Carson', 29 March 1999, www.tome.com/time/time100/scientist/profile/carson.html

3. Office of the Press Secretary, 'President Bush Delivers State of the Union Address', The White House, 31 January 2006, www.whitehouse.gov/news/releases/2006/01/20060131-10.html

4. Cornwall, Rupert, 'Evangelists' Coalition Demands White House Acts on Environment', *The Independent*, 9 February 2006, p. 28.

5. Britt, Robert Ray, 'Ground Frozen Since Ice Age Thaws and Collapses', 20 December 2005, www.livescience.com/environment/51220_permafrost.html

6. Hansen, Jim, 'On the Edge: Greenland Ice Cap Breaking up at Twice the Rate it was Five Years Ago, Says Scientist Bush Tried to Gag', *The Independent*, 17 February 2006, p. 1.

7. Connor, Steve, 'Sea Levels Likely to Rise Much Faster Than was Predicted', *The Independent*, 7 February 2006, p. 2.

8. Watson, Robert et al., *An Assessment of the Intergovernmental Panel on Climate Change. Summary for Policymakers*, Summary approved in detail at IPCC Plenary XVIII (Wembley, United Kingdom, 24–29 September 2001), www.ipcc-ch/pub/un/syreng/spm.pdf

9. Connor, Steve (above, n. 7)

10. Hansen, Jim, 'On the Edge: Scientist Says "We Don't Have Much Time"', *The Independent*, 17 February 2006, p. 2.

11. Jones, Geraint, 'The Inuit', *The Disappearing World: 100 Things Your Grandchildren May Never See*, Part 2: Planet in Peril, *The Independent*, 18 October 2005, p. 5.

12. Lean, Geoffrey, 'Mr Cameron Heads for Arctic Wastes, and a Cold Wind Blows for the Prime Minister', *The Independent on Sunday*, 16 April 2006.

13. Lean, Geoffrey, 'Air Conditioning for Eskimos as the Arctic Warms up', *The Independent on Sunday*, 27 August 2006, p. 40.

14. Lynas, Mark, 'Meltdown', *Guardian Unlimited*, 14 February 2004, www.guardian.co.uk/weekend/story/0,3605,119981,00.html

15. Murphy, Kim, 'Close-up Amid Global-Warming Debate, Alaska's Landscape Shifts', *LA Times*, 8 July 2002.

16. Lynas, Mark (above, n. 14)

17. Lean, Geoffrey (above, n. 13)

18. 'Arctic Report', *BBC 1 News*, 17 November 2005.

19. Amstrup, Steven C. et al., 'Recent Observations of Intraspecific Predation and Cannabalism Among Polar Bears in the Southern Beaufort Sea', *Polar Biology*, Springer Berlin/Heidelberg, 27 April 2006.

20. Hansen, Jim (above, n. 10)

21. Connor, Steve (above, n. 7)

22. Hansen, Jim (above, n. 10)

23. Parks Canada Agency, 'The Climate is Changing our National Parks', Government of Canada, 4 May 2005, www.pc.gc.ca/docs/v-g/ie-ei/cc/index e.asp

24. Usbourne, David, 'How the West was Withered', *The Independent*, 27 July 2006, p. 24.

25. Saunders, Stephen; Easley, Tom; Spencer, Theo, *Losing Ground: Western National Parks Endangered by Climate Change*, NRDC Report, July 2006.

26. Parks Canada Agency, 'The Climate is Changing our National Parks: Impacts on Arctic Parks', Government of Canada, 20 May 2005, www.pc.gc.ca/docs/v-g/ie-ei/cc/repurcussions-impacts1 e.asp

27. Mountain Justice Summer, 'What is Mountaintop Removal Mining?', http://mountainjusticesummer.org/facts/steps.php

28. Mountain Justice Summer, 'Reclaiming Appalachia' [press release], 15 August 2005, http://mountainjusticesummer.org/actions/mto/press_releases/zeb_mountain.php

29. '1989: Exxon Valdez Creates Oil Slick Disaster', *On This Day: 24 March*, BBC News, http://news.bbc.co.uk/onthisday/hi/dates/stories/march/24/newsid_4231000/4231971.stm

30. 'Exxon Valdez Disaster Haunts Alaska 14 years on', *The Washington Post* and agencies, 16 January 2003, www.smh.au/cgi-bin/common/popupPrintArticle.pl?path=/articles/2003/01/15/1042520672374.html

31. Gumbel, Andrew, 'Burst Oil Pipeline Causes "Catastrophe" in Alaska', *The Independent*, 14 March 2006.

32. Cornwell, Rupert, 'US Congressman Savages BP for "Years of Neglect"', *The Independent*, 8 September 2006, p. 48.

33. Foley, Stephen, 'BP Hopes to Start Prudhoe Oil Flow', *The Independent*, 13 September 2006, p. 43.

34. State of Alaska Department of Environmental Conservation, Home Page, www.dec.ak.us

35. State of Alaska Department of Environmental Conservation, Division of Spill Prevention and Response, www.dec.ak.us.spar/index.htm

36. Kidport Reference Library, 'Social Studies: Alaska State Geography', www.kidport.com/REFLIB/UsaGeography/Facts/Alaska.htm

37. Division of Wildlife Conservation, 'State of Alaska Species of Special Concern', Alaska Department of Fish and Game, 2006, www.wildlife.alaska.gov/index.cfm?adfg=endangered.concern

38. Division of Wildlife Conservation, 'Alaska's Non-endangered Species', Alaska Department of Fish and Game, 2006, www.wildlife.alaska.gov/index.cfm?adfg=endangered.non

39. Cornwell, Rupert, 'America Must End its "Addiction to Oil"', Says Bush', The Independent, 2 February 2006, pp. 34–35.

40. Cornwell, Rupert, 'So Has the President Gone Green? Not Just Yet?' [analysis], The Independent, 2 February 2006, p. 34.

41. Union of Concerned Scientists, 'Global Warming Solutions', 2005, www.ucsusa.org/global_warming/solutions

42. Gumbel, Andrew, 'California Sets Global Example with Historic Deal to Reduce Emissions', The Independent, 1 September 2006, pp. 2–3.

43. Gumbel, Andrew, 'How American Cities Have Bypassed Bush on Kyoto', The Independent, 1 September 2006, p. 2.

44. Grammatico, Michael, 'Major Hurricanes (Category 3 or Higher) to Enter the Gulf Coast (1900–2005)', May 2006, www.geocities.com/hurricaneme/gulfcoast.htm

45. Horizon: The Lost City of New Orleans, BBC 2, 2 February 2006.

46. McRae, Hamish, 'Boom and Bust: A Tale of Two Cities', The Independent, 30 August 2006, p. 31.

47. Nature Conservancy News Room, 'Nature Conservancy Partners Propose Renewed Coastal Conservation in the Wake of Hurricane Katrina', Letter to the President from Presidents and CEOs of The Nature Conservancy, National Wildlife Federation, Environmental Defense, and National Audubon Society, 12 September 2005, www.nature.org/pressroom/press/press2083.html

48. Gumbel, Andrew, 'Mississippi Turning', The Independent, 20 September 2006, pp. 26–27.

49. Drye, Willie, 'Mild US Hurricane Season Defied Predictions', National Geographic News, 30 November 2006, http://news.nationalgeographic.com/news/2006/11/061129-hurricane-season.html

50. BirdLife International, 'Objective: The Important Bird Areas in the Americas', 2006, www.birdlife.org/action/science/sites/american_ibas/index.html

51. BirdLife International, 'Fifth Festival for Caribbean Birds', 20 April 2006, www.birdlife.org/news/news/2006/04/cebf.html

52. 'US, Jamaica Sign US$16m Debt-for-Nature Swap Deal', The Jamaica Observer (internet edition), 1 October 2004, www.jamaicaobserver.com/news/html/

53. The Nature Conservancy, 'The Nature Conservancy Contributes to $16 Million Jamaica and US Debt-for-Nature Swap', 2006, www.nature.org/pressroom/press/press1621.html

54. The Nature Conservancy, 'Caribbean', 2006, www.nature.org/wherewework/caribbean

55. Cornwell, Rupert, 'Canada Signs Deal with Loggers to Save Ancient Rainforest', The Independent, 8 February 2006.

56. Ibid.

57. 'Conflict to Consensus: British Columbia Protects Great Bear Rainforest', Environment News Service, 8 February 2006, www.ens-newswire.com/ens/feb2006/2006-02-08-08.asp

58. Medicine Eagle, Brooke, 'Sacred Ecology and Native American Spirituality', www.medicine-eagle.com/6_4.html

Chapter 7: South America

1. Walker, Barry, 'The Birds of the Manu Biosphere Reserve', Barry Walker Manu Expedition, 2000, www.andeantravelweb.com/peru/amazon/manubirdwatching.html

2. Connor, Steve, 'Earth's Final Frontiers', The Independent, 9 February 2006, p. 40.

3. Hebert, John R., 'The Map That Named America: How the Library of Congress Acquired the 1507 Waldseemuller Map of the World', http://usembassy.state.gov/posts/in1/wwwhspjanfeb065.html

4. BirdLife International, 'BirdLife IBA Factsheet: PE125 Manu', 2006, www.birdlife.org/datazone/sites/index.html?action=SitHTMDetails.asp&sid=14920&m=0

5. Walker, Barry, 'The Birds of the Manu Biosphere Reserve: The Greatest Concentration of Species on Earth!', 7 February 2006, gorp.away.com/gorp/location/latamer/peru/manubio.htm

6. 'Tropical Rainforest', www.blueplanetbiomes.org/rainforest.htm

7. Raintree Nutrition, 'Rainforest Facts: The Disappearing Rainforest', 2006, www.rain-tree.com/facts.htm

8. 'The Jungle Beat', This World documentary series, BBC 2, 17 November 2005.

9. 'Monkey Puzzle Forests', The Disappearing World: 100 Things Your Grandchildren May Never See Part 2: Planet in Peril, The Independent, 18 October 2005, p. 3

10. McCarthy, Michael and Buncombe, Andrew, 'The Rape of the Rainforest… and the Man Behind It', The Independent, 20 May 2005.

11. 'La Selva Jungle Lodge Highlights: The Butterfly Farm', www.laselvajunglelodge.com/experince/experiences1.html

12. Philips, Tom, 'Brazil to Call for Global Fund to Save Rainforest and Cut Climate Change', The Guardian, 20 October 2006.

13. Conservation International, 'Amazonia', 2006, www.con/CIWEB/regions/priorityareas/wilderness/amazonia.xml

14. Lean, Geoffrey, 'Our Rivers are Drying to Death', *The Independent on Sunday*, 12 March 2006, p. 17.

15. Sauven, John, 'The Odd Couple', *The Guardian Unlimited*, 2 August 2006, http://environment.guardian.co.uk/conservation/story/0,,1834909,00.html

16. Howden, Daniel, 'How the Amazon's Indigenous People are Holding Back the "Arc of Destruction"', *The Independent*, 11 August 2006, p. 33.

17. Lean, Geoffrey, 'Climate Crisis: A Year to Live', *The Independent on Sunday*, 23 July 2006, pp. 28–29.

18. Lean, Geoffrey and Pearce, Fred, 'Amazon Rainforest "Could Become a Desert"', *The Independent on Sunday*, 23 July 2006, p. 12.

19. Marinebio.org, '*Inia geoffrensis* - Amazon River Dolphin', http://marinebio.org/species.asp?id=337

20. Amazon Conservation Association, 'Amazon Rivers Program', www.amazonconservation.org/home/amazonrivers.html

21. Rainforest Portal, 'Action Alert: Massive Gas Pipeline to Pierce the Amazon', Ecological Internet, 22 March 2006, www.rainforestportal.org/alerts/send.asp?id=amazon_pipeline

22. Ibid.

23. Ibid.

24. Conover, Ted, 'Peru's Long Haul: Highway to Riches or Ruin?', *National Geographic*, June 2003, www.magma.nationalgeographic.com/ngm/0306/feature5

25. Butler, Tina, 'Asphalt and Soya Dreams: Two Oceans, Two Countries and the Transoceanica', 7 April 2005, http://news.mongabay.com/2005/0417a-tina_butler.html

26. Greenpeace International, 'Soya Traders Agree to a Moratorium on Amazon Deforestation Following Customer Pressure' [press release], 25 July 2006, www.greenpeace.org/international/press/releases/soya-traders-agree-to-a-moratorium…

27. Galapagos Conservation Trust, 'Explore Galapagos', 7 February 2005, www.cnn.com/EARTH/9803/12/galapagos

28. Galapagos Conservation Trust, 'Why Conserve the Galapagos?', 2005, www.gct.org/why.html

29. Howden, Daniel, 'Darwin Finch Could Disappear from Galapagos Islands', *The Independent*, 22 September 2006, p. 39.

30. Galapagos Conservation Trust, 'The Isabela Project Achieves the Impossible', July 2006, www.gct.org/jul06_2.html

31. Galapagos Conservancy, 'Conservation Challenges', www.galapagos.org/conservation/challenges.html

32. Butler, Rhett A., 'Amazon Deforestation Slows in Brazil in 2005', 5 December 2005, http://news.mongabay.com/2005/1205-amazon.html

33. McCarthy, Michael and Buncombe, Andrew (above, n. 10)

34. Greenpeace International, 'Soya Blazes a Trail through the Amazon', 12 December 2003, www.greenpeace.org/international/news/soy-blazes-through-the-amazon

35. Sauven, John, 'The Odd Couple', *The Guardian Unlimited*, 2 August 2006, http://environment.guardian.co.uk/conservation/story/0,,1834909,00.html

36. Greenpeace International (above, n. 26)

37. Regalado, Antonio, 'The Ukukus Wonder Why a Sacred Glacier Melts in Peru's Andes', *The Wall Street Journal*, 17 June 2005, p. A1.

38. Lynas, Mark, *High Tide: How Climate Crisis is Engulfing Our Planet*, Harper Perennial, 2005, p. 208.

39. Enever, Andrew, 'Bolivian Glaciers Shrinking Fast', BBC News, 10 December 2002, http://news.bbc.co.uk/1/hi/sci/tech/2559633.stm

40. Ibid.

41. 'Melting Glaciers Threaten Peru', BBC News, 9 October 2003, http://news.bbc.co.uk/1/hi/world/americas/3172572.stm

42. 'Satellite Watches Disaster Hazard', BBC News, 17 April 2003, http://news.bbc.co.uk/1/hi/sci/tech/2951093.stm

43. Science Daily, 'Race to Halt Global Amphibian Crisis Boosted by Rediscovery of Endangered Colombian Frogs', Source: Conservation International, Science Daily, 6 June 2006, www.sciencedaily.com/releases/2006/06/060606183033.htm

44. Mongabay, '"Extinct" frog rediscovered in Colombia', Source: Conservation International, Mongabay, 18 May, 2006, http://news.mongabay.com/2006/0517-ci.html

45. Ibid.

46. Greenpeace International (above, n. 26)

47. BirdLife International, www.birdlife.org/worldwide/index.html

Chapter 8: Antarctica

1. CIA, 'Antarctica', *The World Factbook* [online edition], CIA, 13 June 2006, www.cia.gov/cia/publications/factbook/geos/ay.html

2. Zoom School, 'Antarctica: Map and Geographic Information', EnchantedLearning.com, 2000–2005, www.allaboutnature.com/school/Antarctica/Map.shtml

3. Ibid.

4. Welch, Charles, 'Antarctica', www.solcomhouse.com/Antarctica.htm

5. CIA (above, n. 1)

6. 'Newton Ask a Scientist: Coldest Temperature', Environmental Earth Science Archive, Office of Science, US Department of Energy, August 2006, www.newton.dep.anl.gov/asksci/env99/env040.htm

7. NSIDC, 'Antarctic Ice Shelves and Icebergs in the News: Antarctic Ice Shelf Collapses, March 2002' [animation of Larsen B breakup, 31 January to 7 March 2002], National Snow and Ice Data Center, http://nsidc.org/iceshelves/larsenb2002/animation.html

8. Fricker, Helen Amanda; Scambos, Ted; Bindschadler, Robert et al., 'An Active Subglacial Water System in West Antarctica Mapped from Space', Express Research Articles: 10.1126/science.1136897, *Science* magazine, American Association for the Advancement of Science, published online 15 February 2007, www.sciencemag.org/scienceexpress/recent.dtl

9. Welch, Charles (above, n. 4)

10. Maw, Marianne, 'Sierra Club Honours Antarctica Activist' [press release], 15 November 2004, www.asoc.org/Documents/Earth%care%20Release111504.pdf

11. Atkisson, Alan, 'The Antarctica Project', Context Institute, Spring 1991, p. 35, www.context.org/ICLIB/IC28/ Barnes.htm

12. Australian Government Antarctic Division, 'Full Text of the Antarctic Treaty, 1961', www.aad.gov.au/default.asp?casid=1187

13. Greenpeace Antarctica, 'Greenpeace Applauds Antarctic Protection Victory' [press release], 14 January 1998, http://archive.greenpeace.org/comms/98/antarctic/press/14january98.html

14. Australian Government Antarctic Division, 'Introducing the Madrid Protocol', www.aad.gov.au/default.asp?casid=825

15. British Antarctic Survey, 'Protocol on Environmental Protection to the Antarctic Treaty, Article 11: Committee for Environmental Protection', British Antarctic Survey, www.antarctica.ac.uk/aboutantarctic/treaty/protocol.html

16. Greenpeace Antarctica, 'Historic Antarctic Protection Agreement Becomes Law' [press release], 16 December 1997, http://archive.greenpeace.org/comms/98/antarctic/press/16december97.html

17. Turner, John et al., 'Significant Warming of the Antarctic Winter Troposphere', *Science*, 30 March 2006.

18. Roach, John, 'Antarctica's Atmosphere Warming Dramatically, Study Finds', National Geographic News, 30 March 2006, http://news.nationalgeographic.com/news/2006/03/0330_060330_antarctica_2.html

19. Fildes, Jonathan, 'Unexpected Warming in Antarctica', BBC News, 30 March 2006, http://news.bbc.co.uk/2/hi/science/nature/4857832.stm

20. Turner, John et al. (above, n. 17)

21. Roach, John (above, n. 18)

22. Connor, Steve, 'Ice Bubbles Reveal Biggest Rise in CO_2 for 800,000 Years', *The Independent*, 5 September 2006, p. 6.

23. Ibid.

24. Gleason, Karin L., 'Science: The Antarctic Ozone Hole', NOAA, updated 3 March 2006, www.ozonelayer.noaa.gov/science/ozhole.htm

25. Simpson, Sarah, 'A Push from Above: The Ozone Hole May be Stirring up Antarctica's Climate', *Scientific American*, August 2002, www.sciam.com/article.cfm?articleID=00078FDB-D9ED-1D29-97CA809EC588EEDF&sc=1100322

26. US Environmental Protection Agency, 'The Antarctic Ozone Hole', 8 March 2006, www.epa.gov/ozone/science/hole/index.html

27. 'Record Amount of Ozone Lost over Antarctica', Deutsche Presse-Agentur, Reuters, 4 October 2006, www.smh.com/au/news/world/record-amount-of-ozone-lost-over-antarctica/2006/10/03/1159641325829.html

28. Zehner, Klaus, 'European Space Agency: Statement', Frascati, Italy, 2 October 2006.

29. Marshall G.J.; Orr A.; van Lipzig N.P.M. et al., 'The Impact of a Changing Southern Hemisphere Annular Mode on Antarctic Peninsula Summer Temperatures', *Journal of Climate*, 2006, Vol 19: 5388*5404.

30. Lean, Geoffrey, 'Cracking up: Ice Turning to Water, Glaciers on the Move – and a Planet in Peril', *The Independent on Sunday*, 22 October, 2006, pp. 28–29.

31. Dinar, Athena, 'First Direct Evidence that Human Activity is Linked to Antarctic Ice Shelf Collapse' [press release], British Antarctic Survey, 16 October 2006, www.antarctica.ac.uk/News_and_Information/Press_Releases/story.php?id=293

32. Ibid.

33. Greenpeace, 'Antarctic Report: Short Background on Antarctica', http://archive.greenpeace.org/comms/98/antarctic/report/background.html

34. Welch, Charles (above, n. 4)

35. CIA (above, n. 1)

36. Ramesh, Randeep, 'Blow to Plan for Polar Conservation Zone as India Joins the Cold Rush: New Research Base Would Add to Human Pressure on Isolated Area, Environmentalists Fear', *The Guardian Unlimited*, 11 August 2006, http://environment.guardian.co.uk/conservation/story/0,,1845043,00.html

37. Sladen, W.J.L.; Menzie, C.M.; and Reichel, W.L., 'DDT Residues in Adelie Penguins and a Crabeater Seal from Antarctica:

Ecological Implications', *Nature*, No 210, 1966, pp. 670–71.

38. Cherry-Garrard, Apsley, *The Worst Journey in the World*, Hunt & Roskell, 1922.

39. Olliver, Narena, 'Emperor Penguin', New Zealand Birds, Ltd, 2005, www.nzbirds.com/birds/emperorpenguin.html

40. West, Peter, 'Giant Icebergs, Unprecedented Ice Conditions Threaten Antarctic Penguin Colonies', National Science Federation, 26 December 2001, www.nsf.gov/od/lpa/news/press/01/pr01108.htm

41. Ibid.

42. Ibid.

43. Williams, Jack, 'Sea Ice Threatens Some Antarctic Penguins', *USA Today*, 28 December 2001, www.usatoday.com/news/science/cold-science/2001-12-28-penguins.htm

44. McCarthy, Michael, 'Albatross', *The Disappearing World: 100 Things Your Grandchildren May Never See*, Part 2: Planet in Peril, *The Independent*, 18 October 2005, pp. 6–7.

45. RSPB, 'Save the Albatross', 2006, www.onceextinct.com/squid

46. WWF-Australia, 'WWF-Australia and Peregrine Shipping Announce New Partnership for Albatross Conservation', 27 October 2005, www.wwf.org.au/News-and-information/News-room/View-news/197

47. West, Peter, 'Emperor Penguin Colony Struggling with Iceberg Blockade', National Science Federation, 7 November 2002, www.nsf.gov/od/lpa/news/02/pro291.htm

48. Funded by the National Science Foundation, Gerald Kooyman and Paul Ponganis of the Scripps Institution of Oceanography in La Jolla, California, will research the health of Cape Crozier's emperor penguin colony and compare notes

with David Ainley of H.T. Harvey & Associates, of San Jose, California, who has conducted a long-term study on adelie penguins and is monitoring the effects of the icebergs on their colonies.

49. British Antarctic Survey, 'Tourism and Non-governmental Activities', National Environment Research Council/British Antarctic Survey, 2004, last updated 11 September 2006, www.antarctica.ac.uk/About_BAS/Cambridge/Divisions/EID/Environment/framework/tourismnga.html

50. Pfeiffer, S. and Peter, H., 'Ecological Studies Toward the Management of an Antarctic Tourist Landing Site (Penguin Island, South Shetland Islands)', *Polar Record* (2004), 40: 345–353, Cambridge University Press, published online by Cambridge University Press, 12 October 2004.

51. British Antarctic Survey (above, n. 49)

52. Kelly, Annie, 'Polar Crises: Cold Logic', *The Guardian Unlimited*, 1 February 2006, http://society.guardian.co.uk/societyguardian/story/0,,1698833,00.html

53. British Antarctic Survey (above, n. 15)

54. ATCM Recommendation XVII-1 (1994) provides 'Guidance for Visitors to the Antarctic'. Further, site-specific guidance for visitors is currently being developed.

55. Landau, Denise, 'About IAATO', Letter from the Executive Director, www.iaato/about

56. 'New Sea Life Species Discovered in Antarctica', Spiegel Online International, 26 February 2007, www.spiegel.de/international/0,1518,468742,00.html

57. 'New Sea Life Species Discovered in Antarctica: Photo Gallery', Spiegel Online International, 26 February 2007, 13 photos, www.spiegel.de/international/0,1518,468742,00.html

58. Alfred Wegener Institute for Polar and Marine Research, 'Antarctic Research within the International Polar Year IPY 2007/2008', 20 December 2006, www.awi.de/en/news/press_releases/detail/item/antarctic_research_within_the_international_polar_year_ipy_20072008

59. 'Antarctic Ice Melt Reveals Exotic Creatures', Reuters, 26 February 2007, www.cnn.com/2007/TECH/science/02/25/antarctica.icecreatures.reut

60. 'New Sea Life Species Discovered in Antarctica: Photo Gallery' (above, n. 57), photo 7.

61. Murray, C. and Jabour, J., 'Independent Expeditions and Antarctic Tourism Policy', Polar Record (2004), 40: 309-317, Cambridge University Press, published online by Cambridge University Press, 12 October 2004.

Chapter 9: Europe

1. EU, 'Activities of the European Union: Environment', Europa, 2006, http://europa.eu/pol/env/index_en.htm

2. European Organisation for the Exploitation of Meteorological Satellites, 'Drought in Europe', 7 March 2006, www.eumetsat.int/Home/Main/Media/News/005280?1=en

3. Bisgrove, R. and Hadley, P., *Gardening in the Global Greenhouse: The Impacts of Climate Change on Gardens in the UK*, Technical Report 2002, The UK Climate Impacts Programme, Oxford, 2002.

4. House of Commons Hansard, Written Answers for 18 Jan 2007 (pt 0003), Houses of Parliament, 2007, www.publications.parliament.uk/pa/cm200607/cmhansard/cm070118/text/70118w003.htm

5. Byrne, Patrick, 'Beauty Spots May Go to Save Land', BBC News, 15 January 2004, http://news.bbc.co.uk/1/hi/england/essex/3401011.stm

6. Howden, Daniel; Buncombe, Andrew; and Huggler, Justin, 'From Alaska to Australia, the World is Changing in Front of Us', *The Independent*, 15 September 2006, p. 2.

7. 'Inside Out: Protecting London', BBC London, 20 October 2005, www.bbc.co.uk/london/content/articles/2005/10/20/insideout_flood_feature.shtml

8. Churchill, Winston, 'Sinews of Peace', Speech made at Westminster College, Fulton, Missouri on 5 March 1946, www.historyguide.org/europe/churchill.html

9. Pohl, Otto, 'Gorbachev Pushes Plan to Turn Iron Curtain into Parkland', *The New York Times*, 26 July 2003, p. 1.

10. Woodard, Colin, 'Iron Curtain – Minefield to Greenbelt', *Christian Science Monitor*, www.csmonitor.com/2005/0428/p14501-sten.html

11. Pohl, Otto (above, n. 9)

12. Goossens, Y. and Meneghini, G.P., 'European Parliament Fact Sheets 4.9.9. Industrial Risks: Dangerous Substances and Technologies', European Parliament, September 2006, www.europarl.europa.eu/facts/4_9_9_en.htm

13. The Wildfowl and Wetlands Trust, 'Peter Scott', www.wwt.org.uk/about/Peter%20Scott.pdf

14. EUROPA, 'Emission Trading Scheme (EU ETS)', *Environment*, updated 23 March 2007, http://ec.europa.eu/environment/climat/emission.htm

15. EUROPA, 'Emissions Trading – National Allocation Plans', *Environment*, updated 19 January 2007, http://ec.europa.eu/environment/climat/emission_plans.htm

16. UNFCCC, 'The Mechanisms Under the Kyoto Protocol: The Clean Development Mechanism, Joint Implementation and Emissions Trading', http://unfccc.int/kyoto_protocol/mechanisms/items/1673.php

17. EUROPA, 'Emissions Trading: Commission Sets Out Guidance on National Allocations for 2008–2012' [press release], Brussels, 9 January 2006, Reference: IP/06/o9, http://europa/eu/rapid/pressReleaseAction.do?reference=IP/06/9&format=H

18. 'EU Emissions Trading Scheme', EurActiv.com, updated 23 March 2007, www.euractiv.com/en/sustainability/eu-emissions-trading-scheme/article-133629

19. EUROPA, 'Chemical Accidents (Seveso ii) – Prevention, Preparedness and Response', *Environment*, 28 November 2006, http://ec.europa.eu/environment/seveso/index.htm

20. Haigh, N. and von Moltke, K., 'The European Community: An Environmental Force', *EPA Journal*, Vol 16, No 4, 1990, pp. 58–60.

21. Zwingle, Erla, 'Meltdown: The Alps Under Pressure', *National Geographic*, February 2006, www7.nationalgeographic.com/ngm/0602/feature6/index.html

22. WWF, 'Tourism in the Alps, Hard Choices Ahead', 23 March 2006, www.wwf/about_wwf/where_we_work/europe/what_we_do.alps/index.cfm?uNewsID=64940

23. 'Green Resort Guide: Verbier', Ski Club of Great Britain Ltd, 2007, www.skiclub.co.uk/skiclub/resorts/greenresorts/resort.asp?intContactID=44950

24. UN World Meteorological Organisation, 'European Winter – One of the Warmest on Record', 11 December 2006, www.wmo.ch/news/news.html

25. Organisation for Economic Co-operation and Development, 'OECD Warns Climate Change is Threatening Europe's Skiing Trade', 13 December 2006, www.oecd.org/document/22/0,2340,en_2649_201185_37825494_1_1_1_1,00.html

26. Marven, Peter, 'Edelweiss', *The Disappearing World: 100 Things Your Grandchildren May Never See*, Part 2: Planet in Peril, *The Independent*, 18 October 2005, p. 13.

27. 'Eiger Sheds Rock Mass', Swissinfor/Swiss Radio International, 14 July 2006, www.swissinfo.org/eng/front/detail/Eiger_sheds_rock_mass.html

28. Dousset, B., 'Surface Temperatures Variability of the Paris Basin During the 2003 Heat Wave, Derived from Satellite Multi-sensors Observation' [Abstract], NOAA, www.cosis.net/abstracts/EMS05/00514/EMSO5-A-00514-1.pdf

29. Dorozynski, Alexander, 'Heat Wave Triggers Political Conflict as French Death Rates Rise', BMJ Publishing Group, 23 August 2003, No 327, p. 411, www.bmj.com/cgi/content/full/327/7412/411

30. Dhainaut, Jean-Francois; Claessens, Yann-Erick; Ginsburg, Christine et al., 'Unprecedented Heat-related Deaths During the 2003 Heat Wave in Paris: Consequences on Emergency Departments', *Critical Care*, Vol 8, No 1, BioMed Central Ltd, 2004, pp. 1–2, www.pubmedcentral.nih.gov/articlerender.fcgi?artid=420061

31. 'No Relief for Sweltering Europe', BBC News, 9 August 2003, http://news.bbc.co.uk/1/hi/world/europe/3138763.stm

32. Meehl, Gerald A. and Tebaldi, Claudia, 'More Intense, More Frequent, and Longer Lasting Heat Waves in the 21st Century', *Science*, Vol 305, No 5686, 13 August 2004, pp. 994–97, www.sciencemag.org/cgi/content/full/305/5686/994

33. Ibid.

34. USInfo, 'Northlands: Fragile Ecosystems', US Department of State's Bureau of International Information Programs, http://usinfo.state.gov/products/pubs/biodiv/north.htm

35. 'Methane Bubbles Climate Trouble', BBC News, 7 September 2006, http://news.bbc.co.uk/2/hi/science/nature/5321046.stm

36. Environmental and Energy Study Institute, 'Rapid Thaw of Siberian Permafrost Threatens Major Methane Release', *Climate Change News*, 12 August 2005, www.eesi.org/publications/Newsletters/CCNews/8.12.05%20CCNews.htm

37. 'Study Says Methane a New Climate Threat', The Associated Press, 7 September 2006, www.heatisonline.org/contentserver/objecthandlers/index.cfm?id=6056&method=full

38. 'Methane Bubbles Climate Trouble' (above, n. 35)

39. McKie, Robin and Christian, Nick, 'Siberian Thaw to Speed up Global Warming', *The Guardian Unlimited*, 10 September 2006, http://observer.guardian.co.uk/world/story/0,,1869000,00.html

40. Arctic Council, 'Program for the Conservation of Arctic Flora and Fauna', Conservation of Arctic Flora and Fauna (CAFF), http://arcticportal.org/en/caff

41. Norway, The Official Site of the United States, 'New Act Protects Svalbard Wilderness', Norway Portal, 28 June 2002, www.norway.org/News/archive/2002/200202svalbard.htm

42. IPCC, 'Climate Change 2001 – Working Group II: Impacts, Adaptation and Vulnerability', Intergovernmental Panel on Climate Change, Chapter 13 Europe: 13.2.1.3. 'Coastal Zones', www.grida.no/climate/ipcc_tar/wg2/499.htm

43. Marven, Peter, 'Europe's Mediterranean Coastline', *The Disappearing World: 100 Things Your Grandchildren May Never See*, Part 2: Planet in Peril, *The Independent*, 18 October 2005, p. 38.

44. United Nations Economic Commission for Europe, 'Convention on Long-Range Transboundary Air Pollution:

Protocol on Persistent Organic Pollutants (POPs)', 2006, www.unece.org/env/irtap/pops_h1.htm

45. Stockholm Convention on Persistent Organic Pollutants, Stockholm, 22 May 2001, www.pops.int/documents/convtext/convtext_en.pdf

46. EUROPA, 'POPs – Persistent Organic Pollutants', *Environment*, 16 October 2006, http://ec.europa.eu/environment/pops/index_en.htm

47. IPCC (above, n. 42)

48. Traufetter, Gerald, 'Dutch Answer to Flooding: Build Houses that Swim', *Der Spiegel*, 26 September 2005, www.spiegel.de/international/spiegel/0,1518,377050,00.html

49. Hall, J.; Reeder, T.; Fu, G. et al., 'Tidal Flood Risk in London Under Stabilisation Scenarios', 2005, www.stabilsation2005.com/posters/Hall_Jim.pdf

50. ThamesWEB, 'Flood Defence: Living with the Tide', www.thameweb.com/topic.php?topic_name=Flood%20Defence

51. '10-mile Thames Flood Barrier Plan', BBC News, 10 January 2005, http://news.bbc.co.uk/1/hi/englan/london/4162905.stm

52. NOVA, 'TV Program Description: *Sinking City of Venice*', original PBS broadcast date 19 November 2002, www.pbs.org/wgbh/nova/venice/about.html

53. Bras, Rafael L.; Harleman, Donald R.F.; Rinaldo, Andrea et al., 'Obsolete? No. Necessary? Yes. The Gates Will Save Venice', *Eos*, Vol 83, No 20, American Geophysical Union, 14 May 2002.

54. American Geophysical Union, 'Scientists Debate Wisdom of Plan to Save Venice from Flooding' [press release], American Geophysical Union, 8 May 2002, www.agu.org/sci_sco/prrl/prr10218.html

55. Parfitt, Tom, 'Belarus Cuts off Russian Pipeline in Bitter Gas War', *Guardian Unlimited* Special Report: 'Oil and Petrol', 9 January 2007, www.guardian.co.uk.oil/story/0,,1985743,00.html

56. Parfitt, Tom, 'Russia Turns off Supplies to Ukraine in Payment Row, and EU Feels the Chill', *Guardian Unlimited* Special Report: 'Russia', 2 January 2006, www.guardian.co.uk/russia/article/0,,1676556,00.html

57. EUROPA, 'Treaty Establishing the European Atomic Energy Community (Euratom)', European Union, last updated 7 December 2004, http://europa.eu/scadplus/treaties/euratom_en.htm

58. Friends of the Earth Europe, 'Twenty Years after Chernobyl Disaster: "Nuclear Power? NO Thanks"' [press release], 25 April 2006, www.foeeurope.org/press/2006/joint_25_April_Chernobyl.htm

59. 'Q&A: Common Agricultural Policy', BBC News, 2 December 2005, http://news.bbc.co.uk/2/hi/europe/4407792.stm

60. European Commission, 'CAP Reform – a Long-term Perspective for Sustainable Agriculture', Agriculture and Rural Development, 26 June 2003, http://ec.europe.eu/agriculture/capreform/index_en.htm

61. Department for Environment, Food and Rural Affairs, 'Explanatory Memorandum to the Common Agricultural Policy Single Payment Set-Aside', 14 December 2005, www.opsi.gov.uk/si/em2005/uksiem_20053460_en.pdf

62. UNICEF, 'Over a Million Children in the Ukraine Live with Legacy of Chernobyl', 26 April 2004, www.unicef.org/uk/press/news_detail.asp?news_id=276

63. Swiss Agency for Development and Cooperation, 'Chernobyl 20 Years on: Lest We Forget', 2006, www.deza.admin.ch/index.php?navID=65935&langID=1

64. Scottish Green Party, 'Election: Chernobyl Anniversary – Greens Condemn Nuclear Power as Expensive, Dangerous and Dirty', Scottish Green Party, 26 April 2005, www.scottishgreens.org.uk/

65. World Health Organisation, 'World Health Organisation Report Explains the Health Impacts of the World's Worst-ever Civil Nuclear Accident' [press release], 13 April 2006, www.who.int/mediacentre/news/releases/2006/pr20/en/index.html

66. Greenpeace, 'Chernobyl Death Toll Grossly Underestimated', 18 April 2006, www.greenpeace.org/international/news/chernobyl-deaths-180406

67. 'EU Energy Summit: A New Start for Europe?', EurActiv, 13 March 2007, www.euractiv.com/en/energy/eu-energy-summit-new-start-europe/article-162432

68. Castle, Stephen, 'EU Ministers Deadlocked on Binding Target for Green Power', Independent News & Media Limited, 9 March 2007, http://news.independent.co.uk/europe/article2341339.ece

69. Castle, Stephen, 'Open Skies Pact "Will Worsen Climate Change"', The Independent, 22 March 2007, p. 24.

70. Ibid.

71. Grice, Andrew, 'Blair Hails "Historic Day" in Battle Against Climate Change', The Independent: 'The Climate Has Changed: A Special Issue on the Bill that Makes Action on Global Warming a Reality', 14 March 2007, p. 2.

72. Ibid.

73. Paterson, Tony, 'Bruno, the Problem Bear, Outstays Bavarian Welcome', Independent News and Media, 10 June 2006, http://news.independent.co.uk/europe/article754393.ece

74. Paterson, Tony, 'The Killing of Bruno: Act of Cruelty, or Bear Necessity?', Independent News and Media, 27 June 2006, http://news.independent.co.uk/europe/article1099175.ece

75. Schulman, Mark, 'Beware of Bear: Return of the Brown Bear to Switzerland', WWF, 24 November 2005, www.panda.org/news_facts/newsroom/features/index.cfm?unewsID=50840

76. WWF Global Species Programme, 'Slovenia to Embark on Massive Bear Hunt', 14 February 2007, www.panda.org/about_wwf/where_we_work/europe/what_we_do/mediterranean/news/index.cfm?uNewsID=94120

77. Cove, James and Rodgers, James, 'Concern over Europe "Snow Crisis"', BBC News, 17 December 2006, http://news.bbc.co.uk/2/hi/europe/6185345.stm

78. 'Insomniac Russian Bears Drop off at Last', The Scotsman, 9 January 2007, http://news.scotsman.com/latest.cfm?id=45412007

79. von Bredow, Rafaela, 'Surviving a False Spring', Spiegel Online International, 19 January 2007, www.spiegel.de/international/0,1518,460744,00.html

80. Dick, Gerald, 'Conflicting EU Funds: Pitting Conservation Against Unsustainable Development', WWF Global Species Programme, Wien, 2006, http://assets.panda.org/downloads/eu_conflicting_funds_report.pdf

81. EUROPA, 'Nature and Biodiversity Homepage: EU Nature Legislation', http://ec.europa.eu/environment/nature/home.htm

82. 'Animal Detail' page, Trotters World, 2006, www.trottersworld.com/lynx.html

83. Standing Committee of the Convention on the Conservation of European Wildlife and Natural Habitats, 'Recommendation No. 94 (2002) on Urgent Measures for the Conservation of the Iberian Lynx (Lynx pardinus)', Convention on the Conservation of European Wildlife and Habitats, adopted by the Standing Committee on 5 December 2002, www.lcie.org/Docs/Legislation/Rec94_2002.pdf

84. Standing Committee of the Convention on the Conservation of European Wildlife and Habitats, 'Recommendation No. 101 (2003) on the Implementation of the Pan-Alpine Conservation Strategy for the Lynx (PACS)', Convention on the Conservation of European Wildlife and Natural Habitats, adopted by the Standing Committee on 4 December 2003, www.lcie.org/Docs/Legislation/Rec101_2003.pdf

85. Mapes, Terri, 'Wildlife in Scandinavia – Animals in the Scandinavian Wilderness', About Inc, 2007, http://goscandinavia.about.com/od/knowledgesafety/p/scanwildlife.htm

86. Council of Europe, Convention on the Conservation of European Wildlife and Natural Habitats, Bern, 19.IX.1979, http://conventions.coe.int/Treaty/EN/Treaties/Html/104.htm

87. Dick, Gerald, 'The Status of the Wolf (Canis lupus) in Europe: Amendments: Switzerland Proposal to Pass Cani lupus from Appendix II to Appendix III of the Convention', Convention on the Conservation of European Wildlife and Natural Habitats Standing Committee, 26th meeting, Strasbourg, 27–30 November 2006, Global Species Programme, WWF International, p. 5, www.coe.int/t/e/cultural_co-operation/environment/nature_and_biological_diversity/nature_protection/sc26_int04_en.pdf

88. Tisdall, Jonathan, 'Norway's Wolf Claim Unsupported', Aftenposten English web desk, 28 January 2005, www.aftenposten.no/english/local/article958181.ece>

89. Dick, Gerald (above, n. 87)

90. McCarthy, Michael, 'Mediterranean Monk Seal', The Disappearing World: 100 Things Your Grandchildren May Never See Part 2: Planet in Peril, The Independent, 18 October 2005, p. 46.

91. WWF, *Fish Dish: Exposing the Unacceptable Face of Seafood*, September 2006.

92. Kelbie, Paul, 'Appetite for Fish Spells Disaster for Europe's Stocks as Species Dwindle', *The Independent*, 29 September 2006, pp. 30–31.

93. Beard, Matthew, 'EU Urged to Limit Tuna Fishing as Sushi Demand Threatens Stocks', *The Independent*, 25 September 2006, p. 12.

94. WWF (above, n. 91)

95. Douse, Andrew, *Sea Eagle Project: Possible East Coast Translocation*, Scottish Natural Heritage, Report SNH/06/11/12, www.snh.org.uk/…/14%20Nov%2006/Sea%20eagle%20-%20possible%20east%20Coast%20Translocation.pdf

96. Ross, John, 'Sea Eagles Soar to Recovery', *The Scotsman*, 24 November 2006, http://news.scotsman.com/topics.cfm?tid=270&id=1740502006

97. RSPB Scotland, 'Scotland's White-tailed Eagles Hit Double Century', 27 July 2006, www.rspb.org.uk/scotland/action/doublecentury.asp

98. Grice, Phil, 'Reintroducing the Sea Eagle to England', English Nature General Committee of Council, December 2005, www.english-nature.org.uk/About/meetings/GCP0536.pdf

99. Struww-Juhl, Bernd, 'On a Mission to Protect White-tailed Sea Eagles', American Association for the Advancement of Science, 3 August 2001, http://sciencecareers.science,ag.org/career_development/previous_issues/articles/1050/on_a_mission_to_protect_white_tailed_sea_eagles

Chapter 10: Oceania/Australasia

1. Boehm, Peter, 'Global Warning: Devastation of an Atoll', *The Independent*, 30 August 2006, p. 26.

2. Karoly, David; Risbey, James; Reynolds, Anna, 'Global Warming Contributes to Australia's Worst Drought', Study, 2002, www.ecovoice.com/au/issues/issue%2020/EV20pg3Sphere02.pdf

3. Perry, Michael, 'Drought Driving Australian Farmers to Suicide', *The Independent*, 20 October 2006, p. 39.

4. Preston, Dr Benjamin and Jones, Dr Roger, *Climate Change Impacts on Australia and Benefits of Early Action to Reduce Global Greenhouse Gas Emissions*, Consultancy report written for the Australian Business Roundtable on Climate Change, CSIRO, Canberra, Australian Capital Territory, 2006.

5. 'The Future Eaters: About Tim Flannery', Australian Broadcasting Corporation, 1998, www.abc.net.au/science/future/abouttim.htm

6. Archer, M.; Flannery, T. F.; Ritchie, A. et al., 'First Mesozoic Mammal from Australia – an Early Cretaceous Monotreme', *Nature*, No 318, 28 November 1985, pp. 363–66.

7. Flannery, Tim, *The Future Eaters: An Ecological History of the Australasian Lands and People*, Grove Press, 1994.

8. Davies, Anne, 'Sydney's Future Eaten: The Flannery Prophecy', *Sydney Morning Herald*, 19 May 2004, www.smh.com.au/articles/2004/05/18/1084783517732.html

9. Peatling, Stephanie, 'Australia Tops Greenhouse Pollution Index', *Sydney Morning Herald*, 19 June 2004, www.smh.com.au/articles/2004/06/18/1087245110190.html

10. Australian Greenhouse Office, Kyoto Protocol, Australian Government Department of the Environment and Heritage, 2005, www.greenhouse.gov.au/international/kyoto

11. WWF-Australia, 'Wetland Watch', www.wwf.org.au/ourwork/water/wetlandwatch

12. WWF-Australia, 'Wetland Watch', last updated 24 October 2006, www.panda.org/about_wwf/where_we_work/asia_pacific/where/australia/index.cfm?uProjectID=AU0071

13. NOVA: Science in the News, 'Key Text: Sun and Skin – a Dangerous Combination', Australian Academy of Science, March 1997, www.science.org.au/nova/008/008key.htm

14. Ibid.

15. Australian Museum, 'Indigenous Australia: Introduction', 2004, www.dreamtime.net.au/indigenous.index.cfm

16. Australian Government, 'Atmosphere Theme Report', *Australia State of the Environment Report*, Commonwealth of Australia, 2001, www.ea.gov.au/soe/2001/atmosphere/atmosphere03-9.html

17. Environment Centre of the Northern Territory, 'Securing the Long-term Protection of the Daly River', July 2006, www.ecnt.org/pdf/land_daly_securing_jul06.pdf

18. WWF-UK, 'Papua New Guinea to Allocate 12 Protected Areas', 26 October 2005, www.wwf.org.uk/news/n_0000002021.asp

19. The Convention on Biological Diversity, Secretariat to the Convention on Biological Diversity United Nations Environment Programme, 2006, www.biodiv.org/default.html

20. Australian Government Department of the Environment and Heritage, 'About the EPBC Act', Commonwealth of Australia, last updated 1 September 2005, www.deh.gov.au/epbc/about/index.html

21. Australian Government Department of the Environment and Heritage, 'Great Barrier Reef World Heritage Values', last updated 5 February 2006, www.deh.gov.au/heritage/worldheritage/sites/gbr/values.html

22. WWF-Australia, 'Plan to Protect the Great Barrier Reef Recognised as World's Best', 24 October 2005, www.org.au/news/n244

23. Australian Government, '25 Years of Whale Protection', Commonwealth of Australia, www.aad.gov.au

24. Australian Government Department of the Environment and Heritage, 'How is Australia Protecting Whales?', www.deh.gov.au/coasts/species/cetaceans/protection.html

25. Australian Government Department of the Environment and Heritage, 'Commercial Kangaroo and Wallaby Harvest Quotas', 2006, www.deh.gov.au/biodiversity/trade-use/publications/kangaroo/pubs/2006-commercial-harvest-quotas.pdf

26. WWF-Australia, 'Gardeners Unknowingly Adding to Australia's 4$ Billion/Year Weed Problem', 25 October 2005, www.wwf.org.au/news/n245

27. Marks, Kathy, 'Drought Drives Australian Camels to Go on Rampage', Independent News and Media Ltd, 15 March 2007, http://news.independent.co.uk/world/australasia/article2359077.ece

28. Department of Primary Industries and Water, 'Tasmanian Devil', Government of Tasmania, 18 October 2006, www.dpiw.tas.gov.au/inter.nsf/inter.nsf/WebPages/BHAN-5358KH?open

29. Department of Primary Industries and Water, 'Disease Affecting Tasmanian Devils', Government of Tasmania, 14 November 2006, www.dpiw.tas.gov.au/inter.nsf/WebPages/LBUN-5QF86G?open

30. US Fish and Wildlife Service, '2000 Federal Register Index', Federal Register Documents, 2000, www.fws.gov/policy/frsystem/title.cfm?title=Endangered%20and%20threatened%20species&doc_type=final&date=00

31. Trivedi, Bijal, 'Koalas Overrunning Australia Island "Ark"', National Geographic News, 10 May 2002, http://news.nationalgeographic.com/news/2002/05/0510_020510_TVkoala.html

32. Girges, A.A.; Hugall, A.F.; Timms, P. et al., 'Two Distinct Forms of Chlamydia Psittaci Associated with Disease and Infertility in Phascolarctos cinereus (koala)', Infection and Immunity, Vol 56, No 8, August 1988, pp. 1897–1900.

33. Conservation International, 'Biodiversity Hotspots: New Zealand', 2007, www.biodiversityhotspots.org/xp/Hotspots/new_zealand

34. Kiwi Conservation Club, 'The Moa', Royal Forest and Bird Protection Society of New Zealand, 2006, www.kcc.org.nz/birds/extinct/moa.asp

35. CIA, 'Tuvalu', The World Factbook [online edition], last updated 18 November 2006, www.cia.gov/coa/publications/factbook/geos/tv.html

36. Australian Bureau of Meteorology, www.bom.gov.au/fwo/IDO60101/IDO60101.200604.pdf

37. Botanic Gardens Trust, Sydney, Australia, 'Wollemi Pine: Facts and Figures', Department of Environment and Conservation (NSW), www.rbgsyd.nsw.gov.au/information_about_plants/wollemi_pine/facts_and_figures

38. Botanic Gardens Trust, Sydney, Australia, 'Wollemi Pine: Where to See It', Department of Environment and Conservation (NSW), www.rbgsyd.nsw.gov.au/information_about_plants/wollemi_pine/where_to_see_it

39. Botanic Gardens Trust, Sydney, Australia, 'Wollemi Pine: Protecting It', Department of Environment and Conservation (NSW), www.rbgsyd.nsw.gov.au/information_about_plants/wollemi_pine/protecting_it

40. Hayes, Dr Mark, 'Tuvalu Mo Te Atua (Tuvalu for the Almighty) Part 3', Tuvalu Special News Feature, 2005, www.tuvaluislands.com/news/archives/2005/2005-02-22_tmta3.htm

41. Marren, Peter; Jones, Geraint; McCarthy, Michael et al., The Disappearing World: 100 Things Your Grandchildren May Never See, Part 2: Planet in Peril, Supplement, The Independent, 18 October 2005, p. 33.

42. Kirby, Alex, 'Pacific Islanders Flee Rising Sea', BBC News, 9 October 2001, http://news.bbc.co.uk/1/hi/sci/yech/1581457.stm

43. History Group of the New Zealand Ministry for Culture and Heritage, 'Nuclear Free Legislation – Nuclear Free New Zealand', www.nzhistory.net.nz/politics/nuclear-free-anzus

44. Mark Oliver and agencies, 'Australia Switches on to Light Bulb Change', Guardian Unlimited Special report: 'Australia', 20 February 2007, www.guardian.co.uk/australia/story/0,2017429,00.html

Index

Picture Credits

Lion Publishing

Commissioning editor: Morag Reeve

Project editor: Julie Frederick

Designer: Nicholas Rous

Picture researcher: Kate Leech

Production manager: Kylie Ord